Stepping Up to the Plate

Stepping Up to the Plate

Building a Liberal Pluralistic Israel

by Rabbi Robert (Bob) Samuels

Rabbis Press
Central Conference of American Rabbis
5777   NEW YORK   2017

Emet M'Eretz Titzmach
"Truth Will Spring Forth from the Land"

Library of Congress Cataloging-in-Publication Data

Names: Samuels, Robert, 1933-2016, author.
Title: Stepping up to the plate : building a liberal pluralistic Israel / by Rabbi Robert (Bob) Samuels.
Description: New York : Rabbis Press ; Central Conference of American Rabbis, 5777-2017. | Includes bibliographical references and index.
Identifiers: LCCN 2017016207 (print) | LCCN 2017017830 (ebook) | ISBN 9780881232974 | ISBN 9780881232981 (pbk. : alk. paper)
Subjects: LCSH: Samuels, Robert, 1933-2016. | Reform Judaism--Israel--Biography. | Reform Judaism--Israel--Haifa--Biography. | Jews, American--Israel--Haifa--Biography. | Jewish educators--Israel--Haifa--Biography.
Classification: LCC BM197 (ebook) | LCC BM197 .S22 2017 (print) | DDC 296.8/341--dc23
LC record available at https://lccn.loc.gov/2017016207

Copyright © 2017 by Rabbis Press, a division of CCAR Press.
Printed in the United States of America. All rights reserved.

Portions of this book may be copied for educational purposes by members of the Central Conference of American Rabbis, for use in that member's congregation or institution. No portions of this book may be sold or distributed without the express written permission of the Central Conference of American Rabbis.

10 9 8 7 6 5 4 3 2 1

CCAR Press, 355 Lexington Avenue, New York, NY 10017
(212) 972-3636
www.ccarpress.org

Table of Contents

List of Abbreviations	viii
Foreword	ix
Personal Tribute to Rabbi Robert Samuels	xii
Dedication	xvi
Acknowledgments	xvii
Preface	xviii

CHAPTER ONE: ROOTS

Part 1	***"Bobby"***	**1**
	The Table	1
	The Bike	4
	Uncle Roy	6
	The Badges	7
	The Window	8
	First Base	10
	Mazal	11
Part 2	***Pioneering: It's in the DNA***	**13**
	1800: From Holland to Virginia	13
	1841: A Pioneering Spirit, from Virginia to Texas	17
Part 3	***Call Me Tex***	**21**
	Seventeen Years Old and On My Own	21
	Mentors at Brandeis	23
	Inspired Learning from the Best	24
	Sports at Brandeis and a Big Decision	28
	Social Life and Leadership	29
	My Lifelong Partner	30
Part 4:	***A Pioneering Spirit, from Boston to Cincinnati to Jerusalem***	**32**
	Stirrings of Zionism	32
	Developing My Jewish-Israeli Identity	38

CHAPTER TWO: RABBI BOB

Part 1:	***Aliyah***	**47**
	1962: From Chicago to Haifa	47
	Beginnings at the Leo Baeck School	50
	Building a Diverse Student Population	57
	My First Year at Leo Baeck	59
	Fundraising: The Early Years	62

	The Shock of Death, the Need for Memory, and the Faith to Hope	64
Part 2:	***Family***	**68**
	Our Homes in Israel	68
Part 3:	***Beginnings of Reform Judaism***	**78**
	Bar and Bat Mitzvah	78
	A Boy Scout World Jamboree	79
	Building Congregations: A Strikeout and a Score for the Reform Movement	82
	MARAM, The Council of Progressive Rabbis in Israel	84
	Or Hadash, A New Light Shines on Zion	88
	The Reform Movement Struggles	95
	Progressive Judaism Takes Root	97
	The HUC-JIR Israeli Rabbinic Program	98
	Full Gas in Neutral	105

CHAPTER THREE: BOLD THRUST IN EDUCATION

Part 1:	***The Challenge***	**106**
	The Gap Between the Facilities and the Vision	106
	Grappling with Power	106
Part 2:	***Raising $1 Million and More***	**112**
	Competing for Dollars	112
	"All My Money Will Go for Your Children in Israel"	114
	Giants of Industry	117
	Another Attempt at Entrepreneurial Funding	122
Part 3:	***The Leo Baeck Education Center***	**126**
	Committing to a Life in Israel	126
	The Reform Movement Wakes Up	128
	Our New Campus	131
	The Yom Kippur War Alters Our Paths	135
	Succession	139

CHAPTER FOUR: REALIZING THE VISION

Part 1:	***Education for Values***	**141**
	An Israeli Educator	141
	The Amana Social Contract	145
	A New Beginning: Vision and Goals	148
	Symbols	150
	Finding Role Models	151
	The Gifted	152
	Reading Critically and Writing Intelligently	154

	Using the Sources for Teaching Values	155
	Creative Curriculum	156
	A Culture of Giving	157
	The Dworkin Camp: 1,000 Days Together	159
Part 2:	**Fulfilling the Mission**	**161**
	Making a Home for the Dispossessed	161
	Softball in Israel	171
	With Our Arab Neighbors	172
	Europeans Looking for Reconciliation	176
	Can a Person be Authentically Jewish and Democratic?	177
Part 3:	**K'hila**	**180**
	Initiating and Defining	180
	Building Community Connection	181
	The Community Center	182
	Leo Baeck Comes Into Its Own	187
	The Sports Center	188
	The Lorry Lokey Center	191
	Ohel Avraham	193
	The Congregation	200

CHAPTER FIVE: CONTINUING THE VISION

The Successor	**204**
The Leo Baeck Spirit	205
Democracy and Civil Rights for All	209
Religious Coercion	213
Conversion	217
Midrash and Halachah	222

OUR ETHICAL WILL   224

Glossary of Common Hebrew Terms   228

LIST OF ABBREVIATIONS

CCAR: Central Conference of American Rabbis

CDC: Community Development Corporation

EIE: Eisendrath International Exchange Program

HUC-JIR: Hebrew Union College-Jewish Institute of Religion

IDF: Israel Defense Forces

IEF: Israel Education Fund (funded by UJA, operated by the Jewish Agency)

IMPJ: Israel Movement for Progressive Judaism

MARAM: Council of Progressive Rabbis (*Moetzet Rabbanim Mitkadmim*)

NFTY: National Federation of Temple Youth (American Reform Jewish Youth Movement)

NSCI: North Shore Congregation Israel

UAHC/URJ: Union of American Hebrew Congregations, now Union for Reform Judaism

UIA: United Israel Appeal

UJA: United Jewish Appeal

WUPJ: World Union for Progressive Judaism

FOREWORD

Rabbi Michael Marmur
Jack, Joseph and Morton Mandel Provost,
Hebrew Union College-Jewish Institute of Religion

As a child, Robert Samuels learned that every day is an opportunity to make a change in the world, to make a mark. That formed him as a person, and as a Jew. I can still hear him now, posing the question he learned in his formative years, in his unique voice accented with shades of Houston and Hosea: What did you do today to fix the world? Countless men and women, captains of industry and army generals, rebels and reactionaries were witness to the force of nature known as "HaRav Samuels." They were all addressed by this searching and loving question.

Bob always wanted to counter darkness with light—the light of learning, of understanding, of equality, of community. He believed that if you give people the chance to act with agency and choice, in most cases they will do the good and decent thing. He believed that Zion will be redeemed by education.

Biblical principles were not clichés for Bob, but rather sublime expressions of great truths:

Love your neighbor as yourself (Leviticus 19)

Speak the truth to each other, and render true and sound judgment in your courts; do not plot evil against each other (Zechariah 8)

To act justly and to love mercy and to walk humbly with your God (Micah 6)

Nation shall not lift up sword against nation, nor shall they learn war any more (Isaiah 2).

Bob drew inspiration from the prophets of Israel, but he was not like them. My colleague Arnie Gluck notes that "historically, the prophets were outsiders, marginal people, alienated from society because of their extreme and unrelenting demands. They were not builders of institutions, and with the rarest of exceptions, they were… ineffective. Not so Bob Samuels."

Bob was a builder. The Hebrew word for builder, *banai*, is an anagram of the word for prophet, *navi*. He developed an approach that all his students should learn from—applied prophecy. He would ask: Have you been a witness to injustice? Take part in improving the situation, take responsibility, create an alternative. Have you identified a need? Find a solution. Move things and people. Persuade whoever you need to persuade—students, donors, leaders, bureaucrats—that there is no thing worth doing more than the right thing. Bob built an institution, but even more he helped individuals build themselves up—building and being built. Do you have the potential to do something in the world? Come closer, from every class and race and identity, and we will find a way to realize that potential. Somewhere within you—so Bob believed—there is a treasure, a song bubbling up, a light breaking through, a scientific breakthrough in the offing, a mitzvah bursting to get out. Bob the Builder built a platform upon which the inner beauty of the individual could come to expression. He built sound boxes, sounding boards.

Rabbi Samuels sought a blend of the best of liberal Judaism with the best inherent in Israel. He dreamt of a different future for Jews and Arabs. He combined vision with criticism, analysis with activism, world-healing with fence-mending. His approach, practical prophecy, struck roots in Haifa. At the Leo Baeck Education Center we used to call it *leobaeckiut*, "Leo Baeck-ness," but it was really Bob-ness—Isaiah and Thomas Jefferson and popular Israeli songs all bundled up together, commitment to social solidarity alongside striving for personal excellence.

Bob was not particularly impressed by futile erudition. Being smart was not as important as translating vision into action. In the words of the prayer book: to understand, to comprehend, to hear, to learn, to teach, to keep, to do, to make real. And in Bob's version, also to build.

Bob was addicted to tomorrow. He knew how to celebrate every single day, but he also saw each day as the start of the one on the way. Every day is part of the countdown, the march to the future. He saw today as an opportunity to build tomorrow. In the words of Amos:

The days are coming…
…and I will bring my people Israel back from exile.
They will rebuild the ruined cities and live in them.
They will plant vineyards and drink their wine;
they will make gardens and eat their fruit. (Amos 9)

Bob's fellow builder, Annette, worked tirelessly with him on another great construction project—the Samuels family. The roots they have set down continue to yield remarkable fruits.

I have the privilege of serving the Hebrew Union College. Over the years we have educated many eminent individuals. Bob Samuels takes pride of place among the finest of them.

As a person, a patriarch, a professional role model, a planner, a pioneer, a child of prophets, Bob was a builder. This book tells his story. Reading it can do what Bob always managed to do in his life. Even if we are disheartened and out of new ideas, even if the next step seems unclear, it builds us up.

A PERSONAL TRIBUTE TO BOB SAMUELS

Rabbi Charles A. Kroloff
Past President,
Central Conference of American Rabbis

Bob Samuels was my cherished friend and my hero. Hence, this is both my personal and rabbinic tribute to an *ish tzadik,* a righteous man.

Bob Samuels's entire life was powered by the ideals of the Hebrew prophets. This book is laced with references to Amos, Isaiah, Jeremiah, and Micah, who fueled his life of service. Bob died at the conclusion of Shabbat Kedoshim whose Torah portion captures the principles by which he lived his life:

"Do not turn to idols or make molten gods for yourself."
"You shall leave the fallen fruit of your vineyard for the poor and the stranger."
"You shall not insult the deaf or place a stumbling block before the blind."
"Do not profit by the blood of your neighbor."
"You shall not take vengeance. Love your neighbor as yourself."
(Leviticus, 19:4, 10, 14, 16, 18)

Bob translated those iconic dicta into real life actions. *Tikkun olam* and *g'milut chasadim* (improving the world and extending loving kindness) pervaded every fiber of Bob's being, motivating his every action as rabbi, educator, husband, father, grandfather, and friend.

He and Annette adopted families from the Ethiopian community, helping them overcome bias and deprivation. Bob embraced the residents of nearby Druze villages who cherished him as one of their own. He was adored by Russian *olim* whom he helped to feed, clothe, and educate. To his Arab neighbors he was their trusted friend who assisted them with financial aid, educational support, and wise counsel. For those of us who care about Arab-Jewish relations, Bob was a model whom we would do well to emulate.

He not only taught Torah; he lived it with every fiber of his being, every day of his life.

Bob and Annette made *aliyah* to Israel in 1962 and never looked back. They were Zionists without peer. They committed themselves to raising their family in the Jewish homeland and to strengthening the moral fabric and humane spirit of Israel.

I have often struggled to craft a contemporary English translation to *Pirkei Avot* 2:6: *U'vamakom she'ein anashim, hishtadel l'hiyot ish.* Thanks to Bob, I now have it: "In the place where no one stands up to do what is right, be the one who steps up to the plate."

Bob stepped up to the plate by fusing Zionism with Progressive Judaism. He believed unwaveringly that without liberal Judaism Israel was destined to devolve into a pre-Enlightenment fiefdom ruled by autocratic extremists.

As early as 1962, Bob shared with me his vision of what the fledgling Leo Baeck School might become: a comprehensive educational center that would bring together children of all ethnic and economic backgrounds, educating them to be informed citizens committed to the finest progressive values of Judaism and humanity. He accomplished this goal—and more—because he was not only a visionary, but he knew how to transform vision into reality. It didn't hurt that he was also one of our movement's finest fundraisers and a brilliant strategist endowed with a large measure of *chutzpah*.

Theodor Herzl taught us: *"Im tirzu, ayn zo agadah.* If you will it, it is no dream." Herzl's legacy lived in Bob's soul. He dreamed great dreams, and then went out to make them real.

HaRav Samuels established not one, but two synagogues in Haifa: Or Chadash and Ohel Avraham. The latter was named for our revered professor of Jewish ethics at Hebrew Union College, Cincinnati, Abraham Cronbach, who believed that the world could be healed through "felicitous human relationships." Bob exemplified that philosophy, engaging each of us directly and intensely, the embodiment of Martin Buber's I-Thou relationship.

Bob understood that Progressive Judaism would flourish in Israel only if we produced exceptional leaders. Here, too, he stepped up to the plate, mentoring dozens of women and men who became rabbis, cantors, and lay leaders of our movement in Israel (and in North America too). He believed that the rabbinic program at Hebrew Union College in Jerusalem was the indispensable engine for building pluralistic Judaism in Israel. When his daughter-in-law, Ayala Ronen Samuels, was ordained there in 2013, he told me, "my cup runneth over." Bob and Annette have generously supported the mission of our Jerusalem campus.

Bob was a force of nature. I have never known anyone with as many talents, as determined a spirit, and as much energy as Bob. A star first baseman for Brandeis University's baseball team, he literally stepped up to the plate helping to introduce the American pastime to Israel. His team competed against Israel's finest and proudly ran the bases against a contingent from the United States Sixth Fleet! His fortitude translated into an ability to endure lengthy intercontinental flights with the required focus and stamina to solicit a donor, two hours after landing, for a million dollars.

His love of architecture combined with his superior hand/eye coordination enabled him to serve as general contractor and skilled craftsman in building their gracious home in Ein Hod. His splendid works of art, often inspired by biblical personalities who fueled his spirit, adorn that residence.

Bob was a sharp, insightful critic of the occupation and of Israel's right-wing political leaders. Because he was such an *ohev Yisrael*—such a lover of Israel—his critique carried credibility and impact. Advocating non-stop for the two-state solution, he never hesitated to speak his mind and act on his prophetic principles, and we loved him for that. He earned the respect of Israel's leaders and his rabbinic colleagues worldwide. Haifa University awarded him its Carmel Award of Merit posthumously on June 9, 2016.

He spoke with eloquence and taught with uncommon wisdom. He was self-reflective, self-critical, and cheerleader-in-chief for the achievements, musical and beyond, of Annette and their three children.

Bob was blessed to share his life's journey with his beloved Annette for nearly sixty-one years. Their loving respect for each other and their shared visions are the stuff that exhilarating stories are made of. Their roots go back to their happy, values-laden childhoods in Houston, Texas. They are blessed with amazing children, Ami and Ayala, David and Amy, Tamar and Yigal, all of whom live close by in Israel. Their nine grandchildren, Peleg, Amos, Gilad, Maya, Iris, Eli, Lior, Noam, and Ido, infused with Bob and Annette's talents, spirit, and values, are now making their own contributions to *amcha* and to the human family. Bob cherished his brothers, Vic and Tom, and their families so profoundly that he frequently rearranged his commitments in order to spend an abundance of quality time with them in the States.

The strongest indicator of the character of a man is how he handles adversity. When he was diagnosed with cancer in 2014, Bob Samuels stepped up to the plate for the last great contest of his life, and he responded in the way that he lived his entire life: by embracing every moment with strength and courage, love for family and friends, gratitude for those who were present for him in his time of need, and with his unyielding enthusiasm for life.

In that period of twenty months after his challenging diagnosis, he, with Annette, made four trips abroad, delivered a riveting hour-long talk, after a twenty-hour flight, to the National Association of Retired Reform Rabbis in Florida, advised every branch of our Movement, including the Leo Baeck Center, on how to plan for the future, continued to help people in need, and completed this inspiring autobiography.

On February 29, 2016, Bob and Annette took my wife, Terry, and me on a pilgrimage to the many places we jointly hold dear: Kfar Galim (site of the Reform Movement's first Summer-in-Israel youth program, which Bob helped me direct), lunch on the Mediterranean, Ein Hod, their son David's workshop, and, of course, Leo Baeck. He was quite ill that day, but physical limitations never constrained his spirit, not then, not ever.

Cantor Jeff Klepper wrote this about his mentor: "He was always asking questions, always searching for a better way. His impact on Israel and Progressive Judaism was profound, but it was the sparkle in his eye, the way he loved you with that big Texas heart, that gave you strength and hope for the future."

Toward the end, Bob and I spoke several times a week. At the conclusion of every call, it was he who gave me strength and hope for the future.

Y'didi Hayakar, my cherished friend, you have blessed us all: your family, your friends, your students, the citizens of Israel, your fellow human beings. And you continue to bless us *l'dor v'dor,* from generation to generation.

DEDICATION

I dedicate this book to my parents, Elsie and Irving Samuels, who gave me a democratic home to grow up in, setting me on my way.

I dedicate this book to Dr. Leo Baeck, who has been my inspiration for how to live and how to die; to Rabbi Meir Elk, who treated his young American colleague with great respect and was, in short, a mensch; and to Dani Fessler, who absorbed all the critical values as a child, worked as a young adult, and is now leading the Leo Baeck Education Center toward a brilliant future.

I dedicate this book to my wife, Annette, who has been my life partner and my base after every triumph and every storm. She has anticipated my every thought, mood, and situation in life and has helped me step up to the plate.

My illness has shown me the complete dedication and readiness to step up to the plate of all my children, their spouses, and my grandchildren. They have absorbed the values of tradition and anti-tradition, and they are ready for leadership. I dedicate the future to them.

ACKNOWLEDGMENTS

There have been so many named and unnamed partners along the way. I acknowledge you have had a part in the long tradition of liberal education and *k'hilah* (community). Thank you. To all of my baseball players who have stepped up to the plate smashing homers and hitting singles, you cheered up my days and, further, my faith. To my granddaughter, Iris, who masterminded the technology and shared my fervor about many topics as we worked together. As I sit here on my sick bed, I cannot be more grateful to Amy Fields, my daughter-in-law, for having sat by my side to organize and write the final chapters of this book. She was generous, creative, and she wouldn't let me off the hook.

PREFACE

In Texas in the 1940s, many Jews had Christian friends. Roy Wilson was Protestant, and he was my Dad's friend. "Uncle" Roy loved kids, and he always seemed to be around to teach us "things." The *big* thing was baseball. At eight, I started Little League at Cherryhurst Park, and Uncle Roy was always there. He taught me the ratio between length and weight of my bat, how to properly rub Neatsfoot oil on my glove, and the rules: "Learn all the rules, Bobby," but not just the ones in the Baseball Rule Book. No, here were some of Uncle Roy's rules: you need to know when to be tough and when to be nice, how to act when you're playing well, and how to take it when you aren't. For Uncle Roy, the game of baseball taught you a way of life. "When you *step up to the plate* to hit the ball," he said, "everything must come together: knowing what this pitcher throws, the situation on the field, your skill, your courage, your strength, your determination, and your desire. So, Bobby, always *step up to the plate* with the confidence that you'll hit the ball and with the knowledge that if you succeed three times out of ten, you'll be a star."

Nine years later, as Brandeis University's first baseball team ran out onto the newly finished ball field, our coach, Walter Mahoney, challenged us: "Boys, hitting a baseball is one of the hardest skills in sport. But the whole team depends on what you do at the plate. So, that's what we have to practice. You have to really want it! So, *step up to the plate* and hit! If you can do that, our team will win, and you can succeed at anything you want to do in your life."

I love baseball, and I got quite good at it. This book is about how I've tried to *step up to the plate* and "hit the ball" throughout my life. It is about my vision of a better world and my batting average in creating conditions for that world.

CHAPTER ONE
ROOTS

PART 1
"Bobby"

The Table

It all happened around the table. My parents were die-hard democrats. Not democrats with a big D, active in a political party, but democrats in the true sense of the word. They believed in giving their children responsibilities and privileges. They expected a lot of us three boys, Bob, Tom, and Vic, and the dinner table is where we learned about those expectations. All of us were free to go about our business throughout the day—working, playing, learning, doing our chores—and our parents never interfered in our decisions regarding the right thing to do whether at home, in the street, in school, in the community center, on the playing field, at the YMCA or the Scout troop. But at 6:00 P.M. we had to be sitting at the dinner table because the family would have its "democratic" meal.

Here's what made it democratic. Mom dished out everything she had prepared on each plate. It was always a balanced meal. She was a wonderful cook, but some of her dishes might not have been to your liking. If there was something you didn't like, you ate it anyway, sometimes by breathing only through your mouth, so as not to taste it. You did that for two reasons: first, because we were poor, and you knew how hard it was for our parents to put a well-balanced meal on the table, and secondly, you definitely did not want Mom to say, "Eat your food, son. Think of all those poor children in China who have nothing to eat." No one around the table wanted to hear her say *that* again.

Once everyone had his meal in front of him, Pop would say, "OK, Bobby (or another family member's name), it's your turn." We all knew what that meant. We expected it. So each of us bowed our head, and the one called on had to give thanks for our food and create an extemporaneous prayer, blessing the family and whatever else he had thought of during the day. We all got good at creative prayer. Sometimes God got in, but more often not. I often wondered how God could hear us, but then it was such a warm feeling to be in the bosom of that family, I came to believe that God was that togetherness of our little family around that table. Pop taught us to be positive, non-critical of others during our blessing, and he never corrected us at the table. If he wanted to point out something regarding our blessing, he would always do it gently and kindly sometime in the coming days.

After the prayer, we would eat with animated conversation and in a joyous mood, unless something very sad had happened in the family, the community, or the country that day. When Pop thought the time was ripe, he would say again, "Okay, (someone at the table), what happened today?" We all knew that he was *not* looking for a news story. What he expected from us was an account of what we had done for someone else that day. It was an astounding 24/7 ethical mitzvah system. You could not bear the shame of saying, "Nothing happened today, Pop." This was not only against the rules, it was against family honor. So knowing that at 6:00 P.M. everyone, including the parents, had to be ready if called upon, you prepared for the moment every day.

The range of help that the five Samuels gave the family and the community because of that simple dinner table question was a lesson deeply ingrained in the developing child and young adult. By the time I left home at the age of seventeen to go to a university two thousand miles away, I had internalized how to use hand, heart, and conscience to help others or make life better in some small way.

What did we actually say in response to my father's query? "Pop, we have a new kid in our class." (He was in fact a 1943 refugee.) "Eric is Jewish, but he barely speaks English. He came from Europe. His clothes look funny, and he's always off in a corner by himself. So today I asked Eric to show me his notebooks. He's actually a nice kid, so we went through the lessons together, and I taught him some English words." (Eric went on to become a highly regarded professor of physics.)

"Today, Pop, I was at a Scout meeting. Some of the kids in my troop have a hard time with our rope knots, and we had to do them before the Scoutmaster. So, we went behind the Scout house, and I showed them how to memorize five different knots."

"This morning Mr. Potter on Bonnie Brae Street told me to stop delivering his paper because he lost his job. I told him that I would continue to put a paper on his porch every morning until the end of the month, no charge, and that I hoped he would get another job by then."

I always wanted Pop to call on me. I was proud to be an ethical mitzvah (good deed) doer. *Mitzvah asseh ben adam,* the *doing* of an ethical mitzvah, and not just *talking* about it, was what we were taught was the essence of being Jewish and being American.

And what about the Friday night, Erev Shabbat, table? What did we do to make Shabbat significant? Every week, Mom came home from the butcher with a wide piece of brown paper the length of the icebox door (later, the refrigerator). I sat down with my drawing board to make a matrix with the days of the week horizontally and the names of the five of us vertically. Daily tasks were assigned to each person and inserted into the matrix. Each day of the week, we knew what our family task was because it was written up there on the fridge. Each night, Mom would evaluate how well each of us had done his task and carried out his responsibilities that day, and she would stick on a gold, silver, or bronze star accordingly.

Erev Shabbat was "count the stars" night in our family "court." One of the five of us was chosen to be the *av beit din*, the judge of the week. The butcher paper was taken down to the table, and we had a frank and spirited evaluation according to our stars for each day. The family court determined how each of us had performed his appointed tasks. The family consensus was respected and accepted. On the basis of this evaluation, tasks were assigned for the next week. Each of us got some jobs we really wanted, and some we preferred not to get. The tasks for the new week were inscribed on the new butcher paper and taped to the refrigerator door, serving as the basis for the following week's work schedule. If one of us could not perform his task for some reason, we negotiated with another family member to exchange with us on a *quid pro quo* basis. I don't remember our mother ever telling us what to do; it was written on the refrigerator door. This was a brilliant pedagogic tool to help the family function as a team and without rancor.

When the court process was over on Friday night, our mother, a true Southern lady born in Savannah, Georgia, would stand up and put on her white gloves. This was the sign that we were going to synagogue, to Temple Emanu El, the Reform congregation served by Rabbi Robert Kahn. Have no illusions that this was a simple matter, for the junior high and senior high school football and basketball teams often had games on Friday night. We three boys were avid athletes and sports enthusiasts. Our parents understood this and never had a problem if we asked to go to the sports event rather than to synagogue. If I did go to the football game, I never felt overpowering joy that I was missing the Friday night service. In fact, I missed it, because it was so beautiful and so spiritual.

The Bike

We were a poor family. For the first fourteen years of my life, we had no car. That first seven-year-old coupe was given to my dad in 1947, two years after the end of World War II. During the war, Pop had worked as a riveter, building Liberty Ships at the Brown Shipyard. In fact, that's why we moved to Houston. He wanted to enlist in the military when America went to war, but he was rejected because of poor eyesight. He told us how important it was for America to build those ships fast, as the American fleet had been sunk at Pearl Harbor. We had moved from Corsicana to Houston in 1941, and just after Pearl Harbor in December, Pop started working at the shipyard on the midnight shift. With no car, Pop left home at 10:00 P.M. every night and walked an hour to Main Street where he caught a bus that took another hour to get to the shipyard. This meant that he arrived home at 10:00 A.M. every morning, when we were already at school.

With no car, it was important for me, as the oldest son, to have a bike. So, at age eight, I bought a second-hand bicycle from a kid in my third grade class. My bike became the transport vehicle for our family purchases for six years. I went on errands to the grocery store, to the hardware store, for ice to put in our icebox, and for early morning bread. These and other family purchases were initially all made possible by my second-hand bicycle. But I quickly decided to work toward a better bike and had my eye on a new Schwinn. At age nine, I got my first job selling *The Saturday Evening Post* and *Liberty* magazines in front of the Mellie Esperson building in downtown Houston. It was the busiest corner in Houston, which was still a small city in 1942.

"*Get your Saturday Evening Post and Liberrrrrrty magazinesssssss!*" I sang out hundreds of times, literally putting a magazine in people's hands. I made enough money to buy that Schwinn, the Cadillac of 1942 bikes. Now I could get a real job. I applied to become a paperboy, delivering the morning newspaper, the *Houston Post*. I was assigned a route of 250 subscribers. So from age ten to graduation at age seventeen, I awoke every morning at 4:15 A.M. At 4:30 A.M. the papers were delivered to the Weingarten Supermarket near our home. The warm bread was also delivered to Weingarten's, providing a hearty snack. Accompanied by my faithful dog, Taffy, I sat there folding 250 papers to throw onto the porches of my subscribers. Often my brothers, Tom and Vic, would help me with the larger Sunday paper when I had to make two rounds. I rewarded them with waffles at a neighborhood café.

I was already a young entrepreneur, handling all the tasks of getting new customers, receiving the right number of papers, delivering on time, managing the monthly payment collection, and paying for the papers so that I made a profit. In the early years, on the way home after finishing my route around 6:30 A.M., I would buy ice the size of my two saddlebags, so that every morning we had fresh ice to keep our food cool. My bike was not only transportation to school, baseball practice, the Scout house, bar mitzvah lessons, youth group and friends' visits, and delivering the groceries, but also our family wheels until my high school graduation in 1950.

I often took care of my younger brothers, Tom and Vic. Tom was four years younger than I was, and Vic was four years younger than Tom. We were all athletes, and despite the age difference, we played football, baseball, and street ball in the yards and in the street in front of our house. I was often responsible for them when our parents went out or when both were working in the afternoon. I would take them to the movies, baseball games, the zoo, to play miniature golf, or to swim in the neighborhood municipal pool. We three boys had a wonderful childhood and adolescence together with much in common, and that has continued throughout the years.

I had many jobs during my high school years and during the summers while attending university. I sold popcorn and peanuts at the rodeo, circus, and wrestling matches. I sold Fuller Brushes door-to-door. I delivered Pepsi-Cola and fruit drinks in an eighteen-wheeler to all of the out-of-town distributors. I had a Coca-Cola route in downtown Houston for a summer.

I was taught to be independent, to make judgments for myself, and to be a responsible individual. As a result, by age seventeen, I was secure and confident at home and away from home.

Uncle Roy

For us kids, "Uncle" Roy and "Aunt" Doris, a nominally Christian couple without children, were family. In addition to teaching us how to play baseball, Uncle Roy also taught us to drive. We didn't have a car, but he did. He parked his 1938 Ford in the middle of the dead-end street beside our house.

Uncle Roy always had the time and the patience to teach neighborhood kids to fix whatever broke to maintain our bikes, to build a tree house, or to learn the Cub Scout Manual. But that wasn't all. When I was eight years old, long before I could see over the steering wheel, he gave me my first "driving" instructions. "Okay, Bobby, put your left foot on the clutch and the right on the accelerator. Left down all the way…I know your leg is not long enough. Scoot down. Alright now, left foot up slowlyyy... right down slowlyyy... try again, you'll get it."

Tragically, Roy contracted tuberculosis. In those years, when a person got a communicable disease, he had to be isolated so as not to spread the disease. What were Roy and Doris to do once he had to be isolated? Leave it to Mom and Pop. They came to the rescue, as they did for so many others through the years. They had a tiny two-room house built in the backyard behind our home at 1736 Colquitt Street. Every day, one of us would deliver food and supplies to their porch and then stand outside Roy's window for a conversation.

From inside the closed house, Uncle Roy taught me the principles of baseball. He did not just teach me the necessary skills of throwing, catching, batting, running, and sliding, but rather, he taught me the principles of teamwork, justice, honesty, companionship, hard work, consistency, the challenges of victory, and the acceptance of defeat. Uncle Roy became my Jiminy Cricket. He always wanted to know how baseball practice went, how the game went, how I was hitting, how I was playing defense, what I was studying, how I liked my teachers, and whether my newspaper subscribers were treating me with respect. Uncle Roy died in 1952, but as I grew into adolescence and beyond, I continued to see him with my inner eye of conscience and heart.

When Pop became a CPA and opened his own accounting office, Aunt Doris served as his loyal bookkeeper for thirty years. My parents stuck by her throughout their lives, and my brother Vic cared for Aunt Doris through many years of old age. Uncle Roy and Aunt Doris have always been a symbol for me of the education I received from my parents, teaching me that reaching out to others, irrespective of their family, religious, or ethnic background, is a supreme Jewish mitzvah.

The Badges

When I was nine, I joined the YMCA and the Scouts. Other enrichment programs, such as summer camps and music lessons, cost money. The Y was free and had marvelous programs for kids like me, with workshops such as woodwork and ceramics and sports like swimming and boxing. Camping in the wild with the companionship of my fellow Scouts was formative. The Cub Scouts was perfect for me. I was a Cub Scout and then a Boy Scout from ages nine to fourteen. I loved it. As a Cub, I became a Webelos (*W*olf, *B*ear, *L*ion, *S*cout). Once I became a Boy Scout, I lived for getting those merit badges. I became a Star Scout (five badges), a Life Scout (ten badges), and almost became an Eagle Scout (twenty-one badges). I was a member of Troop 29 at the South Main Baptist Church, the only Jew in the troop. One boy was Catholic, and all the rest were Baptists. They welcomed me because I was a good athlete, and Ralph Davala, the Catholic, because he was a good swimmer. That Baptist Scoutmaster must have been without prejudice because I never felt an anti-Semitic moment in that troop. He was also a fine mentor, advising me on which merit badges to work for: citizenship, leadership, personal fitness, family life, camping, and sports. The ones I worked hardest for were service to the community and to the nation, the subject of many conversations at our family table.

As one of the few Jews at Sidney Lanier Junior High School, I began to realize that my baseball buddies and other classmates were friendly on the ball field and at school, but I was never invited to their homes or their parties. It was insidious anti-Semitism, so I began to gravitate toward Jewish kids. When I finished junior high in 1947, I decided to continue at San Jacinto, the senior high that most of the Jewish kids attended, and to join a Jewish youth group. I left the Scouts and became an active member of AZA 136, the young men's fraternity of the B'nai

B'rith Youth Organization (*Ahavah, Tzedakah, Achdut,* fraternal love, benevolence, unity). I practiced and played baseball every afternoon from 2:30 until 5:30 and was the only Jewish boy on the team. It was the boys in my youth group and the girls in the corresponding sorority, the B'nai B'rith Girls (BBG), who became my social world for those three formative high school years. Annette, my wife of sixty-one years, was a member of that BBG club and was the "sweetheart" of my youth group in the eleventh grade.

The Window

When Temple Beth Israel was founded in 1854, it was a traditional congregation. But by the twentieth century it had become Reform. It practiced Reform Judaism in its classical mode, i.e., mixed seating, no head covering, Protestant-like hymns in English ("God is in His Holy Temple, Earthly thoughts are silent now..."), Sunday services as well as Shabbat, mixed Jewish-Christian professional choir, and rabbinic robes. When we arrived in Houston in 1941, Beth Israel was a genuine American Reform congregation. Rabbi Henry Barnston and his successor, Rabbi Judah Schachtel, were known throughout the United States as anti-Zionists. In 1945, these men were among the leaders of a group of rabbis, congregants, and congregations to form the American Council for Judaism, a militant anti-Zionist Jewish organization against the creation of a Jewish state.

They believed that God had scattered the Jewish People for the purpose of spreading the concept of monotheism throughout the world. Jews were to live a highly ethical life and to be "a light unto the nations." Our People had gone through three stages, the first being a nomadic tribal tent-life in the period of the Patriarchs and the Judges (1750 BCE to 1000 BCE). The second was a national life under Kings and Priests (1000 BCE to 70 CE). The third stage was life after the Temple was destroyed in the first century CE, after which Jews were scattered throughout the Babylonian and Roman Empires. Historic Judaism has seen this loss of homeland as the greatest tragedy of the Jewish People because we lost our sovereignty. Since then, the majority of Jewish communities have prayed for the restoration of the Kingdom of David in the Land of Israel. Most Jews have believed that God destroyed our independent Land because of our sins but would never abandon us and would someday send a messenger, the Messiah, to create a national home once again for the Jewish People. However, Jews who were emancipated in the French and American revolutions at the end of the eighteenth century appreciated Western European and North American citizenship. Many believed theologically that we have been spread throughout the world to bring God's word to the nations. It was the task of the Jews of North America, so thought these classic nineteenth-century reformers, to spread the message of universal peace by living an exemplary life. This would hasten the Messianic Age, when "the lion will lie down with the lamb" and "Nation will not lift up sword against nation, nor learn war anymore." The Jews of Temple Beth Israel believed this. America was their Zion; Washington was their Jerusalem. They were content, and they believed God was declaring a new period in Jewish history and in the history of humankind.

When the horrors of the Holocaust became known in 1945, toward the end of World War II, the controversy between the Beth Israel stance and those who wanted a Jewish homeland for Zionist reasons or as a haven for Jews who were in lands where they were being persecuted became critical. Many of the members of Beth Israel no longer believed in the ideology of the "Dispersion of the Jewish People to spread God's Word." These families decided to break with Beth Israel and its anti-Zionist and anti-traditional stance to form a new congregation, to become known as Temple Emanu El. My parents were among the first to join that fledgling congregation.

Today, Houston's Temple Emanu El is a powerful congregation in one of the great religious buildings of North America. When I was a developing adolescent in the 1940s, it was a fledgling congregation struggling to make a name for itself. The congregants of Emanu El worshipped in the small Central Presbyterian Church on Montrose Street. The church directors arranged to remove all Christian images for our Shabbat prayers.

I loved that little sanctuary and decided to become a bar mitzvah there. Once a week in the seventh grade I had to leave baseball practice early to ride my bike to my Hebrew lesson with Mrs. Paula Victor, a survivor of Auschwitz, who came to live her remaining years in Houston. She looked like an immigrant, she acted and talked like one, and I loved her and her lessons. Rehearsals for the bar mitzvah ceremony were led by Rabbi Alan Green, the interim rabbi, until Rabbi Robert Kahn returned from the war, where he served with distinction as a chaplain in the South Pacific.

Once, while waiting for the rehearsal to begin, I was playing with a yo-yo outside the church building, practicing a loop-de-loop, throwing the yo-yo out in front so that it does a 360-degree "around-the-world" and comes back to you. As I threw the yo-yo out, the string broke, but the yo-yo continued its trajectory, crashing through one of the stained glass windows. (Sixty-eight years later, I still create stained glass, which must be a result of some sub-conscious guilt I haven't yet overcome.) Broken window notwithstanding, both Rabbi Green and Rabbi Kahn officiated as I became Emanu El's first bar mitzvah.

The leaders of this new congregation had a passion for a warmer, more traditional Judaism. This passion, together with my personal relationship with Rabbi Kahn and a secular teenager's discovery of a Jewish world, all profoundly affected me more than any of us realized, as my life would soon reveal.

First Base

In addition to participating in Scouts as a boy, I played baseball from ages eight to twenty-two, at first in Little League at Cherryhurst Park, then in junior and senior high school, and subsequently in college. I am left-handed, which gave me a decided advantage as a first baseman. Throughout my baseball career, I was an all-conference first baseman. First base, my position, turned out to be a triple entendre.

I learned three values about "first" base.

First, on defense, my job was to ensure that opposing hitters would not reach first base successfully. In order for that to happen, I needed the assistance of all eight of my teammates on the field. Baseball is a game of total coordination among all nine players. Every time a batter comes to the plate, you move according to how you think that person is going to hit the ball. Once the ball is on its way, all nine defensive players must move in a smooth and intelligent direction in order to fulfill the task of getting that person out or limiting his advance. If there is an error, the other players must move in such a way as to help correct the error and keep the runner from advancing.

Any manager of a public or private institution or business knows that only through such coordination of all factors can a goal be achieved. If it is not achieved, there should be a correction in such a way that those responsible are pleased they have backup. One must look for partners, rejoice in their success, and overcome all attempts to aggrandize one's own ego, whether in sports, business, politics, marriage, education, or culture. I have based my management style throughout my life on these principles I learned as a child on the baseball field.

Second, on offense, first base is key. As a person driven to succeed and skilled to do so stage by stage, I learned early on that reaching that first plateau was the sign of imminent success. In achieving one's dreams and visions, a person must start by getting to "first base." Just getting safely there, you are on your way to "scoring." This was proven true by the Oakland A's Major League baseball team when they demonstrated that "on base percentage" was the single most important factor in winning games.[1] I was never a power hitter, but I quickly figured out how to size up the positioning of the defense and then hit to a place on the field that would maximize my chances of getting to first base.

It has taken me thirty-seven years of building an educational institution by "stepping up to the plate" on a daily basis and sizing up the political, economic, and social chances of "getting to first base." We have had many failures ("outs"), but many more successes in reaching "first base" and beyond.

Third, in nature, life grows slowly. Planting a garden takes patience as we watch the first sprouts of the oak tree emerge from the earth and wait until we get shade from that tree. Meanwhile, there are setbacks, such as wind, drought, insects, and disease that hamper its straight-line development into a beautiful mature tree. Patience is a requisite in life. Initially we must get to "first base," work hard all our lives to touch all the bases, and finally succeed in getting "home," the perfect metaphor for my life as an educator.

Mazal

What luck I had at age eight when we moved to Houston. Lewis Levy, my relative, had been the first Jewish resident in Houston, moving there from Galveston in 1840. He had been among the founders in 1854 of the first Jewish congregation in Texas, Houston's Temple Beth Israel. So it was only natural that when we moved to Houston in 1941,

---

1. "On base percentage": the percentage of times at bat that a hitter gets on base, including hits, walks, errors, and hits by the pitch. The team manager just doesn't want you to make an "out."

Pop would take his eight-year-old son to Beth Israel to register me in the religious school. But the 1941 leaders of the congregation refused to accept me because Pop couldn't pay the congregational dues and my tuition.

Why was this fortunate? Because Pop decided to teach us himself. "Sunday morning in the park with Pop." He would take us to the train yard to ride on a locomotive engine with the engineer or on a bus ride through Houston. One Sunday a month we would go to Hermann Park, the largest public park in Houston. We would play on the swings, slide down the sliding board, and then sit on a bench and learn about the prophet Amos or a psalm. This quiet, gentle soul laid his hands on his developing son. Micah and Isaiah became my heroes, demanding of the ancient Hebrews to stop their evil ways and begin living an ethical life. Reading Psalm 8, I realized I was just "a little lower than the angels and crowned with honor and with glory." Pop and the park had a profound influence on my soul and on the rest of my life.

There are many successes in life that can be attributed to one's personality, skills, and efforts. But everyone needs *mazal,* luck. We don't choose our parents, and we don't choose our time and place. My home training and my *mazal* would help carry me forward as I left Houston at the age of seventeen to make my way in the world.

I had *mazal* to be born to those parents, who struggled financially all their lives but knew how to impart to their children the basics of justice, compassion, love, and an upstanding life.

I had *mazal* to be born in America, not Europe, in 1933, the year Hitler came to power.

I had *mazal* to be born with the DNA of a heightened spatial sense for learning and fine-tuned coordination that allowed me joy in sport.

And I had another kind of *mazal,* to be born into a family with a long history of pioneering. It was in our DNA.

CHAPTER ONE
ROOTS

PART 2

Pioneering; It's in the DNA

1800: From Holland to Virginia

I like to reflect on the first generation of my family in America, Abraham and Rachel Levy, born in Amsterdam in the eighteenth century. In 1789, when the French Revolution heralded a new day of freedom and justice for Europe, Abraham was twenty years old. How disappointed he must have been with the executions of thousands of workers and peasants beheaded during the Reign of Terror under Robespierre and the crowning of Napoleon as Emperor in 1804. When Napoleon placed his brother to rule over a puppet kingdom in Holland, Abraham and Rachel saw that Europe was in chaos and incapable of giving the people the power of self-government. The French Revolution's promise of "Liberty, Equality, Fraternity" was but a distant dream.

Abraham began to read about the settlement and recent history of the new United States. He had read about the American Revolution thirty years before and about the preamble to the Declaration of Independence, stating that "all men are created equal, that they are endowed . . . with certain unalienable Rights . . . that among those are Life, Liberty and the pursuit of Happiness." Oh, how Rachel and Abraham wanted those rights for their children!

He read about George Washington's acceptance of the presidency and about his home in Virginia. When he received the text of Washington's 1780 letter to the Jewish congregation in Newport, Rhode Island, he was amazed at the content:

> *The citizens of the United States all possess alike liberty of conscience... May the children of the stock of Abraham continue to merit and enjoy the good will of all, while everyone shall sit under his vine and his fig tree, and there shall be none to make him afraid.*

Then he read how Washington had refused to continue as president in order to make clear that America would never have leaders who had absolute power and "divine rights."

From Abraham's last will and testament, we know that George Washington became his hero. He left in his will a statue of Washington in addition to one of Moses, and he asked that his tombstone be carved exactly like Washington's. George Washington, Thomas Jefferson, and James Madison, all of Virginia, were building a country freer and more equal than that of Napoleonic Holland.

Abraham read some of the essays of Alexander Hamilton and James Madison (later to become *The Federalist Papers*) describing the checks and balances between the states and the federal government and about the restraints placed on the power of a national leader. He realized the difference between the ability of America to limit that power and the inability of Europe to do so. Europe no longer offered the promise of freedom for Abraham and his family.

There was a "Jewish" reason to consider leaving Amsterdam. His Jewish Portuguese family had been in Holland now for 300 years, since the Church expelled them from Portugal in 1497. Holland had been a haven, an accepting society. But 300 years later the Jews still lived in a ghetto, with special laws curtailing their equality.

And the rabbis, oh, the rabbis! How intolerant they had become of those seeking a life of freedom and a religion free of superstitions and constricting laws. How those rabbis coerced their flock. Look what they had done to Baruch Spinoza, the greatest philosopher of the seventeenth century, excommunicating him for having elevated reason over creed.

Then there was Uriel Acosta. The rabbis forced him to lie on the floor of their great synagogue in Amsterdam and stepped on him as a symbol that their ideas of Jewish tradition were truth, rather than his identification with the social protests of Israel's pre-exilic prophets. Abraham and Rachel loved Jewish tradition, but their Amsterdam Jewish community was too coercive and too fundamental.

They looked across the ocean to America with its promise of "liberty and equality for all." Rachel had already given birth six times, and the youngest was still just a baby. Their older children were aged fourteen, thirteen, nine, eight and five. Could they make the difficult journey with such a young family? Where should they go? Who would help them? How would they make a living?

I imagine Abraham asking Rachel: "Are you with me? Will you go with me to America? Can you manage the children when I get a job? We can sell our home for the cost of the voyage and settling in America. I have heard that there are now six Jewish congregations there already. Come with me to a city there where Jews have already established a community."

Rachel, now thirty-four years old, whose first child, Lewis, was born when she was twenty, might have responded: "I will go and leave my beloved Bernard family, for I want my children to live in freedom. But you must promise me that when we are settled, you will work to make it possible for me to care for the children."

In 1811 Abraham Levy wrote to the Beth Shalome Congregation in Richmond, Virginia, declaring that he was considering bringing his family from Amsterdam to live in their city. The congregation responded that they already had one hundred members, a few families had roots in Holland, and the Levys would be welcome. They wrote:

"You can open any kind of dry goods store. And we have customers who are moving out West. Jacob Cohen of Richmond's 'Cohen and Isaacs' hired a frontiersman named Daniel Boone to survey their holdings in the territory of Kentucky. They are looking for intelligent, literate, urban merchants to help them develop their trade. You will be able to support your family here in the great State of Virginia. Our President, James Madison of Virginia, wrote ten amendments to our Constitution, the first of which says 'Congress shall make no establishment of religion nor prohibit the free exercise thereof.' That means that we Jews have the same freedom of religion as our Christian neighbors, and Christianity will never become a political or military force in this country."

In 1815, in the spirit of biblical Abraham and Sarah, my ancestors went forth from their country, their birthplace, and their family's traditions, from Amsterdam, Holland, toward "the Land that I will show you," toward Richmond, Virginia.

After they sold their Amsterdam home, Rachel announced she was again pregnant, so they altered their plans and sailed only to England, where Isaac was born and Lewis got married. Thus, with children aged one to nineteen, they once again pulled up stakes and set sail for the New World.

As the ship sailed up the James River toward Richmond, Abraham brought them together on deck to show them the reason they were making this difficult journey. There was Jamestown, the first settlement of Europeans in the New World. And just behind it was The College of William and Mary at Williamsburg. He told them this was the birthplace of the Statutes of Religious Freedom in America and the concept of the separation of church and state; that it was here that President James Madison had written the Bill of Rights. Then he told them about Yorktown at the mouth of the York River, just north of their voyage, where Washington had defeated the British army to win the American War of Independence.

The ship docked at the Richmond terminal in October with its brilliant fall foliage. The Levy family's faith in this pioneering journey was reinforced by the sight of the magnificent Virginia State Capitol at the top of the hill. It was designed by the state's genius architect, Thomas Jefferson, based on classical Roman temple architecture.

They were immediately welcomed by Kahal Kodesh Beth Shalome Synagogue. The Jewish community now numbered more than 130 members. Its presence in Virginia had been a primary reason for the Levys' decision to settle in Richmond, and they quickly became active members. Abraham was to become one of the forces behind the development of the congregation. One source says he was a religious man: "Mr. Levy helped them buy a new Temple (he put up most of the money) and used it as a residence!" Two of his sons, Jacob and Isaac, became presidents of Beth Shalome.

Abraham went into the dry goods business, starting as an itinerant salesman in the western part of the state, but within two years he opened his own store in Richmond. That store produced the income to support several children, grandchildren, and beyond. During their years in England, the Levy family had learned English, which made it possible for them to integrate quickly into both the Jewish and the general communities in Richmond.

Not long after their arrival, Abraham was invited, with other Virginia newcomers, as guests of former President James and First Lady Dolly Madison to Montpelier, their western Virginia plantation home. Abraham told his host how important his essays on democratic government had been to him in deciding to move his children to America, and especially to Virginia.

Abraham kept his word to Rachel that he would make it possible to care for their children in the New World. Virginia was then a slave state. Four of the first five presidents were from Virginia, and all of them had large plantations that used slave labor. So it was not surprising that Rachel and Abraham solved the problem of caring for their large family in similar fashion. Abraham's "woman Peggy" cared for the children and then served Rachel and Abraham long after the children had grown and left home. Regarding Peggy, Abraham wrote in his will, "…My personal estate, except for my woman Peggy, shall be sold by my executor…My woman Peggy has been a faithful servant, and to secure her comfort the remainder of her life, I authorize her to choose which of my children she will live with. I give her to the child she may so select on condition she shall be treated with kindness and humanity, and to secure her comfort, I do hereby give to the child taking Peggy the sum of one hundred dollars."

Just imagine, five thousand miles at sea with seven children, including a baby. It took a pioneering spirit and a readiness to face the unknown to make such a journey. But make it they did, never looking back. And they succeeded. In retrospect, with the increase in both secular and religious anti-Semitism and the eventual annihilation of virtually all the Dutch Jews by the Nazis, that pioneering move by Abraham and Rachel Levy in 1814 saved what was to become thousands in our family from suffering and death. Even more profoundly, that journey to Virginia has produced amazing people in the succeeding nine generations.

1841: A Pioneering Spirit, From Virginia to Texas

As a boy and youth growing up in Houston, I did not know that my family had been there for one hundred years before we arrived in 1941. Born in Holland in 1799, my great-great-great-grandfather, Lewis A. Levy, was the oldest of Abraham and Rebecca's children. In 1817, while the family was temporarily residing in England, this eighteen-year-old took Mary Bernard, a seventeen-year-old Dutch-born cousin, to be his bride. After arriving in Richmond, Lewis worked with his father selling dry goods to the farmers and plantation owners in western Virginia. By 1825, the Levys had opened their first store. Abraham Levy and Sons (later Levy Brothers) on Main Street was a landmark well into the twentieth century.

Lewis and Mary wanted their own independent life. In 1826 they left with their four children in order to establish a business in the thriving sugarcane industry in New Orleans, Louisiana. The French had begun to grow sugarcane in Louisiana in the 1750s, and by the time of the Louisiana Purchase in 1803, huge areas of the territory had been planted. Our family spirit of pioneering emerged once again, as Lewis saw the possibility of a fine business in this former French and Spanish territory with its new culture and different life. The Levys settled in, and my great-great-grandmother, Elizabeth, was born there in 1838. Lewis's business thrived during the twelve years they lived in New Orleans.

In 1831, Lewis was joined by his brother, Dr. Albert Moses Levy, who had recently been widowed and had left his infant daughter in Richmond to be raised by his brother and sister-in-law, Jacob and Martha. Dr. Albert, as he was known, tried to establish himself as a surgeon in New Orleans. He was unhappy with his life as a single man, so in October 1835, he answered the urgent call of Stephen F. Austin and Sam Houston for volunteers to join the Texas settlers in their struggle for independence from Mexico.

Every volunteer was promised a plot of land following the war. In response, a group of Americans met in a coffee house on October 13, 1835, in New Orleans and formed the "New Orleans Grays," the first out-of-state volunteers to fight for Texas independence. The two Levy brothers attended that meeting. Dr. Albert decided to pick up stakes and join the volunteers. He tried to convince his brother, Lewis, to join him, but Lewis's growing family and business kept him there. The Grays quickly headed West, with thirty-six men, muskets, and four cannons, to join the Texian army (referring to residents of Mexican Texas). They marched 250 miles to Gonzales, where the rag-tag Texians pushed back the Mexican army. Dr. Albert, the only physician, was appointed Surgeon General of the entire Texian army. He marched to Bexar (San Antonio) and fought in the battle to take the city, which was won on December 11, 1835. He was cited for bravery. Here, in a letter to his sister, is his description of the five days of battle:

> *After regular storming of the Alamo for five days and nights, we achieved a victory unparalleled in history, obtained by 225 disorganized and undisciplined men armed with muskets and bayonets against a well-fortified fort with thirty pieces of cannon. Our men fought like devils. I worked in the ditches addressing the sick and the wounded. I crossed a street where more than 200 muskets shot at me. I cheered the men and assisted the officers for five days and nights, running about without a coat, dirty and ragged, but, thank God, escaped uninjured.*

Dr. Albert did not take part in any further ground battles and was not in San Antonio for the battle the Texians lost at the Alamo. Instead, he was sent to Matagorda, on the Texas coast, to sail on the Texas schooner *Independence,* which fought the Mexican fleet trying to blockade the coast. The *Independence* was captured, and he was imprisoned in Mexico. He escaped with the help of sympathetic jailers, swam across the Rio Grande River, and walked the 175 miles from the border to Matagorda.

After Texas declared independence from Mexico in 1836, five years before it became a state, Dr. Albert was awarded a grant of some two thousand acres of land "for enrolling himself in the ranks of free men assembled to oppose tyranny and oppression." In March 1836, he settled in Matagorda, halfway between the Mexican border and the basin that was soon to be known as the city of Houston, named after Sam Houston.

Lewis Levy remained in New Orleans. In 1838, however, he and Mary fled New Orleans during a horrible yellow fever epidemic, moving with their seven children to Galveston, Texas. Because of Dr. Albert's contribution to the Texas War of Independence, General Sam Houston, now the president of the Texas Republic, offered to sell Lewis fifteen acres in newly founded Houston for twenty-five cents an acre. Thus it was in 1840 Lewis and Mary became the first permanent Jewish residents of Houston. Their land started at Allen's Landing, where the White Oak Bayou bends into the Buffalo Bayou to form what was to become downtown Houston.

Lewis became one of the distinguished businessmen in the early history of the city, opening shop as a merchant and dealer in land certificates. He became a leader in Houston, organizing a collection for victims of the yellow fever epidemic in New Orleans. He was the first chairman of the Houston Hebrew Benevolent Society, dedicated to the care of poor Jews throughout Texas. He spearheaded the establishment of the Houston Jewish Cemetery and was instrumental in the formation of Beth Israel, Texas's first Jewish congregation. He also assisted in procuring from Europe the first Texan capable of acting as *chazan* (cantor), *shochet* (ritual slaughterer), *mohel* (circumcisor), and *baal korei* (Torah chanter).

In 1850, as a result of the oppression of Jews in the Austro-Hungarian Empire, Lewis Levy wrote a letter to the *Asmonean,* a Jewish newspaper in New York. The following are excerpts from that letter:

> *Ever since...the establishment of the Christian church as the religion of a State, the Jews have suffered persecution in those countries where the church was established by law...But a change has come over the world. In almost all parts of Europe, the Jew has of late had some respite from his suffering, and his equality to the rest of the citizens has been acknowledged. Only where despotism governs is it considered good policy to oppress the Children of Abraham....Austria dares to lay the burden of the expenses of the Hungarian War upon the shoulders of the oppressed Jews of that empire. But who can force them to stay in these countries?...America will bid them welcome!...A whole continent would be open to them to settle where they choose...They can buy in their own name the very day after their arrival as much land as they choose; their children are not forced into the military; they have the right after five years to give their votes in the choice of all civil offices; and the taxes to be paid on their property are merely nominal to support the most liberal government upon earth....In our own State thousands of acres of land can be bought...for the small sum of from 25 cents to $1 per acre... Indeed, I would not exchange my 15 acre lot, with the house on it, and the garden around it, which I possess in the city of Houston, for all the thrones and hereditary dominions of the Emperors of Austria or Russia.*

Thirty-two years had passed since he sailed up the James River to establish a family in the new land. He had learned the lessons of those giants of Virginia and brought them to the frontier of Texas. Lewis Levy, immigrant Jew, was now a proud and wise Jewish American leader.

It is sobering to consider that if the Jews in the Austro-Hungarian Empire had heeded his call, they, too, would have flourished as America developed. Instead, ninety years later, Adolf Hitler murdered most of those who remained. But in 1861, Lewis Levy, sixty-two years old, died as an honored pioneer of the City of Houston. Mary lived to be eighty-eight. Her grave in Brenham, Texas, is considered a Texas Heritage Site by the Daughters of the Texas Republic. Lewis and Mary's descendants have lived in freedom and security for 176 years throughout Texas in Austin, Bastrop, Beaumont, Brenham, Chapel Hill, Corsicana, Dallas, Elgin, El Paso, Galveston, Houston, Lubbock, Luling, Schulenburg, and Wichita Falls.

CHAPTER ONE
ROOTS

PART 3
Call Me Tex

Seventeen Years Old and On My Own

I did not plan on becoming a pioneer in the tradition of my ancestors, but there it was, right on the table. My acceptance into the freshman class of Brandeis University for the fall of 1950. In high school I had studied three years of mechanical, machine, and architectural drawing, and I had already been accepted into Rice Institute (later to become Rice University) in Houston with the aspiration to study architecture and engineering. My whole life had been centered around Houston.

That was not to happen. Dr. Abram Sachar, the president of the newly founded Brandeis University near Boston, came to Houston in the spring of 1950 looking for a student. He wanted "geographic distribution" in the next freshman class, as the two first classes were too heavily weighted with second-generation Eastern European Jewish students from Boston and New York. Several people recommended me to him, and in one conversation, he changed my life.

He hit me in four crucial places—financial support, Judaic studies, baseball, and a pioneering adventure. Dr. Sachar offered me a full scholarship for room, board, and tuition; he convinced me that the best scholars in Jewish Studies were already at Brandeis; he promised me a serious experience in baseball; and he pointed out that Boston was a different culture two thousand miles from home. I was intrigued with the offer. My parents, who always backed whatever direction my life took, gave me their blessings, and I decided to give it a try. So, on September 5, 1950, this seventeen-year-old naïve and idealistic teenager boarded the train with one Samsonite suitcase for what was to become my first great pioneering experience.

Arriving on campus, quite apprehensive, I was greeted by C. Ruggles Smith, the Director of Admissions and a New Englander wearing a bow tie. I had never met a C. Ruggles Smith type before. He was formal but friendly, commanding but comforting, efficient but encouraging. He told me that my dorm room was in "Ridgewood." He would take me there, warning me not to be alarmed or discouraged; it was the name for a new dormitory complex not yet finished. We walked to what turned out to be the "Ridgewood construction site." Workers frantically finishing construction was my first sight of my new home. Beyond the bustle was a strikingly beautiful, modern set of buildings with a central courtyard set in the woods. I loved the architecture and moved from apprehension to excitement as we approached my room.

"Where is the door?" I asked C. Ruggles.

"They haven't arrived yet," he responded.

I set down my suitcase and surveyed the room. The bed was there, but in three separate pieces. I looked for a not-to-be-found desk and chair, but by this time, I had already gotten the picture. So, I thanked the admissions director for his personal welcome, and then he departed.

Immediately following, Harry Berkan, my upper-classman roommate, entered the room. "Samuels?" he inquired.

"You can call me Bob," I responded.

"Oh, no, we've decided to call you Tex. We wondered what a Texan that wanted to study here would look like. All we know about Texas is what we see in Western movies." I understood immediately why Dr. Sachar had recruited me, and I felt a responsibility as a Texan to represent an authentic America with deep roots in a culture different from my new home in New England.

Brandeis was a magical place. The university was small, rural, and bursting with nature's fall colors. It had an authentic Irish medieval castle with pie-shaped dorm rooms in a turret, a dining room transformed from a dissecting room in its former life as a medical school, a wishing well, and a huge barn for the library. The campus was being built daily with energy and urgency. There were only 171 students in the freshman class and even fewer in the two classes ahead of us.

Mentors at Brandeis

Houston's San Jacinto High School was a large municipal school that was probably a six on a scale of one-to-ten in regard to academic excellence. It was too easy for me. I had a job every morning from 4:30 to 6:30, and I was on the baseball field every afternoon from 2:30 to 5:00. In an excellent school, more demanding of its better students, I would not have been able to spend so much time outside of studying and reading. I did all my homework in a forty-five-minute study hall. Yet when I graduated at age seventeen, I was among the top twenty students in a class of four hundred. That school did not demand enough of its students.

Consequently, when classes began at Brandeis, I quickly realized I was out of my league. My classmates from Boston Latin and from New York's Bronx Science were right in their element. They had already read many of the texts in the social sciences and humanities that were a revelation for me.

I realized that if I were to survive, I would need to find a method of study that would help me catch up on the learning material, absorb and integrate the knowledge required. I went to Dr. Sachar, who was delighted I had turned to him. He suggested I outline each subject, searching for the essence, and then discuss it with fellow students in the class. Dr. Sachar offered to critique one of my outlines for a humanities course. This was seminal mentoring by the university's president of a talented but undereducated freshman. It was a key learning strategy I developed at Brandeis and honed throughout my life. Whenever I have been faced with an intellectual, managerial, social, or economic problem, solutions have come to me by carefully analyzing the issue in a one-page outline and then discussing it with colleagues and/or my wife.

How fortunate I was to also have a true intellectual Jewish mentor in Professor Nahum Glatzer. With only one elective course in my freshman year, I chose a course in the Judaic Studies Department, "Job and the Problem of Suffering." I did not know then that the instructor was one of the brilliant German Jewish intellectuals who had been saved in the 1930s by Dr. Avraham Biran, the outstanding founder of the prestigious Reali School in Haifa, nor that Dr. Sachar had invited him, together with other German-trained scholars, to join the fledgling first faculty of this new university. Dr. Glatzer spoke in a low voice and in measured syllables with a distinct German accent. But as we studied Job, Isaiah, the New Testament, Milton, Dostoevsky, Baeck, and Buber, Dr. Glatzer's scholarship and deep humanity emerged and triumphed.

As I progressed in my knowledge in Judaics, Dr. Glatzer became my teacher, guide, and friend. Often he would invite me to his home to discuss a new book by Abraham Joshua Heschel, to elicit my doubts that God answers prayer, or to help me frame my intellectual autobiography. "I love learning Bible, Dr. Glatzer," I once told him, "But Talmud is too esoteric for me." "Forget Jewish Law for now," he said, "but look for the universal ethical principles in the midrash." I have been searching for and teaching Judaism's universal ethical principles in our rabbinic texts ever since. Dr. Glatzer was, indeed, my teacher and my mentor in every sense.

Inspired Learning from the Best

In that first year, all 170 freshman students sat at the feet of Professor Max Lerner, who had become famous writing for the *New York Post,* due to his keen observations of social and intellectual trends in America. Each week he distributed mimeographed pages he had written on "America as a Civilization," material that several years later would become a bestseller by that name. Dr. Lerner sat on the edge of the stage in Seifer Hall with his omnipresent "book-ends," Dr. Leonard Levy, a civil libertarian, and Dr. Bernard Rosenberg, a critic of American culture and American Jewry. They delved into the issue of the day and then opened it up to discussion.

Afterwards, I sat in the library or, if it was a clear day, by the "wishing well," analyzing those presentations. The conflict became clear between the basic correctness of America's political and economic system, which would provide more and more opportunities for my fellow students and me, while the same processes often uncovered bitter ideological conflicts: wide disparities between conservatives and liberals, rich and poor, and whites and blacks; religious bigotry; corruption and lawlessness. Dr. Lerner and his colleagues challenged my sense of social responsibility and justice. It was here that I began to develop my life-long admiration for an American civilization that aspires to provide every person with a life of freedom, respect, and satisfaction. However, this sometimes conflicts with the need for restraints against egotism and the abuse of power.

Dr. Leonard Levy, still in his twenties, was destined to become one of America's preeminent scholars on civil liberties. He taught a course on the Bill of Rights, concentrating on the First Amendment "Wall of Separation" between religion and state, on the freedom of speech, and on the Fifth Amendment's guarantee against self-incrimination. My life has been particularly influenced by the lack of that Wall of Separation in Israel. I have had to fight the politicization of religion, religious inequality, and coercion throughout my career here.

Professor Frank Manuel taught eighteenth-century intellectual history. Dr. Manuel sat on the edge of his desk, his partially amputated leg, a casualty of the 1948 War of Independence, swinging back and forth, and his deep voice proclaiming the rights of man. He taught us that seventeenth-century Baruch Spinoza's revolutionary pantheism, for which he was persecuted by the Amsterdam rabbis, was the wellspring for such seventeenth- and eighteenth-century philosophers as John Locke, Jean Jacques Rousseau, David Hume, and Montesquieu. Their humanistic thought slowly became the philosophic bedrock for the Enlightenment Period. Their ideas countered long-standing theological beliefs, released Europeans and Americans from the dictates and coercions of medieval religion, led to the American and French revolutions, and eventually brought about the collapse of the monarchies and the birth of nation–states based on the will of the individual, the rights of man, and the governmental separation of powers.

Frank Manuel was a bitter man, frustrated by the failure of those new nation–states to gather the political will necessary. Nonetheless, his keen intellect and his knowledge of the authors of modern thought, the creators of the Emancipation, helped me begin a lifelong search for the sources of truth and a human contract based on equality despite differences. Throughout my managerial career, I have often seen him almost lift himself off the table as he demanded honesty and human freedom, a reminder that I am a link in a very long chain of struggle for social justice. Then I return to the sources and renew both the vision of those intellectually brave thinkers and of my own resolve not to compromise principles learned long ago at my family table.

I have often thought of the permanent contributions that Brandeis made to my life. One of them, certainly, is the ability to write (readers will judge this for themselves). Not having the background to pass off the freshman course in English composition, I sat in Dr. John Wight's class not knowing what to expect. He gave us an assignment to write a one-page essay on any subject, so I did mine on "Baseball as a Metaphor for Life." Two days later, my paper was in my mailbox with more red marks than blue. It was a disaster in syntax, form, spelling, punctuation, and content. I had to rewrite it and turn it in with my next weekly essay. They were returned two days later, again full of red-marked corrections. Thus it was throughout the entire year. Often, in addition to the new weekly essay, I would be correcting up to five previous ones until I slowly began to improve. By January, as the trees lost most of their leaves, my essays began to lose their red marks. By May, the essays started to get compliments. I often thought of the sheer quantity of essays Dr. Wight had to work on in a period of five or six days. I am, however, profoundly grateful to him and to Brandeis for teaching me English composition well enough to be able to write and to review and advise my Leo Baeck English teachers and administrators.

Brandeis was a place of culture. Here, too, the university would mold me by directing my artistic and cultural tastes. I had naturally grown to love the shapes and concepts of architecture. Each new building erected during those four exciting years inspired me to pigeonhole the architect, engineer, or contractor who appeared as the buildings named Shapiro, Ullman, Usen, Usdan, Hamilton, Marcus, Olin-Sang, and Schwartz began to appear on campus, often replacing utilitarian names like the library, classroom #5, and auditorium.

My exposure to culture continued through Professor Leo Bronstein, a remarkable interpreter of art. He was a bit strange in behavior but very artistic and knowledgeable about a wide variety of forms and national traditions of art. His lectures have been part of my artistic palate in each art museum and gallery I have visited over the years.

But it was two singular musical personalities who have made a lasting imprint on my soul. On meeting Dr. Sachar on the campus one day, he asked me if I played a musical instrument. When I answered in the negative, he suggested I take the "Introduction to Music" course with Edwin Bodky, then the only music professor. I signed up for the course without realizing the personality of the musician Dr. Sachar had brought to Brandeis to inaugurate a music department. Dr. Bodky was a short, stodgy man with a thick German accent who had a prodigious knowledge of classical music. He was an outstanding harpsichordist and pianist. He would stand on the stage facing the piano with his head turned to the right toward the class, then rush to the piano and play *anything* mentioned in our lesson. He was full of energy, a mentor for the few musicians in our class, but also kind and encouraging to those of us who were music initiates. When I turned in an emotional interpretation of a Mozart symphony, Dr. Bodky graded it as seriously as if I had found an undiscovered Mozart composition. He was so anxious to impart his love of music and so kind. He loved us, and we returned his love with respect and admiration.

The other musical personality was perhaps the twentieth century's best-known American musician, Leonard Bernstein. As the academic year 1951–52 began, we students did not know that Dr. Sachar had recruited him the previous summer at the Tanglewood Music Festival in the beautiful Berkshires of Western Massachusetts. Bernstein had just been appointed the musical director of the New York Philharmonic and was thus not able to accept Sachar's invitation to be an on-campus faculty member. Realizing this, Dr. Sachar suggested he visit Brandeis once a month and develop a creative arts festival for the first commencement in June 1952. When Bernstein agreed, Dr. Sachar charged into action, as was his wont, getting a donor to fund the building of a creative arts amphitheater and that first festival. It made Brandeis one of the most exciting places to be a student. Once a month Bernstein would appear on campus, coming directly from Logan Airport, as 300 students anxiously awaited this intoxicating musical genius. He would jog down the aisle, leap onto the stage, run to the open piano, hit one chord, look out at us, and smile. There was electricity in the air as he would identify the chord and then proceed to use it as the base for musical literature through the ages. He was charming, brilliant, creative, and charismatic. One felt that he was experimenting with the vast body of musical knowledge within. It was the most exciting that learning could be. I was torn between taking notes and watching him dance while elegantly playing pieces from Bach to Broadway on the piano. Those magical moments made life at Brandeis an even rarer treat.

Dr. Sachar was a genius. While his faculty was still small, he decided to enrich our experience by bringing a group of amazing personalities to campus to speak to the senior class. Those evenings were unforgettable as Margaret Mead, Robert Frost, Leo Szilard, Archibald MacLeish, Nathan Straus, Jr., Norman Thomas, Ludwig Lewisohn, and others told us of the turning points in their lives, the important decisions they had to make, their successes and their failures. We gathered on the floor in the Castle commons room. Dr.

Sachar moderated, briefly introducing each personality in historic context. Faculty members in that person's field would have been invited by Dr. Sachar to give us a reading list, to sit with us during the evening, and then to form a faculty-student panel to discuss the evening's issues and values the following week.

Alvin Johnson, the 80-year-old non-Jewish economist who founded the New School for Social Research, told us of how he had saved German Jewish scholars from the Nazis. *Norman Thomas,* six-time Socialist candidate for the Presidency, pacifist, and founder of the ACLU, told us why he objected to America going to war in both World Wars I and II; why he believed the Jewish People should recreate themselves, but that Zionism as an anti-Arab structure would fail. In spite of his defeats, he told us he was optimistic. "I am not a champion of lost causes," he said, "but of causes not yet won." *Leo Szilard,* the Hungarian physicist who conceived of the nuclear chain reaction in the year Hitler came to power, came to America, and created the Manhattan Project, told us of how he had unsuccessfully pleaded with President Truman's administration to do an atomic *test* explosion to be observed by the Japanese in order to get their surrender before Hiroshima. *Margaret Webster,* the highly successful first female producer and director of Broadway theater and opera, anguished over the trauma of Senator Joseph McCarthy's hounding of her. *Nathan Strauss, Jr.,* told us of the powerful pull of the Jews of Palestine on his father and how he, the son, had brought Anne Frank's father to work at Macy's before World War II. *Robert Frost* assured us that "The Road Not Taken" was only a description of a winter's trip through the snow of New Hampshire and was not meant as a metaphor for life's choices. We told *him* that once he gave us the poem, it was ours from which to learn and extrapolate life, irrespective of his original intent.

So it was that Brandeis University put before us giants of society to reflect on their journeys and to see ourselves through their choices, their experiences, and their values. These encounters provided me with life-changing experiences.

Sports at Brandeis and a Big Decision

At my Houston interview, Dr. Sachar had promised me that I would be challenged and that I would find satisfaction on the baseball diamond at Brandeis. How could he promise this when prior to 1950 there were no practice fields on campus? But Dr. Sachar seemed to fulfill *all* his impossible promises during the twenty years of his founding presidency. He convinced Benny Friedman, the immortal Michigan quarterback, to become Director of Physical Education, and lo and behold, upon my arrival on campus, the baseball field was under construction. Friedman hired one of the groundskeepers as our coach, but Walter Mahoney was indeed a baseball *maven*. Baseball is a springtime sport, so I decided to go out for a fall sport, soccer, in order to stay in shape until the ground cleared of snow and the beautiful trees on campus began to produce leaves once again, a sign in America that the "national pastime" was up and running for a new season.

I played both soccer and baseball all four years, had endless energy, ran hard on the soccer field, but starred on the diamond. Baseball may be the only skill that is natural for me, perhaps because I started it so early in life with Uncle Roy. Upon graduation, I was offered a contract with the Philadelphia Phillies farm system, but I had decided to enroll in the Reform rabbinic seminary, Hebrew Union College-Jewish Institute of Religion (HUC-JIR), and they pressed me to begin my studies. There was no financial incentive in signing to play with other good college baseball players in those days, so professional baseball passed me by. Semi-pro and amateur leagues have given me much pleasure through the years, but those intensive practices and games at Brandeis were pure joy for me.

Social Life and Leadership

Brandeis was so new and so raw in those early 1950s. There were few social clubs, but if you wanted one, all you had to do was get a couple of friends to join you, so all of a sudden Brandeis had a French Club, or a Mountain Climbing Club, or a Sno-Ball Dance, or a Quarry BBQ or a Theater Group ("Hi-Charlie").

Beginning my sophomore year, I roomed in an off-campus house with Bill Marsh, a very talented cartoonist. He decided to run for student body president. Living so far from home, I was *always* on campus, and "Tex" became well-known. Students saw me play baseball and soccer. They saw me in student theatrical productions. They saw me driving students around campus and into Waltham for pizza in my 1935 Plymouth coupe with a rumble-seat. My classmates liked me, so they elected me to the position of class president alongside Bill Marsh.

And so it was that our Ridgewood cottage room became the hub for student politics on campus. Bill and I worked with the administration to help solve students' problems and logistical issues on campus. We dovetailed with the editors of the *Justice*, the student newspaper, to test the student temperature on issues such as race, social justice, and sexuality, to ensure that if the *Justice* published some concern, it was not going to blow up in our faces. My close relationship with Dr. Sachar was instrumental in finding the fine line between voicing our opinions on significant academic, political, economic, and social problems and taking responsibility for that voice.

The class presidency brought with it the high honor of leading the processional at our graduation and speaking on behalf of the class at the 1954 commencement exercises. Here is an excerpt from that speech:

> *Our eighteenth-century philosophers who gave us the Enlightenment agreed with our eighth- and seventh-century (Before the Common Era) Pre-Exilic Hebrew Prophets that leaders have the responsibility to see that all of God's creatures are treated with respect and decency; that they stamp out corruption, greed, and avarice from their own lives; that they lift up the fallen and free the captives; that they give bread to the hungry and shelter to the homeless. Many of our leaders live such lives, such as our Brandeis President, his counselors and advisors, his faculty, and his workers. We have been blessed to be their charges these four years. But many leaders do not have those universal values, and they stain the Land. It will be our task to go forward with the knowledge and principles we have imbued within these academic halls, on these playing fields, on this precious piece of New England land called Brandeis of Waltham; to internalize what we have learned—to use our heads, our hearts, and our hands, as we wrote in our yearbook, to carefully take our world apart and to put it back together in a new and better way; to leap into the breach, in whatever field we master, and to make a difference. We go forward from this day to make a difference.*

I left Brandeis ready to make a difference.

My Lifelong Partner

Twelve-year-old Annette Colish attended my bar mitzvah, but I didn't know it. I was a Jewish American whose family had been in Texas for over a hundred years; she was an American Jew whose father was a

Conservative rabbi born in Lithuania. I was a Boy Scout in a Baptist troop; she was a Zionist who went to Jewish camps. I went to the Saturday Morning Fun Club at the Alabama movie theater; she went to Shabbat morning services at her father's Conservative synagogue. I went to the YMCA on Sunday morning to attend free activities; she went to religious school. But at age fourteen, I joined a Jewish youth group, and there we met.

As a teenager, I became more Jewish, and there she was. I loved my father, who was teaching me Jewish ethics; she loved her father, who was a symbol of Jewish tradition and Zionist fervor. It is a tale of mid-twentieth century American Jewish kids, living in freedom with the power of choice. We could perpetuate our parents' way of life, and we could change or abandon it. As we moved into full adolescence in our high school years, it was this freedom to choose that brought Annette and Bob together. We loved our teenage life; we loved to dance; we loved the great outdoors; we loved sport; we loved to learn; and we grew to love each other. That love took time, and it took a change of venue. I went East to college, then she went East to college. I dated other girls, she dated other boys, and we dated each other. Something way down deep was happening. I was learning and experiencing being more Jewish, learning to love and respect her father and his deep Jewishness. Annette was learning to love my parents and yearning for the deep joy and happiness she found in the Samuels family. American freedom to love whom you wanted in spite of differences in background and culture pulled us together. We were happy together; we learned from each other; we meshed. We had tender sex; we trusted each other; we felt the warmth and tingle of touch. She loved my stepping up to the plate; I loved her musical talent on the violin. It was a good start for a lifelong romance. Both of us were daring, ready for something new.

Both of us had pioneering DNA. We reveled in challenge. It was our birthright; it had been in my family for 150 years, beginning with my ancestors' pioneering journey across Europe to the fledgling country of America in 1800.

CHAPTER ONE
ROOTS

PART 4
A Pioneering Spirit, From Boston to Cincinnati to Jerusalem

Stirrings of Zionism

I entered Brandeis University in 1950, the third class of Brandeis. The University had been founded two years earlier, in 1948, the same year that the Jewish *yishuv* (settlement) in Palestine, having won the War of Independence, established the first Jewish State since the Romans destroyed the Temple in Jerusalem 1,878 years before. Many Jewish American World War II veterans had gone to Palestine as volunteers to fight in the War of Independence. They were called *Machal, (Mitnadvey Chutz L'aretz),* a Hebrew acronym for "foreign volunteers."

When the Israel-Arab armistice was signed, many of these *Machal* veterans returned to the States where Congress had passed the G.I. Bill. The United States showed its gratitude to the veterans who had helped defeat the Nazis and the Japanese by offering these men and women a free university education. This wise act of a grateful nation provided an opportunity for thousands of veterans to acquire an education and at the same time produced young men and women who would go on to create a sound middle-class economic and social base for America.

Four of those young men came to Brandeis to study in those first years. As a child, I was profoundly affected by World War II: the stories about heroism and death; the collecting of metal, rubber, and tinfoil for the war effort; the Jewish refugee family living next door; my father working all night building ships for the war; the war films we watched. As a teenager, I became aware of the Jewish fight for independence in Palestine and the desperate attempts of the Jewish refugees to get to Palestine. There I was at Brandeis, in the dorms, the dining rooms, and the local pizza pub with those veteran Jewish fighters who fascinated me with their first-hand stories from Israel. They retold their experiences of breaking through the Arab barrier around Jerusalem, flying David Ben-Gurion into besieged Jerusalem via a Piper Cub, and freeing an encircled kibbutz from the Egyptian army marching toward Tel Aviv.

In May 1951, during my freshman year, David Ben-Gurion visited the Brandeis campus. He was introduced by Dr. Sachar as the most powerful leader of the Jewish People and the most important leader in the creation of the new Jewish State. Zionism was a powerful force then. Following the realization that a third of our People had been annihilated in Europe, the Western world felt an obligation to help the Jewish People settle the 600,000 refugees left in Europe and the hundreds of thousands of Sephardic Jews living in Arab countries in North Africa and the Middle East.

Ben-Gurion said that Israel and Brandeis had been established simultaneously, and it was wise for young American Jews to study at Brandeis, "but only in order to prepare for *aliyah*, for once the Jewish State has been established, the only place for Jews today is in our own culture in our own Land." I listened thoughtfully. It had been a Reform rabbi, Judah Magnes, who had been the first Chancellor of the Hebrew University, established in Jerusalem in 1925. I determined that I would go there to experience this miracle of Jewish rebirth and to study at the University.

In June 1954, following graduation from Brandeis, I began my rabbinical studies, spending the summer in an *ulpan* (intensive Hebrew language course) sponsored by HUC-JIR. The *ulpan* took place in Towanda, a tiny town in the rolling hills of Pennsylvania. My teacher, Stephen Schafer, was a senior rabbinic student at the time and one of the few devoted Zionist students. He encouraged me to go to Israel to study in a Hebrew-speaking environment. He believed I needed that kind of Hebrew background in order to be a serious graduate student in Jewish texts. My non-Zionist professors at HUC-JIR disagreed. They counseled that I must finish my Bachelor of Hebrew Letters degree of two years of study before I would be allowed a leave of absence, so I went to Cincinnati in the fall of 1954 for my first year of rabbinic studies. The College felt that a good grasp of Biblical and Rabbinic Hebrew would enhance my Israeli experience. Subsequent history, however, has shown that Rabbi Schafer was correct. Now, and for the past forty-five years or more, the College has demanded that all incoming students spend their first year of rabbinic studies in Israel.

I used those two years to prepare for my first trip to Israel. On June 12, 1955, Annette's graduation day from Harvard, her father, Rabbi Nathan Colish, and my rabbi, Robert Kahn, officiated at our wedding at Temple Emanu El in Houston.

Two days later in Cincinnati we began Camp Cincio, a summer day camp for Jewish boys that Joe Goldman, a rabbinic school colleague, and I founded with an initial investment of $25 each. It was an instant success. The following summer we added a similar camp for girls called Camp Cinciette and combined the two camps, now one hundred children, for two four-week sessions. The kids and their parents loved the combination of outdoor activities along with programs of Jewish content.

I did not realize it at the time, but between that camp and the seventh grade class I taught at the Isaac Mayer Wise Temple Sunday School, I was gathering experience for what was to become my life-long passion, creating educational experiences combining the values of the Emancipation, Jewish tradition, and a Buberian I-Thou relationship for Jewish learners. We taught the kids about the American and Jewish values of freedom, justice, learning, worship, and social responsibility. The campers were encouraged to excel in learning, help other campers, respect common people that we met along the way, and take leadership roles. The kids expected the four weeks to be just fun, but we also strove to inculcate values for life. Throughout my career, I have searched for similar methods for teaching the values of the Hebrew prophets and the eighteenth-century philosophies: social justice and loving human relationships.

Joe and I each made enough profit to carry us through the next academic year. During the second year, Annette and I had additional jobs, and we saved the summer money for our 1956–57 year in Israel. HUC agreed to my leave-of-absence, so in September 1956, having completed my Bachelor of Hebrew Letters degree, we sailed from New York to Naples on the *SS Independence* and then to Haifa on the new Israeli ZIM ship, the *SS Israel*. It was to become a two-year honeymoon that changed our lives.

We were the first married couple from HUC-JIR to go to Israel for a study year. We registered for an *ulpan* in Givataim, a sleepy village-type suburb of Tel Aviv with unpaved roads and chicken coops behind most houses. The *ulpan* was ill-suited for us both. Annette was a beginning Hebrew student, but with her musical ear and excellent university training, she wanted to progress faster than the new immigrants in her class. For me, having studied grammatical and Biblical Hebrew for two years in Cincinnati, I was put in an advanced class. I knew Hebrew grammar and could almost read texts, but I couldn't speak the language. My fellow students were Israelis who had been in the country for several years, spoke Hebrew well, but did not know how to read and write.

We decided to leave the *ulpan* and go up to Jerusalem where we found a *sabra* (Israeli-born) graduate student, Menachem Regev, who was ready to teach us an hour lesson each day. We prepared together and separately some six hours for that daily lesson. We read *LaMatchil*, the easy-Hebrew newspaper; we listened to the news broadcast in easy Hebrew; and we read prose sections of the Bible and short stories of Nobel Prize laureate S.Y. ("Shai") Agnon. We wrote a composition almost daily. Little by little, we began to hear and speak Hebrew with understanding.

We lived with an Orthodox family in Rehavia, a section of Jerusalem where many of the European Jewish intellectuals lived. The family consisted of a father, mother, three sons, and a daughter. The father was a rabbi, the head of a yeshiva. He knew I was a Reform rabbinic student and was very tolerant and accepting. The family needed the rent, so they gave us one of the three rooms in the apartment. All the children slept in one room, and the parents slept in the living room. The cot-sized bed we slept on sagged so much we put our trunk beneath it for support. The family had a boiler that was heated once a week by kindling a fire under it so that each member could shower before Shabbat. I joined the YMCA in order to take a daily shower. We heated our room with a "Friedman," a heater in the middle of the room that used kerosene supplied from a donkey-driven cart. We bought old bicycles to transport us around the city. These were one-speed, non-gearshift bikes, making it a challenge to climb the hills of Jerusalem. We had our daily hot meal at the Mensa, the student restaurant of the Hebrew University on Mamilla Street. It was an old Turkish building located next to the ten-meter high wall that separated West from East Jerusalem. For us, that was the end of Jerusalem.

Just after our arrival in 1956, the Sinai Campaign of October-November was launched. President Dwight Eisenhower and his Secretary of State, John Foster Dulles, surprised by the surreptitious bonding of England, France, and Israel, sent ships to pick up American citizens in the Middle East. Only a few American students were in Israel then, but most of them left. We decided to stay. We tried to volunteer but were told we were not needed. So we quickly went to Tzahala, a suburb of Tel Aviv, to help the Renov family with four children whose father was a pilot. We dug a huge hole in the sand behind their house to be used as a shelter in the event of an air raid.

There had been eighteen students that year in the American Students-in-Israel program of the Hebrew University, twelve of whom left. The university upheld its commitment to the six that remained. Annette and I joined them on many of their trips around the country. Readers who have participated in the Hebrew University Year-in-Israel in subsequent years will be amused to learn that in that 1956–57 academic year, the few *tiyulim* (tours) with Geography Professor Carmi were done in one large taxi.

These were tough economic years for the struggling new nation. Israel was just emerging as an agricultural country. During the Mandate (1920–48), the British had helped to develop infrastructure the *yishuv* needed, but when the State was established, it was still a very poor society. Flour, sugar, coffee, and meat were in short supply. It was a period called *Tsena* (Austerity). A resident was issued a book of stamps that in turn allowed the purchase of moderate quantities of items in short supply. We lived on a diet of eggs, tomato and cucumber salads, bread, cheese, and tea. We were given stamps for only one hundred grams of (bad) coffee per month. People dressed modestly and ate modestly.

Ben-Gurion led the nation in living humbly. Very few people had private vehicles. As prime minister, he was driven around in a ten-year-old Studebaker and, on principle, he never wore a tie. President Yitzchak Ben-Zvi lived in a simple apartment and refused to have the State build him a presidential residence as long as thousands of new immigrants were living in tents and tin huts. Israelis were beginning to research and develop products, but one lived a simple life of milk products from *Tnuva* (dairy company) and clothes from *Atta* (clothing company). The government owned most companies.

Generally, the disparity between the haves and have-nots was insignificant. Government ministers worked in the kitchen during weekend meals in their kibbutz dining halls. Although television did not get to Israel until the 1960s, other sophisticated activities were prevalent throughout the country: bookstores, lectures, concerts, folk dancing and singing nature, archeology and newspapers. Every political movement had its own ideological press.

Israel had only 600,000 Jews when it was established. By the time Annette and I arrived in 1956, the new country had already absorbed some 400,000 survivors from the camps and the forests in Europe and 800,000 Arabic-speaking Jews from North Africa and the Middle East. The process was in full swing. Israel's predominantly Ashkenazic population was dedicated to absorbing *all* these immigrant Jews. Jews in the free world, shocked by the Holocaust, were ready to finance their absorption. Moshavim (co-operative agricultural villages) were established for immigrants. Housing units were built in the cities, and development towns sprang up in the Galilee and the Negev. Schools, universities, clinics, hospitals, museums, and concert halls were mostly joint projects of the Jewish People in Israel and in the Diaspora.

It was a heady time. Could the remnants of this People recreate itself in a post-war world and establish a true democracy in the midst of an Arab people and land mass? Could Israel give equality to the hundreds of thousands of Arabs who had become citizens of the *Jewish* State? Could Ashkenazic Jews share leadership and give equality of opportunity to Sephardic Jews? These were the questions that dominated Israeli conversation in the 1950s. Annette and I *lived* those questions for two years.

Albert Einstein wrote a book on Zionism in which he offered this definition:

> *Zionism is the movement to restore in Palestine a nation which will both gather in all Jews who live in countries where they are not wanted and also develop a Jewish culture which will counter the inevitable process of assimilation of Jews who live in lands that offer them freedom.*

Einstein's definition wedded the Zionism of both Theodor Herzl and Ahad HaAm. We saw that Israel was not there to answer the needs of Holocaust survivors alone, but rather to challenge Jews to recreate our language and create an old-new culture that would contribute a revolutionary new mode of national living in the world.

Based on Israel's Declaration of Independence, we had every reason to believe that the ethics of the Hebrew prophets would be a guiding light for Israel's leaders and would shine the lamp of human liberty brightly. We believed that our sages would revive our ancient texts to create a new Jewish-democratic culture. We felt that with the need to give equal rights, privileges, and responsibilities to Israel's Arabs and to Jews from Arab lands, Israel would show other nations how we not only recreate Hebrew, but would use that language to instill in a People the words and values of social justice, civil rights, and civil liberties.

I had preached in my High Holy Days congregation in Schulenburg, Texas, on the deep significance of the Montgomery Alabama Bus Boycott, which I saw as a huge step in America's centuries-long struggle toward equality and dignity for its black citizens. Could Israel lead the way through the treatment of its Arab citizens? We were thrilled by the spirit of Israel's *chalutzim* (pioneers) and by the "can do!" attitude of Israel's leaders. We felt our background in values and our education had prepared us to participate in and to contribute to the making of Israel's social culture. In short, we were hooked.

Developing My Jewish-Israeli Identity

All societies have pockets of this and pockets of that: older people, younger people, white people, people of color, and the educated and uneducated. Israel was no different. Villages, neighborhoods, and new towns were created to provide housing, education, health facilities, and employment for Jews who came from Morocco's Atlas mountains, from the death camps in Poland, from the neighboring lands of Lebanon and Syria, from the universities in Germany, even a few from faraway North America. It was so clear to us that it was a race against time for this nascent nation to integrate the survivors with those who had been fortunate enough to come to the *yishuv* prior to 1941 and to give a respectable life to the poor and large families from Tunisia, Algeria, Morocco, Egypt, and Yemen. It was a period of the establishment of one kibbutz (agricultural collective) after another and one moshav after another. It was during a period when Hebrew *ulpan* courses were springing up like mushrooms and quickly filled with people who spoke European or Arabic languages. These participants were hoping to survive and develop themselves in the new language and culture that was being formed here.

Yediot Achronot, one of the popular afternoon newspapers, published an entire edition of the Talmud. *Maariv*, the other large circulation paper, published the six volumes of the Mishnah. When an archeologist delivered a lecture on his current excavations, hundreds, if not thousands, came. A whole nation was searching for its history and its roots in the Land. Like the poetry of the psalmist, "Truth will spring forth from the Land" (Psalm 85), the truth of ancient Jewish existence in this Land was literally coming out of the earth daily in the 1950s. Geologists, paleontologists, demographers, and biblical scholars were all searching, searching, searching; and their conclusions made for animated learning and conversation throughout the *yishuv*. It was an intoxicating time indeed, as Israelis laid the foundations for the nation and its culture in the making.

I was never a believer in an anthropomorphic god. I never saw God as a wise, bearded, old man on a cloud, "marionetting" human life and nature from above. Prayer for me had never been a plea to such a God to intervene in time and place on my behalf. Rather than appealing to "He who makes peace in the heavens" in my daily activities, and in prayer and meditation, I connected with two major currents: the stream of events following the horrendous years of the 1940s and the subsequent careful analysis some Israelis were making of life in our old-new Land. The shock for me, at age twenty-three, to encounter people who had been through the fires of hell and the relentless pressure of security in a land where Jews were not wanted by an angry, frustrated, aggressive Arab population, did not help me to develop a belief in a supernatural or a merciful God. As a developing theological student, I felt much closer to Spinoza's pantheism than to the biblical God with whom I could talk, praise, or petition. My spirituality and interest in religion came naturally from my parents' "ethical living" dinner table and Brandeis's "truth even unto its innermost parts." However, I could believe in God as the Oneness of order in the physical universe and as the Source of faith that even scientists need in order to unlock the mysteries of that order. My search was beginning, and it has never abated, to find God not in the heavens but in the miracles of nature and human nature.

The Israel of the 1950s with its socialistic agrarian life was fertile ground for such a search. I found truth in many open fields and hidden corners, in the stories and the lives of people from the four corners of the earth. August 1956 to June 1957 was one of the most formative periods for Annette and me—so much so that we decided to stay in Israel for an additional year. I asked for and received permission from HUC-JIR to extend my leave of absence. My rabbinic school partner at Camp Cincio agreed to give us half the profits from that summer, which I would return to him from the profits of the year following his ordination.

In the summer of 1957 we traveled for 110 days through 14 European countries, starting in Turkey and ending in Scotland. We bought a Lambretta, an Italian motor scooter, which we fitted for camping with a tent, ground cover, sleeping bag, rain gear, food container, and box for clothing. We borrowed $500 from Rabbi Kahn's "Good Works Fund," and that lasted us for the entire four months, including the cost of the motor scooter.

We saw a Europe still emerging from the devastation of World War II. We often pitched our tent behind a farmhouse and, through hand motions, were invited in for a hot drink and an exchange of pictures and stories. We stayed in youth hostels along great rivers, in beautiful valleys, and on the crest of high mountains. Our Lambretta slipped on the cobblestone streets of Belgium and couldn't make the steep climb on the unpaved roads ascending from Norway's fjords. Often in the mountains of Switzerland and Norway, we were unable to fold our tent in the early morning because it had frozen during the night. We met wonderful people of all ages and cultures along the way. We put on our one change of nice clothing in order to visit museums and attend concerts. No couple ever had a more meaningful and romantic honeymoon than Annette and I had on the continent of Europe in 1957.

At the end of the summer, Annette returned to Israel where she had two jobs, playing in the Jerusalem Symphony Orchestra and teaching violin at the Jerusalem Conservatory of Music. I stayed in London for the High Holy Days where I served as an assistant rabbi at the St. John's Wood Liberal Synagogue. On the day after Yom Kippur, I put my scooter on a train to Marseilles, then had it lifted onto the *SS Moledet*, a new passenger liner for the Israeli ZIM Shipping Line. It was a summer to remember, but now my real year of academic studies at the Hebrew University was to begin.

By the 1950s, the Hebrew University had collected or had trained the finest Jewish scholars in the world. In the academic year 1957–58, I had the privilege of being able to study Bible and midrash with Nechama Leibowitz, education with Ernst Simon, Kabbalah with Gershom Scholem, history with Yehezkel Kaufmann, Hebrew with Aharon Rozen, and biblical archeology with Yigael Yadin. Annette and I traveled at every opportunity with Israel's legendary guide, Zeev Vilnai, who wrote *the* authentic guidebooks, both in Hebrew and English. Dr. Vilnai became a mentor for my later guiding through Israel.

Zeev and his wife, Esther, had an open house every Shabbat afternoon. There we met some of the intellectuals and the movers and shakers of Israel. Professors Ernst Simon and Hugo Bergman introduced us to the multi-nationalist *Brit Shalom* and *Ichud* political parties they founded together with Professor Martin Buber. Naïvely, I believed that this conception of equal citizenship and pluralism would soon define Israeli society.

My learning experience with Teacher Nechama Leibowitz (she preferred Teacher to Professor) was phenomenal. She introduced me to an expanded understanding of the biblical text through the use of medieval commentators. Weekly, for the general Israeli public, she produced a mimeographed sheet that she called *gilyonot,* questions she asked on the Torah portion of the week by bringing in commentaries on an issue. I, like hundreds of Israelis, would submit my answers to her penetrating questions. Incredibly, she answered *each* respondent *every* week starting in the 1940s and lasting until the 1970s. It was a *tour de force*, but Nechama did it as a supreme mitzvah. She once said that her hundreds of students of every "size, shape, and form" were her children. I took her course at the Hebrew University on "Joseph and His Brothers" and have used her insights into the biblical narrative throughout my teaching career.

When I realized the importance of her midrashic approach to the biblical text, I began to follow her throughout Jerusalem to the Orthodox Women's Teachers' College, the Seminar for Teachers from Abroad, and the Seminar at Ein Kerem. When she realized that I was attending every lesson throughout the city, and she saw that I had a Lambretta, she asked me if I would take her from place to place, rather than her ordering a taxi. One of the beautiful experiences of my life was driving this amazing scholar of all Jewish texts, this very Orthodox woman, with her omnipresent beret tucked down to her neck and her scarf blowing in the wind, on the back of my motor scooter. She also introduced me to her husband (her father's brother) who was totally blind and knew the entire Talmud by memory. For several months I went to their home almost daily where I would read to him articles from the daily newspaper, after which he would give me a Talmud lesson.

Two last comments on that crucial year in my training. First, it was in 1957 that a number of liberal Jerusalemites, mostly *yekkes* (German-born Jews), inaugurated the first Reform congregation in Israel. It was called *HaChugim L'yahadut Mitkademet* (The Circles for Progressive Judaism). The leading figure was Shalom Ben Chorin, whose teenage son, Tovia, served as non-professional cantor (and later became an outstanding rabbi, both in Israel and later in Europe). That congregation was to become known as Har-El. Annette and I attended the first worship service. We felt thrilled and privileged to participate in this pioneering act of introducing Progressive Judaism to non-Orthodox Israelis. Secondly, I became a regular visitor to the Jerusalem bookshops, many of them specializing in Judaica. We spent half our monthly budget on the purchase of Judaica books. I collected enough books to fill a metal trunk, which I took back with me to Cincinnati to launch a serious library in Judaic Studies.

In 1958 we returned to Cincinnati so that I could prepare for examinations in several courses, thereby making up one of the two years spent in Israel. As I studied the material and took the exams, I realized I had acquired the tools for understanding Hebrew texts. Even more important, the experience of living Jewish contemporary life with all its sweetness and all its imperfections had had a profound impact on both my intellectual and spiritual life. I still loved architecture as an art but not as a life direction, for I was now totally immersed in Jewish studies and Jewish life.

Annette and I were considering returning to Israel following my ordination. Consequently, I began inquiring into Reform rabbinic positions in Israel. I was shocked to learn that only two Reform rabbis had made *aliyah*, and that had occurred many years ago. The first was Judah Leib Magnes, ordained in 1900. As a true Zionist, he went to live in Palestine in 1922. Rabbi Magnes was the only one of his generation. He did not go as a rabbi, but rather as an educator-administrator. He became the first chancellor of the Hebrew University and a devoted advocate of the creation of a bi-national state whereby both Arabs and Jews would share national tasks and build a new culture together. The second Reform rabbi to make *aliyah* was Saadia Gelb, ordained in 1946. He came as an illegal immigrant in 1947. Rabbi Gelb settled in Kibbutz Kfar Blum and became a national figure in the Labor Movement. He believed in the equality of the religious movements in Judaism but was never active in securing those rights. Thus I learned I had no predecessors who could be role models for me in bringing the message of Progressive Judaism to Israel.

What about Reform rabbis in America? Would they support my work in Israel? On the HUC-JIR faculty, I found extremely divergent views. Dr. Nelson Glueck, the president, saw Palestine-Israel primarily as a source for his archeological research and was less than encouraging to me. Dr. Eugene Mihaly was a staunch anti-Zionist. Dr. Jacob Marcus was sure I was on the wrong track and stated he would help me get a congregation appropriate to my rabbinic skills as soon as I was ready to forget my "naïve, romantic vision of the Holy Land and contribute to the work of holiness in America." Dr. Ezra Spicehandler, the only true Zionist on the faculty, was very enthusiastic.

The only rabbi in the field in 1958 who gave me a sense of purpose in Israel was Rabbi Samuel Cook, director of the National Federation of Temple Youth (NFTY), the Reform Jewish youth movement. He would become a major influence on me, both as an advocate of informal educational work with youth and as the only link to an educational institution in Israel, the Leo Baeck School.

I did some research on the relationship to Palestine of members of the Central Conference of American Rabbis (CCAR). I learned about the life of Judah Magnes and about the writings of Abba Hillel Silver and Maurice Eisendrath from their visits to *Eretz Yisrael*. Rabbi Silver, ordained in 1915, visited in 1919. He was most enthusiastic about the kibbutz pioneers who were secular intellectuals, who rejected all the dogmas and laws of religious halachah, and who, instead, chose to work the Land with their hands and be productive. Rabbi Eisendrath, ordained in 1926, was changed by his visit in 1935, mainly by the kibbutz pioneers he met. He felt that those labor pioneers were living the ethical values of Reform more than any American Reform Jews were. Rabbi Samuel Wohl, ordained in 1927, became a member of the League for Labor Palestine. In 1935, he convinced 240 out of 300 CCAR members to sign a letter of support for the League.

But it is the Columbus Platform of 1937 that was most telling for me. The CCAR had passed the Platform with the following statement: "In the rehabilitation of Palestine we behold the promise of renewed life for many of our brethren. We affirm the obligation of all Jewry to aid in its up building, not only as a haven for the oppressed, but as a center of Jewish culture and spiritual life..." I took this statement to several rabbis in large Midwest congregations. It was clear they did not see themselves or their congregants in the category of "some of our brethren." It was also clear that now, following the Holocaust and the founding of Israel, they felt an obligation to encourage their wealthy congregants to contribute to the rescue work of the United Jewish Appeal (UJA) and the Joint Distribution Committee, the health work of Hadassah and Israel's cultural and educational institutions. The anomaly was that they did not see the need for contributing to Israel's "spiritual life." The politicization of religion and the opposition to any reform within Jewish life in Israel was a turnoff for those Reform rabbis in 1958.

All this convinced me that were we to return to work in Israel, very few of my Reform colleagues would follow me in making *aliyah*. Their financial support would be to rescue and integrate immigrants and to educate Israel's next generation rather than to support the "spiritual" work through congregations.

The next two years in Cincinnati were a time of great joy. Annette and I started our family. Ami, our first son, was born at the end of the next academic year in 1959. Annette was again pregnant, with David, at my ordination in June 1960.

My studies were meaningful, as I no longer limped through the Hebrew texts in Bible or the Rabbinic and Modern Hebrew literature. During those two years, I had a congregation in Fairmont, in the mountains of West Virginia. I was the director of OVFTY, the Ohio Valley Federation of Temple Youth. I joined the great Rabbi Samuel Cook, the national director of NFTY, as one of his protégés. I volunteered as a rabbinic leader as the Reform Movement opened camps in New York, Pennsylvania, Georgia, Wisconsin, and especially in Zionsville, Indiana, where I was co-dean of a NFTY National Institute and dean of the OVFTY Regional Institute, recruiting faculty and staff and building the leadership training program. At each of these camps, I joyfully led some staff and many campers in the building of an outdoor chapel for youth prayer.

I wrote my rabbinic thesis under the preeminent American Jewish historian, Professor Jacob Marcus, preparing myself in this major. My thesis was on the life, writings, and significance of Judah David Eisenstein, a Hebrew-speaking *maskil* (learned man) who had emigrated to the United States in the nineteenth century and was called the *Ba'al HaOtzrot*, the writer of anthologies on the Bible, the Talmud and the midrash. He wrote an autobiography called *Otzar Zichronotai* (The Treasury of My Memories), a running commentary on Jewish people and events of significance in the United States from 1850 to 1900. I translated this book and some of his articles from Hebrew into English.

I was now competent to do graduate work in Judaics with proficiency in Hebrew, making it possible to delve deeply into and to appreciate my studies in Bible, rabbinics, history, liturgy, homiletics, human relations, and speech. Two of the seminary's professors had a profound influence on my thinking. The first was Biblical Studies Professor Sheldon Blank. He taught me to analyze the writings of the great classical Hebrew prophets, Amos, Micah, Isaiah, and Jeremiah. My Jewish world view is based in large part on my encounter with their passion for social justice and on the theological conceptions of those pre-exilic Hebrew prophets and the history of the Jewish People in the sixth, seventh, and eighth centuries BCE. I understood more clearly the tensions in religion. Between priest and prophet. Between traditions and ethics. Between a world controlled by a powerful God from above through His priestly ministers and a world of humanism where the focus is on caring for the powerless and nurturing felicitous human relationships. This would become a central battle for me as I later entered the social, theological, and political culture of Israel.

The second professor who influenced me deeply was Jewish history Professor Ellis Rivkin. His historiography was based on analyzing various documents of the period being studied in order to ascertain the personal prejudices and positions of those sources' authors and thereby to uncover the inner processes at work that made them take those positions. This literary analysis should lead toward a glimpse into the truth of what really happened in the past. Professor Rivkin's "process theory" reveals an integration of opposing sources, explaining what each writer really believed, which facts were chosen as history, and then a synthesis into an integrated conception of the period and ideas studied.

One of Professor Rivkin's methods of illustrating his theory was to bring the *New York Times* into class in order to read an article on the American-Russian Cold War conflict or technological discoveries of the late 1950s, and to try to ascertain from what was written and what was not written the inner process of life in our times. With the headline of the article against his chest, Professor Rivkin would exclaim, "Boys [no women were accepted yet for rabbinic studies], here it is!" It became clear that what was written did not tell the whole truth. Based on this careful reading, Professor Rivkin would analyze, and then extrapolate from this, the interface between the Pharisees, Sadducees, and the Essenes as reflected in the writings of Josephus, the Mishnah, and the New Testament.

In sum, the careful analysis of biblical life and rabbinic values by Israeli Nechama Leibowitz and American Sheldon Blank revealed a tradition of Jewish and universal ethical values, while Israeli Yehezkel Kaufmann and Americans Nahum Glatzer and Ellis Rivkin helped me to delve into the real struggles and achievements of our People in ancient and in modern times. The discovery of life in every period in *Eretz Yisrael* by Israeli Yigael Yadin and American Nelson Glueck, and the history and analysis of the Jewish experience in North America with Max Lerner, Frank Manuel, and Jacob Marcus, all led me into new conceptions of God, man, nature, prayer, tradition, and ethical living arising from the revolution in thought in the eighteenth century. Brandeis University, HUC-JIR, and the Hebrew University had given me tools in my search for truth as a Jew and as a citizen and had prepared me to become a Jewish leader. The question was where to lead and whom. In June 1960, when President Glueck laid his hands on my head and ordained me a "Rabbi in Israel," he never thought that meant a rabbi in the country of Israel, but so it was meant to be.

CHAPTER 2
RABBI BOB

PART 1
Aliyah

1962: From Chicago to Haifa

At my ordination in Cincinnati in 1960, Rabbi Samuel Cook, the great director and builder of the National Federation of Temple Youth (NFTY), congratulated me and invited me to be co-dean of the National Institute in Zionsville, Indiana, that summer. I told him that Annette and I wanted to return to Israel to help build an infrastructure for Reform Judaism there. He suggested I consider becoming an assistant to Dr. Max Elk, the founder of the Leo Baeck School in Haifa. That interested me. When he told me I was eighteenth on the list, I replied, "Sam, I don't know who all the other seventeen are, but I believe that none of them will go there. Do you have someone who is a true Zionist, wants to be a pioneer, is ready to give up the automatic respect and income that American Reform rabbis get from their communities, and has a partner ready to share in that pioneering task?" He smiled and said, "You've just become number one."

Congregation Har-El in Jerusalem, founded in 1957, advertised for a rabbi three years later. As I approached my ordination, I was given the opportunity to put my name forward. I decided not to do so, as I felt unprepared to be the rabbi and offer sermons to the likes of Martin Buber, Hugo Bergman, Ernst Simon, and other giants of philosophy and education who were members of the congregation. Har-El did employ a Reform rabbi, Jerome Unger, a colleague who was ordained with me in 1960. Rabbi Unger, who was married to a native Israeli, was anxious to move to Israel. However, he left Har-El after one year to join the staff at The University of the Negev in Beer-Sheva (later to become Ben-Gurion University).

Annette and I decided to wait two years to make *aliyah*. I took a position as assistant rabbi in North Shore Congregation Israel (NSCI) in Glencoe, Illinois, an affluent suburb of Chicago. It was a good choice. There were many opportunities for rabbinic experience, and congregants were most welcoming. We arrived in the summer of 1960. Annette was pregnant with our second son, David. The congregation provided us with a beautiful and spacious home, and several professionals offered us pro bono services.

I preached twice a month at Shabbat services, always during our festivals, and every week in the religious school. I helped prepare youngsters and their families for bar and bat mitzvah. I led services for the 1,000-person overflow from the main service during the High Holy Days. I was responsible for the entire 2,000-child religious school, including the 200 tenth grade confirmation students. I wrote a weekly column on the Torah portion for the Temple bulletin. I taught conversion classes; officiated at baby namings, weddings, funerals, and memorials; organized and led adult and teen retreats at the winterized camp of the Reform Movement in Oconomowoc, Wisconsin; and taught two courses each semester in adult education, introducing my suburban Chicago congregants to Modern Hebrew Literature in English translation, Jewish history, and spoken Hebrew.

NSCI was the perfect practical rabbinic environment for a young, energetic ordained rabbi. There were differences, however, with the senior rabbi, Edgar Siskin. I saw the results of one-day-a-week religious education yielding little motivation to learn Judaics and Hebrew. I wanted to experiment with alternative Jewish education, including field trips to such sources of Jewish experience as Israel ("Our Homeland"), New York City ("The Largest Jewish City in the World"), and Western Europe ("Our Roots"), but Rabbi Siskin resisted experimentation for these highly educated but assimilated Reform Jews. Although many of his congregants were ripe for such alternate Jewish experiences, it was only under different rabbinic leadership that they would be exposed to the world of the spiritual uplift of Israel, soul searching retreats, and Jewish Renewal.

At NSCI we made many lifelong friends, several of whom supported my work in Israel. During the two years in Chicago, I was able to "step up to the plate" quite literally by joining a Sunday morning adult baseball team in Highland Park when I could.

In our second year, we began to move from a theoretical *aliyah* to a practical one. Annette was pregnant again, but she joined me in taking up the challenge, and a challenge it was just to get there. Our preparations included starting an exchange program with a small school in Haifa. I found the perfect pioneer for this in my congregation in Chicago and taught him personally in preparation for his junior semester in Israel. Since that initial exchange program, that young man, now Rabbi Dr. Marc Rosenstein, has had a distinguished career in Israel as the pioneer of *Makom Bagalil*, a creative Jewish seminar center in the Galilee. He was also the director of the Israeli Rabbinic Program at the Jerusalem campus of HUC-JIR.

I still needed a job offer. Dr. Elk at the Leo Baeck School agreed in principle and promised a half-time salary as a teacher. I felt moderately prepared for such a position and assumed I would be out of the spotlight and able to ascertain whether the average secular Israeli would be amenable to Progressive Judaism. In the fall of 1961, I went to New York to meet with Rabbi Cook; Rabbi Hugo Gryn, the director of the World Union for Progressive Judaism (WUPJ); and Rabbi Maurice Eisendrath, president of the Union of American Hebrew Congregations (UAHC, now URJ, the Union for Reform Judaism). Rabbi Jay Kaufman, Rabbi Eisendrath's assistant, attended the meeting and proposed that I become an official *Shaliach* (emissary) of the World Union to determine the readiness of Israelis to accept Reform Judaism. He offered to help the World Union raise the $1,000 necessary for the move, with the promise of a combined (Leo Baeck and WUPJ) annual income of $5,000. I agreed to leave my congregation the following summer and begin a journey of exploration in Israel.

Dr. Elk immediately accepted the plan. In our correspondence, he proposed that I take on the following responsibilities: become homeroom teacher for a ninth grade class and teach them Bible, teach midrash (non-legal rabbinic texts) in the tenth grade, be responsible for the student council, develop programs of worship for the students and their families, and take responsibility for fundraising. With these expectations, set up in the winter of 1961–62, I was able to announce to NSCI that I would be leaving Chicago the following summer to live in Israel.

My sermon, "From Israel (NSCI) to Israel (the State of)," was announced in the Temple Bulletin. Many of the families in the congregation were fascinated with the fact that their rabbi, a seventh-generation

American, was about to take on such a venture. They responded positively to my call for funds both for the Baeck School and for developing Reform Jewish programs. I called together a group of wealthy friends in the congregation and asked them to help me raise a $50,000 nest egg to fund the expenses of the fundraising that I would need to do. They presented me with almost $45,000. World Union President Rabbi Jacob Shankman of Temple Israel in New Rochelle, New York, raised the additional amount.

We now had two sons, aged two-and-a-half and one, and Annette was pregnant with our third child, Tamar, born in May 1962. On August 1, the day my congregational contract ended, we flew to Annette's sister in Boston. All of our furniture and belongings had been packed into a "lift," a pre-container wooden box transported by sea. Annette stayed with the children in Boston while I flew to Israel to arrange for an apartment in Haifa, a kindergarten for Ami, and for our belongings and a Fiat 600cc car to be delivered from the Haifa port. When Annette arrived on September 15, all was ready for the family in a centrally located apartment on Mount Carmel, which I had rented for a year. It was now time to "step up to the plate" in a foreign land under conditions for which my training had not prepared me, but my pioneering DNA would guide me.

I consider Annette a heroine. She is a concert violinist with two academic degrees in music from Harvard and the Cincinnati Conservatory of Music. She cheerfully came to Israel with three babies, all in cloth diapers, with no family backup except me to help care for the children and to make a home in a new country, with a new language, and a monthly income of $400. Descending from the airplane, carrying a son on each arm and a daughter on her back, she handled it as if it were the most natural thing in the world. Annette learned the dynamics of Israeli life. She quickly became fluent in Hebrew and never complained there was not enough money for the family's needs. If family is the first mitzvah, she has lived that to the fullest.

Beginnings at the Leo Baeck School

And to what kind of institution did I come? The twelve-year school divided into two distinctly different schools: an eight-year compulsory, free elementary school and a four-year private, tuition-based secondary school. The elementary school had been founded by Dr. Elk in 1938 as a kindergarten. It was one of several social and educational initiatives of Dr. Elk, mainly for the German-speaking immigrants who had settled in Haifa, wisely escaping the ever-increasing bitter discrimination and violent acts against the Jews of Germany in the 1930s. In 1935, Dr. Elk had left his congregation in Shtetin on the northern German-Polish border and within the first year had founded Beit Yisrael, a liberal congregation in Haifa. The congregation quickly became the instrument that Dr. Elk and his colleagues used for the religious, social, educational, and cultural needs of those new German-speaking residents of Palestine. In the fall of 1938, Beit Yisrael opened a kindergarten for five-year-olds, to be followed each year by a new kindergarten until those first children graduated from the eighth grade. Dr. Elk, as headmaster, hired an impressive cadre of teachers and educators who combined a general liberal education with Jewish subjects and experiences.

During the first eighteen years, the elementary school was housed in rented homes at 16, 18, and 47 Hillel Street. It was called The Hillel School, both because of its location on Hillel Street in Haifa's Hadar neighborhood and, more so, because of its liberal orientation, inherited from the world view of the great first-century BCE Rabbi Hillel. In 1946, as the first class of eighth graders was applying to secondary schools, Dr. Elk initiated and incorporated a secondary school (all high schools were privately funded). He formed The Hillel Secondary School, a corporation with a board of directors, and cancelled the organizational connection with his Beit Yisrael congregation. By 1954, the board of the school, looking forward, negotiated with the Haifa Municipality to take responsibility for the elementary school. A contract was signed, Dr. Elk remained headmaster, and the municipality funded the construction of a proper school building on Golumb Street. Dr. Elk and his associate, Elisheva Egozi (who followed Dr. Elk as headmistress of the elementary school in 1959), empowered the seventh and eighth graders to lead the school's social and extra-curricular activities, a leadership program for which the school received the Education Prize from the Ministry of Education. In the center of the new secondary school building were a kitchen and cafeteria-dining room. Home economics and nutrition were taught, and the students helped in the preparation of the food. For many students in those early years, this was their daily hot meal.

In September 1947, the first class of kindergartners from Beit Yisrael enrolled in the ninth grade in what was to become the Leo Baeck

Secondary School. During that year, Rabbi Dr. Leo Baeck made his first and only trip to Palestine, and at the invitation of Dr. Elk, his former student, he visited the school. At the reception for the great rabbi, Dr. Elk requested Baeck's permission to rename the school in his honor.

Rabbi Baeck had been the head of German Jewry before World War II and was a distinguished theologian. From 1933, as the Nazis increased their brutality toward Jews, most of the intellectual leaders of German Jewry found refuge in academic institutions in the West. Rabbi Baeck, too, had received an invitation from Cincinnati's Rockdale Temple, but he refused to leave. He felt an obligation to help get entry permits to countries around the world for as many German Jews as possible, both within Germany and for those lucky enough to flee from the gathering inferno. He did, indeed, save thousands of lives in this heroic mission. Nonetheless, in 1943, the Nazi SS sent him to Theresienstadt in Czechoslovakia. Though erected by the Nazis as a "self-run" camp with intellectuals, artists, and sportsmen, Theresienstadt was a concentration camp where thousands were starved, died, or sent to Auschwitz to be gassed. Baeck was given the daily task of removing the garbage from the camp, but his presence there was inspiring to the inmates. After lights out, this "garbage man" once again became Rabbi Baeck, going into a barracks to lecture on Plato, Maimonides, or an aspect of *The Essence of Judaism,* his most profound and influential book. For those tortured Jews, Baeck became a beacon of intellect, culture, and hope for deliverance.

In May 1945 when the camp was liberated, Rabbi Baeck was still miraculously alive. He joined his daughter, who had escaped to London. After recovering from his physical suffering, he was chosen president of the World Union. HUC invited him to Cincinnati as scholar-in-residence for several months each year until 1953.

While visiting the Cincinnati campus during my junior year at Brandeis, I had the privilege of meeting Rabbi Baeck. I sat in on a class he taught on "Midrashic Texts on Jewish Problems." I did not understand much of the lecture, but I have made midrash my main source for revealing the universality of rabbinic thought. I also had the experience of seeing him as the kindest, most humble man. I shall never forget the feeling of awe from being with this eighty-year-old inspiring rabbi. While walking together down the hall, he reached forward and held the door open for *me*, a twenty-year-old pre-rabbinic student!

Rabbi Baeck's deep learning, his leadership, courage, and spirituality both before and during the war thrust him into the limelight throughout the Jewish world. He became a symbol of the triumph of moral education, ethical living, and human decency in a world gone mad. Many organizations and institutions throughout the world asked to take his name, striving to live by his standards. Dr. Elk's Hillel School in Haifa was one of those institutions. The inspiration of Rabbi Baeck's thought has been a guide for me in internalizing the moral law in our school and community.

By the time of Rabbi Baeck's death in London in 1956, this nascent secondary school in Haifa, based on his spirit of humanism, had graduated six classes. Dr. Elk had recruited two colleagues from his rabbinic seminary in Breslau to join the faculty, as well as several other scholar-teachers who had immigrated to Israel with doctorates in their fields. Rabbi Dr. Pedatzur Daniel taught Jewish and humanistic subjects, Latin, and Greek. In time, Dr. Daniel became vice-principal of the high school, responsible for pedagogy. Rabbi Avigdor Porat was head of Judaic Studies in the elementary school. Eventually, he became the coordinator of Judaics in the first years of the junior high school.

Each of these three rabbis had studied in the same rabbinic seminary, but in fact represented very different modern conceptions of Jewish tradition. Rabbi Daniel was Orthodox, Rabbi Elk was Conservative, and Rabbi Porat was Liberal. Rabbi Daniel would not attend services at the school as he would not travel on Shabbat. Rabbi Elk would take a taxi from his home but would exit the cab two blocks from the school and walk the rest of the way. When Rabbi Porat attended, no one asked or cared how he got there. Rabbi Daniel considered Reform Judaism to be a caricature of religion. He was tolerant of my presence, but not of my religious liberalism. Rabbi Elk was more traditional than I, but accepting and respectful of change. Rabbi Porat and I were similar, and he often sought me out to discuss the weekly Torah portion or how to teach issues of the spirit in a developing secular Israeli society. Rabbi Elk was the glue that held these very different interpretations of Torah together. I was free to teach Bible and Rabbinics with the most modern theological and pedagogic conceptions, and Dr. Daniel was equally free to influence our students toward observance of halachah (Jewish law). Dr. Elk and I often had serious and welcome discussions on what our graduates should know and feel regarding their Jewish and Israeli identities.

Dr. Elk's Judaism was pluralistic and traditional but without coercion. Beit Yisrael had no *ezrat nashim* (section for women, separated by a curtain in the back of the hall). Women did sit in a side section on the same level as the men but with no curtain. Dr. Elk would preach in Hebrew facing the men and then turn to face the women to give a précis of the sermon in German.

Dr. Elk created a Jewish atmosphere in the school. The morning began with the recitation of a psalm. Male students took a *kippah* (head covering) out of their backpacks and donned it while studying Jewish texts. All students studied Bible, Rabbinics, and Jewish thought. All Jewish holidays were taught and appropriate ceremonies prepared.

Prior to my arrival in 1962, the Leo Baeck Board had rented a house at 47 Hillel Street for the high school. It had been built years before by an Arab family and had an exterior winding stair entrance and beautiful oriental floor tiles. In 1955, a contractor received a permit to build a four-floor apartment building above this Arab home. Because the school occupied the house, it was given the option of buying the ground floor and part of the first floor. NFTY provided the renovation funds in order to create five classrooms downstairs, three upstairs, three offices, a teachers' room, and a tiny library.

There were eight classes, two in each grade, ninth through twelfth. The first two years were general studies, emphasizing Hebrew language and literature, science, humanities, and Judaics. In the junior and senior grades, each class was divided into two majors: one equally split between the physical and the biological sciences and a second class with some thirty literature and humanities majors, together with six to ten pupils majoring in Arabic and Middle Eastern studies. Dr. Elk still had the use of the original elementary school building down the street at 16 Hillel. We transformed that space into a physics-chemistry and biology lab. The number of students accepted for each class was dictated by the number of tables and chairs one could squeeze into a room.

Dr. Elk managed the finances, the connection with the elementary school, and the teaching staff. Dr. Elk had contact with the students and their families, but from afar. For the school to be close to the students and their families, Dr. Elk appointed Rachel Zuri, the girls' physical education teacher, as a kind of dean of students and the person responsible for maintenance of the building. Rachel was also the coordinator of the families for the American Student Exchange Program.

By the summer of 1962, the Leo Baeck Secondary School had a board of directors, owned the space it occupied at 47 Hillel Street, graduated its twelfth class, had a superior teaching staff, and offered four curricular majors. Several staff members had come to the school with Ph.D.s from German universities: *Geveret* (Mrs.) Dr. Zavadi, Mathematics; *Geveret* Dr. Zilberstein, English; *Geveret* Dr. Yaakobi, Biology; *HaRav* (Rabbi) Dr. Elk, Judaics; *HaRav* Dr. Daniel, Bible; and *HaRav* Dr. Rafael, Talmud. Several of the other teachers also had second and third university degrees. Under different circumstances my guess is that most of those teachers would have been professors in universities. But here they were, preparing *sabras* and new immigrants with the classic education of a German-Jewish *gymnasia*.

By 1962, the facilities were poor: eight different-sized classrooms for eight classes, a tiny teachers room, no panes on many of the windows, no heating in the winter or air conditioner in the summer, no facilities for physical education (the students ran races down Hillel Street!), two small science labs a ten-minute walk away, a tiny room for the library, and inadequate bathrooms, all suffused with the aroma of cooking from the apartments in the building. But no one complained. The standard of learning was high, the atmosphere was social and friendly, and the times were different. Most students lived in small apartments in Haifa's Hadar neighborhood. Material objects were simple, and people's expectations were for content and character rather than for material objects and wealth. Leo Baeck's simple building fit right in with the spirit of the day.

My work at Leo Baeck began the day after I arrived in August 1962. We arranged my class schedule, a meeting with the American exchange students and their Israeli families, and a discussion regarding the structure and management of Leo Baeck, including its budget and overall finances. Dr. Elk invited me to his home so I could meet several of the teachers. They were all extremely friendly and welcoming, but as we drank our tea and snacked on Frau Elk's cookies, the main conversation hung on whether the Hebrew word for "roots" was *shohrashim* or *shawrashim*. It was very intimidating. This subtle distinction in Hebrew grammar, which so occupied the minds of my

Hebrew colleagues, was a wakeup call. I felt like I was batting for the first time in the Major Leagues. Recognizing that I was in a new civilization and a new culture, speaking a new language, I had to adapt or fail.

Dr. Elk's motivation for hiring me was first and foremost to fulfill a commitment to Rabbi Cook, who had given the youth of NFTY the challenge of aiding this fledgling liberal school in Israel as a foothold for Reform Judaism. "Bricks for Baeck," "From Gehenom To Gan-Eden," and "The Cronbach Chapel" were all creative projects to teach Jewish American teenagers about Israel and develop programs to raise funds for the Leo Baeck School. Dr. Elk accepted me not just as a representative of the Reform Jewish youth of North America, but as a colleague from the very beginning. It was a breath of fresh air and a motivator to work under the leadership of this pioneering progressive rabbi of the generation before me.

I also had great respect for Dr. Elk for another reason. There were three liberal rabbis from Germany who had come to Palestine in the 1930s. Rabbi Elk settled in Haifa, Rabbi Pinchas and Rabbi Philip in Jerusalem. When they were ordered by the Orthodox rabbinic establishment to accept and practice all of Jewish law or not be recognized, Rabbi Pinchas left the country to become a liberal rabbi in Sweden, and Rabbi Philip accepted their conditions in order to be able to serve the members of his congregation in Jerusalem. Only Rabbi Elk stayed true to his convictions, accepting the consequences of his refusal to sign such a coercive contract, knowing this would limit his ability to officiate at life-cycle events for the members of Beit Yisrael. It was a very courageous and valued decision, and I was proud to work under the leadership of such a principled man for twelve years. As a liberal and Zionist rabbi, he was unique in his generation. I believe that a person with a different personality and goals would have soured me, causing me to return to America and the Baeck School to fail.

Dr. Elk immediately put me on Leo Baeck's board of directors, making me a partner with those German-educated board members in maintaining the well-being of the institution. They, too, accepted me as an equal, motivating me to dialogue with them on matters of principle and institutional direction.

I asked Dr. Elk for an office in that converted apartment house, and he granted me one. It was an eight-foot-square space taken away from the bathroom with an open channel along the floor for the rainwater that flowed in from the side of Mount Carmel in the winter rains. This room contained a part of my personal library, my desk, a desk for the chair of the student council, and a desk for my associate, Miriam Bettelheim, who was a brilliant collaborator in fundraising and development. That room became both the social hub for Leo Baeck students and the fundraising center.

A German-trained rabbi who left his cultural home in Europe and an American-trained rabbi who left his, each for very different reasons, found each other in Haifa during the 1960s. Rabbi Elk was in his sixties; I was in my thirties. Our teamwork, based on common intellectual and social goals, was to produce an institution that would transform communities and thousands of Israelis.

Building a Diverse Student Population

One of my tasks in helping to build this liberal school was to meet with the legendary mayor of Haifa, Abba Khushi, who was one of the most powerful leaders of the dominant Labor Movement. The city, known as "Red Haifa," was a main stronghold of Labor. It was important, therefore, to introduce myself and determine the mayor's knowledge and opinion of Reform Judaism. He agreed to meet me during that fall of 1962.

As I was ushered into his office, he rose to greet me stating, "Rabbi Samuels, I want to know all about you."

I gave him a little of my background. He interrupted me to ask: "I was taught that the Reform Movement was anti-Zionist, so what are you doing teaching in a Haifa school?"

I explained that some of the greatest Zionist leaders had been Reform rabbis: Rabbis Judah Magnes and Saadia Gelb had made *aliyah,* and Rabbis Abba Hillel Silver, Stephen Wise, and Arthur Lelyveld had a great influence in the United States on the establishment of Israel. I said that Reform had changed its ideology as a result of the Holocaust and the birth of Israel, and that my purpose was to contribute to social justice in Haifa.

Abba Khushi smiled and asked me how I planned to do that. I responded, "Teach humanism, pluralism, and democracy; bring Jewish American teenagers to live and study at Leo Baeck; educate the children of the *shikunim* [public housing comprised of small apartments for large Sephardic families] and new teenage immigrants who haven't learned Hebrew; encourage teenagers to volunteer wherever help is needed; and give non-Orthodox families an opportunity to practice Judaism in a modern, non-coercive mode."

The mayor jumped out of his chair, pointed out the window toward the port of Haifa, and said, "You see that port down there? That is where our new Israelis arrive. When they come off those immigrant ships, we don't look at the shape of their noses, and we won't look at the shape of their conscience either. Fulfill those tasks, and I will help you." And so he did.

Dr. Elk sent me to the *ma'abarot* (tin shack neighborhoods) in Haifa and the Haifa Bay to find Sephardic students. In the *ma'abarah* in Kiryat Haim I was welcomed into the two-room hut of the Fara'gi family. The parents and all eight children were there. Mrs. Fara'gi told me that Haim, her oldest son, was smart, and I agreed to take him into the ninth grade. Under the direction of a tutor, Haim began to excel in his studies. He graduated with honors and went on to earn two academic degrees. Five more of the Fara'gi kids graduated from Leo Baeck, though by the time the fourth attended, the family name had been changed to Pereg. Atzmon Pereg, the youngest, played soccer with my son, Ami, and became a regular visitor in our home. Upon graduation Atzmon made a ceramic plaque for me, which I am proud to have hanging in my home.

The Fara'gi-Pereg family is a microcosm of what could have been for all the children of the million North African Jews who came to Israel in the early 1950s. A scientific-humanistic education for their children, coupled with love and respect for their North African culture, could have been the base for these proud Jewish communities to understand the values of social democracy and ethical Judaism. Had the children of all the Moroccan, Tunisian, and Algerian immigrants of the 1950s been given this kind of value education, Israel today would be a different country, and I dare say that the Center-Left leaders would still be in power. Israel's leaders eventually came to realize they must do something on a national scale to address the phenomenon called "the second Israel." Leo Baeck had a part in the attempt to correct the second class status of Israel's Sephardic population.

Dr. Elk also told me that he would like to have some Druze students. The Druze are non-Muslim Arabic-speaking people with their own religious traditions, elders, and prophets. They live mainly in the mountainous areas of Lebanon, Syria, and Israel. They are loyal Israeli citizens, serving in the IDF, and are well accepted among the Jewish population. Near Haifa, high on the Carmel Mountain, are two such villages, Isfiya and Daliat-el-Carmel. I decided to search for promising students from Isfiya, the village closer to Haifa.

One of the village leaders, Zaki Zahir, had a son studying in the eighth grade. He was anxious to send him to a high-standard school, so he invited me to his home. Not knowing what to expect, I entered to find a beautifully decorated living room with colorful, soft-filled pillows on benches that circled the room. Over drinks and food served by his wife and 13-year-old daughter, both of whom disappeared after each serving, we discussed the proper education of children both at home and in school. Zaki proved to be quite liberal and knowledgeable, though when asked if he would also send that beautiful adolescent daughter, he thought for a moment and replied, "Not yet!"

There was a large television set in the room, which was strange. Israel as yet had no television. When queried, Zaki said, "I have faith!" I thought to myself: this is pretty much the story of my own life, jumping out in front (stepping up to the plate) without knowing what the result might be. I told Zaki we would take his son, Yoel, into our ninth grade the next year. I asked him if Yoel had a close friend who could join him, as the trip to Haifa from Isfiya was long. He did, and in fact we took in four such students during that first year, 1963–64. During both the ninth and tenth grades, they received an additional ten hours a week of Hebrew lessons to prepare them for their sophisticated studies as juniors and seniors. Once Professor Ezra Spicehandler, the dean of HUC-JIR in Jerusalem, visited and sat in the back of a Talmud class for seniors. When the bell rang, Ezra said to me, "That boy there is a fine Talmud student." It was Yoel Zahir.

They all graduated four years later with full matriculation and have all had both successful professional and solid married lives. In 2014 we had ninety Druze students, fifteen in each grade of our six-year high school, half of whom were female.

My First Year at Leo Baeck

In the beginning of my Israeli rabbinic career, Dr. Elk agreed I could hold High Holy Day services for Leo Baeck students and families in the fall of 1962. As a member of a B'nai B'rith lodge, he arranged for us to use their hall in the Central Carmel. Leo Baeck had 190 students enrolled that September. We had 120 students for our Rosh HaShanah evening service. Two of the Israeli students, who had been chosen to attend the exchange program in the United States, helped me with the arrangements: Gil Nativ, who became an outstanding rabbi, Talmudist, and my partner in creating Reform Judaism for over fifty years; and Mordechai Wertheim (Rabbi Motti Rotem), the first *sabra* Reform rabbi ordained in Jerusalem. He has had a distinguished career in Haifa, Jerusalem, the Caribbean, and, of all places, Texas.

That first academic year was full of tension but much satisfaction. I was the homeroom teacher for a ninth grade class with twenty-seven students. There were twenty-seven because that was the maximum that could fit into a room that had been converted from a bedroom. It was limited in size, both because of the limits of space and vision. Dr. Elk saw the school as the continuation of the elementary school he had founded for the children of the members of his congregation, who were by and large *yekkes*, middle-European Jews who had arrived in Haifa in the 1930s as a result of Nazi anti-Semitism. Subsequent classes would have a mixture of Ashkenazic and Sephardic students, but not this first one. I loved that class, and I stayed in touch with some of them.

As I walked into the room for the first time on September first, the children stood up and applauded me. What a welcome! I had assiduously prepared for this day. I knew *Tanach* (the Hebrew Bible), but my Hebrew was rudimentary. The biblical commentaries I used were mostly in English. I had to master the Hebrew of medieval and modern commentators to the historical prophets, Joshua through Kings, a period of 600 years. I began my preparations in Chicago and spent at least three hours preparing for each class during that first semester.

At the beginning of this first lesson, I told my students that I wanted to be their friend and was there to listen to anything they wanted to share with me. I offered the following trade: "You can see from my Hebrew that I am a beginner. I know *Tanach* and am going to thrill you as we learn about our ancestors. Together we will determine whether each of them was ethical or not, and we will search for the values we believe in. And you know Hebrew. I want you to be my teachers: Bible for Hebrew. Is it a deal?" Generally, teachers neither expect nor tolerate pupils correcting them. I had learned that total honesty and transparency won the hearts of others and that students were aware of almost everything happening in the classroom anyway. It was a value that would become the general environment of the school and community center. I dare say this openness and honesty has been a key factor in the success of our educational and community endeavors. All are equal in value, and everyone has something to contribute, regardless of age, gender, ethnic background, or economic status.

We became very close friends. Those first students were fourteen years old, and I was twenty-nine. That was a huge difference then, but during this past half-century, we have become colleagues, and the difference in knowledge, life experiences, and expectations has closed. One of the true blessings of teaching in the same institution over a lifetime is the affection and respect between all those exploring the world together and then later comparing how the world has responded to each of us.

Every one of those twenty-seven students was in the Hillel troop of the *Tzofim* (Scouts). They all believed in *Hagshama*, fulfillment, which meant that when they graduated high school and finished the army, they would become a member of a kibbutz. I dare say that if the Reform Movement had been truly Zionist and had founded a kibbutz by the 1960s, many of my first students would have become members. Only one of those twenty-seven ninth graders actually did become a lifelong kibbutznik, but this Zionist ideology motivated them to volunteer as workers on a kibbutz for a full week during each of the Sukkot, Chanukah, and Pesach vacations. Our homeroom classes were passionate debates on current events in Israel and in the world and the response of ethical Jews to those events.

I also taught a tenth grade class in *Torah She-ba'al Peh,*[2] preparing a curriculum teaching midrash, which uses a biblical text in order to teach a universal value. Usually the lesson for life is not derived from the text itself, but rather from a thought or value of those wise rabbis of the first five centuries of the Common Era. The value system of *sabras* became clear as we explored such questions as why man was created singly; how righteous was Noah; what was the real sin of the building of the Tower of Babel; why Abraham defended Sodom; why he did not sacrifice Isaac; who were the angels ascending and descending Jacob's ladder; and whether the Red Sea indeed split.

---

2. Rabbinic tradition holds that Moses received two Teachings on Mount Sinai, The Written Law and the Oral Law. The Written Torah or Teachings is all of the books in the Hebrew Bible, and the Oral Torah or Teachings is the Talmud and midrashim. The Oral Torah in Hebrew includes law (halachah) andlore (midrash)

I tested their values in other ways. For instance, they considered it a mitzvah to help their classmates, so if a friend asked for help on an exam, they didn't refuse. This was not an ethical issue for them, but lying was. So I decided to test them on this. Early in the year I gave them a flash test, and as they walked into the room, I wrote on the board the following sentence: "I have neither given nor received help during this examination: signed_____" There were thirty students in the class. I received *nine* different versions of that sentence on their papers. Some said they did not give, others wrote that they had not received, still others admitted to cheating only once. It turned out that *sabras* were "honest" cheats.

At the next lesson I brought in the following midrash: *The Torah notes that Moses, prince of Egypt, had killed an Egyptian who was tormenting a Hebrew slave. The next day Moses intervenes in a quarrel between two Hebrews. One of them challenges Moses: "Who made you a judge over me? Do you intend to kill me as you did the Egyptian?" Moses says to himself, "So, the 'thing' (davar) is known."* But the midrash interprets *davar* as "word," its other meaning, and then states that it stands for *gossip*. According to this interpretation of *davar*, it was because of their slandering each other, their tale-bearing, that the Hebrews were enslaved. After learning the midrash, the class discussed the universal lesson from the text. It turned out that most of the students did not think that *lashon hara* (gossip) was bad, but rather that it was a natural aspect of human nature. I now knew that I had my work cut out for me. For fifty years now we have tried to clarify what is the ethical way, the moral path for Israel's society.

Fundraising: The Early Years

Most of my fundraising in those initial years (1962–65) was done through the rabbis in the congregations of the UAHC. Several of them were Zionists. Many were not, but after 1948 had become supporters of Israel's security and of programs for Israelis struggling economically. Most were interested in our struggle against Israeli religious and political leaders who denigrated Reform Judaism, but they were much more ready to help fund the financially needy than educational or liberal religious projects. They themselves would donate moderately and would find members to donate to Leo Baeck for Holocaust survivors, new immigrants, social justice and pluralism, and scholarships. A few were deeply concerned about the ability of Israeli democracy to include progressive education and progressive Judaism. We created a large network of Reform donors, including the National Federation of Temple Educators (including children in religious schools), NFTY, the National Federation of Temple Sisterhoods (today Women of Reform Judaism), and the National Federation of Temple Brotherhoods (now Men of Reform Judaism). In addition, many members of NSCI with whom we had become close during the two years I served as assistant rabbi provided me with both contributions and other assistance, such as housing while traveling, a rental car, or paying the telephone bill.

Such fundraising was very difficult in those days. Computers and cell phones did not appear until after the 1980s. Through letters, I informed possible donors when I would be in the States. I had a large date book with names, phone numbers, and past donations. I had no one to do my advance bookings. My base was in New York City and in Houston. The headquarters of Reform Judaism was on Fifth Avenue in New York. I always had a desk there from which to make my calls, operating out of the NFTY office, which was *very* keen that Leo Baeck succeed in planting a beachhead for Reform Judaism in Israel.

I felt it was a holy task to bring to Israel *all* the money people entrusted to my care. I tried to set the example for other leaders by sleeping in the homes of friends, eating in inexpensive restaurants, and finding cheap flights and VUSA (Visit USA) flight plans to make multiple flights for a preset fee. My expenses never exceeded 5% of donations. Sad to say, many leaders raising funds for Israel spend thousands of dollars on their own personal luxury at the expense of organizations they represent, moneys meant to do humanitarian work.

Having raised funds before arriving in Israel in order not to be dependent on the World Union for the cost of my trips, I wanted to take the responsibility to another level. Israel was at the beginning of its development. Could I create a business in Israel that would assure Leo Baeck significant funding from the profits and thereby alleviate the necessity for constantly seeking donations in the future? After consulting with wealthy friends both through the Haifa Rotary Club and in the United States, we decided to open a firm in Haifa called CDI, Carmel Development Industries. Haifa had the only deepwater port with its own shipping companies and a large grain silo; the oil refinery and the large electric plant were in Haifa; the Technion was well-established and was the chief source of research for Israel's industrial development; and a new university was being established in Haifa. I felt we could assume Haifa would expand quickly. I went in search of investors to buy Haifa real estate, proposing we incorporate as CDI. We recruited two Haifa friends as voluntary consultants who promised to invest if I could find partners in the States.

That took me back to Glencoe, Illinois, to North Shore Congregation Israel, to meet with four members with extensive resources: Lester Crown, Harold Perlman, Zollie Frank, and Jerome Stone. They liked the idea but felt that Israel was too young for them to invest in. They were ready to donate for the absorption of Jews who needed a home, but not to buy property on speculation that it would increase in value as those Jews settled in Haifa. They agreed on the spot to donate $5,000 each to Leo Baeck, but not to invest in CDI. My first attempt at entrepreneurial funding ended that spring day in 1964 in Jerry Stone's board room.

It is sobering to consider what CDI might have become. Haifa's real estate has exploded during the past fifty years. We purchased our apartment in 1963 for $17,500 and sold it in 1985 for $185,000. In 2015, that apartment was worth $375,000. Investment in CDI in 1964 would have earned those four Glencoe families and Leo Baeck rich rewards through wise buying and selling through the years, but it wasn't to be.

The Shock of Death, the Need for Memory, and the Faith to Hope

One of my favorite students was killed in the Six-Day War. *Asher Eliad* had been a member of my tenth grade class during my first teaching year. He was tall and handsome, diligent and responsive to the lessons on ethics based on Talmudic texts. He wrote poems and played basketball. He was kind and thoughtful. He died at age twenty on the second day of the 1967 war as he ascended the Golan Heights toward Tel Kazir. Asher had lost a friend the day before. He sat in his tent that night and composed a poem of tribute to his comrade in arms. The following morning, as his unit approached their target, a sniper shot Asher in the chest, exactly through that poem in his vest pocket.

We Israelis read daily of the number of casualties in war and terror, but this was my first existential experience with a personal loss. I was thirty-four, unaccustomed to the death of the young. Asher's death shocked me, and it still hurts. Years later, Asher's younger brother, Shlomo, and I brought rounded basalt stones from the spot where he was killed. They surround the olive tree in our commemorative hall at Leo Baeck, which memorializes the twenty-three graduates and students who have lost their lives to war and terror.

Avinoam Taub was killed in 1970 during the War of Attrition on the Suez Canal. Israeli forces had been building a chain of fortifications in an attempt to prevent a massive attack by Egyptian tanks across the canal. Avinoam's unit came under massive artillery bombardment. He, too, was twenty when he died, and he, too, had studied with me as a sixteen-year-old in the tenth grade. Avinoam, a talented teenage sculptor, had studied and created in many artistic styles with grace and sensitivity. His family agreed that Leo Baeck could create a posthumous exhibit of twenty of his sculptures, two of which they donated for permanent exhibition.

Miri Farber was also twenty when she died in 1970. Her mother, Rachel, was a veteran teacher at Leo Baeck. Miri was a gifted student whom we sent to London as a high school junior. I had the privilege of discovering her intellect and deep culture as she trained for that experience. She flowered in England, learning in a fine school and teaching Hebrew every afternoon. Miri lived with the very prominent Wolfson family. Her Israeli family was secular, but the Wolfsons exposed her to traditional Judaism. As a result, she decided upon graduation from Leo Baeck in 1968 to enter the military rabbinate and became a personal assistant to the then-head of the army rabbinate, Rabbi Shlomo Goren. Miri was killed in a tragic traffic accident while traveling to General Goren's office in Tel Aviv. Leo Baeck published a booklet on Miri's writings and life. Miri died just before the first female rabbi was ordained in the United States. I believe that had she lived, she might have studied for the Reform rabbinate at HUC in Jerusalem and become an early leader of Israeli liberal Judaism.

Eitan Fichtenbaum was twenty-one when he died during the Yom Kippur War in 1973. He was an outstanding athlete at Leo Baeck, full of energy and ready to take on any assignment. Eitan carried on these traits in the IDF as an officer of a unit that fought in the Sinai. He lost men, and at the first opportunity returned to the home front in order to be present when the families of his fallen comrades were notified. On the way, deprived of sleep, his vehicle overturned. Israel was robbed of another son with a fine liberal education and an energetic personality who could have changed the world. I was informed while sitting on the sand in the Haifa Bay, frustrated while manning a cannon, searching for non-existent enemy planes and knowing that thousands of our young people were losing their lives. I suddenly saw Eitan's face in my mind's eye and the huge tragedy of our existence hit me, and I cried. I still do. Each subsequent year we invited Eitan's mother, brother, and family to join us as our students played a basketball game in his memory. And each year for twenty-five years, as I dropped the ball on the floor, and we observed a minute of silence, I cried for him and for us.

One more memory: I retired in 1999. Four years later a beautiful seventeen-year-old senior student was killed when a suicide terrorist blew himself and everyone else up on a Haifa bus. *Elizabeth Katzman* was a star performer in our annual school drama production. A sensitive, dramatic, and talented actress, Liz was everything her parents and her teachers would ever want in a developing adolescent. The death of a soldier in combat is hard enough to live with, but the murder of an innocent teen, so ripe to begin a life of love and service, is poignant beyond description. The whole school cried. And once again we searched for a significant memorial. We created a quiet conversation corner near our chapel with an artistic sign.

And it was similar with eighteen other Leo Baeck graduates and students tragically cut down in the dawn of their lives and Israel's independence. It has been a personal wound as I have matured and grown old here in our wounded Land. As I grieve for those whose faces and personalities can be seen only by my inner eye, I grieve too with all the teachers and students and all the families and all the soldiers who knew someone among the 25,000 Israelis killed in war and terror over all these years.

Israel's Memorial Day is in the spring, on the fourth of Iyar, preceding our Independence Day. It is a somber day when family and comrades of the fallen attend ceremonies at all military cemeteries during the national moment of silence at 11:00 A.M. In order for our families to be able to arrive on time, Leo Baeck has an early morning memorial starting at 8:00 A.M. for the families and teachers in our memorial room, followed by a heartrending and poignant ceremony of remembrance and hope in our auditorium, attended by all of our students, the families of our fallen, and hundreds of our graduates who are serving in the IDF.

The loss of those whose minds and souls we touched has made me sensitive as well to all those Palestinians who have suffered loss in our tragic century-old conflict. It is my dream of an ordered, ethical, and democratic land for us and for the entire Middle East that motivates me to encourage our present leaders to inspire our remarkable teachers and staff to dedicate themselves to a better future. In spite of those losses I still have faith that Israelis and Palestinians can regain the moral high ground, so that the Ashers, Avinoams, Miris, Eitans, and Elizabeths, together with the Ahmads, Muhameds, E'ads, Saris, and Hanans alive today, will no longer have to fight and fear that their promise of love and success in life will be aborted before they reach a ripe old age.

CHAPTER 2
RABBI BOB

PART 2
Family

Our Homes in Israel

1 Moriah Street in Haifa's Central Carmel
Upon our arrival in Haifa in September 1962, we rented an apartment on Mount Carmel. With a baby, a one-and-a-half-year-old in cloth diapers, a three-year-old in nursery school, and a $400-a-month income, we took the two-bedroom apartment as is. We had packed our belongings in Chicago in A and B boxes, A for immediate use and B to be unpacked when we moved into permanent living facilities. The Carmel apartment had a balcony where we stored all the B boxes and set out Tamar's red hobbyhorse and Annette's bike, which she used for shopping. It was a perfect landing pad in our new country. We hired a young woman from Tunisia whose family had come from aristocracy but was poor now. She was very intelligent but had no professional skills, worked for minimum wage for us, and knew nothing about childcare or house cleaning. She subsequently became a banker.

I was unaware in 1962 that a home telephone was a luxury and that it took up to six months to get a line. When I was informed of this at the post office, I was shocked.

"I have just come from the States. Everyone there has a phone. I will be teaching here. How can I be in touch with my students?" I asked naïvely.

"Where will you be teaching?" queried the clerk.

"At the Leo Baeck High School."

"I have two daughters studying there!" was his enthusiastic response.

I had a telephone and a line the next week. Such was the Israeli world of *protectzia* (pull), in those days.

But the telephone was not private. You had a "party line" with a neighbor, and the neighbor could cut into your conversation and ask for the line. And it wasn't only the neighbor. The operator who dialed the requested number could cut in or listen to your conversation. Two examples: Following a call to Tel Aviv, the operator called me and said, "I heard you are going to Tel Aviv tomorrow. Can I have a ride?" Another day I called London. During the conversation, the operator cut in, saying, "You have a long distance call from Tel Aviv" and immediately cut me off.

Among our children's belongings was a "little red wagon." They played with it in the inner courtyard in front of our apartment. One day an upstairs neighbor asked me if he could borrow it for a couple of days. Thinking that he wanted to pull his grandchildren around their house, I asked our kids, and we loaned it gladly. Six months later our upstairs neighbor was producing "little red wagons" for sale in Israel for the first time. America was influencing Israel's popular culture long before McDonald's and Pizza Hut.

That first apartment quickly became a meeting place for both Israelis and guests from the World Reform Movement. My students climbed the mountain from their apartments on the Hadar for lessons and to play with our very young and extremely active children. Amateur musicians converged in the evenings to play chamber music with Annette. I was the only American Reform rabbi in Israel, so a steady parade of Movement leaders from North America, Britain, Western Europe, and the Southern Hemisphere dropped in to get a report on the possibilities for Progressive Judaism in an Israel managed by European socialists. Our kids grew up with a stream of English-speaking guests engaged in rich conversation at our humble dinner table.

4a HaTzofim Street, Haifa
In January, we began to search for our own home to rent, build, or buy. We could have bought a 150-square meter home on a half-dunam (one dunam is about a quarter of an acre) plot in the Haifa suburb of Tivon for $25,000 ($750,000 today). Had we resettled in the developing new immigrant town of Upper Nazareth, as requested, we could have built a 200-square meter villa on a one-dunam plot for $20,000 ($500,000 today).

We decided to put our roots down in Haifa. High on the Carmel Mountain a large luxury neighborhood called Denia was beginning in 1962. We were offered a one-dunam plot for $5,000. We quickly decided not to build there for two reasons. It was too far from the Baeck School, and we didn't have the $35,000 needed for the plot and the house to be built on it. A home in Denia today on a full dunam plot would be worth $1.5 million.

We had $17,000 to spend: $5,000 from our Chicago savings and $12,000 from Annette's father, a gift for his daughter and her family. This was his profound joy, because of all his large American Colish clan (nine siblings, their twenty-one children and forty-one grandchildren), Annette was the only one to fulfill his deep Zionist commitment of *aliyah*, the personal ascent and upbuilding of *Eretz Yisrael*. We knew we could purchase an apartment with this sum.

During our two-month search we were shown many options, mostly uninspired "boxes." Suddenly in March we found the perfect place. Shell, the British Petroleum Company, which had built a pipeline from Iraq to the Haifa Bay, had completed a beautiful compound for its senior executives and engineers just before the State of Israel was established in 1948. It consisted of five buildings, each with four apartments of 125 square meters and two additional attic rooms built in each building for their servants. The construction was according to the highest British standards with imported building materials, and the insulation ensured that winter-summer temperature never varied more than five degrees. Behind the empty apartment was a thirteen-dunam practice golf course with lovely small pine and oak trees that Shell had created.

The price was right, as every Israeli who had been shown the apartment fled when told its story. The former occupants were a husband and wife who had a friend who was also the husband's secret mistress. One day the mistress visited the ill wife and poisoned her tea. The wife died; the mistress went to prison; the husband moved to Tel Aviv. Our non-superstitious theology saved us several thousand dollars, as we had no problem living with those "ghosts" in the bedroom.

Annette and I and our children thrived in that home. We volunteered to keep the golf course manicured for twenty-three years. Over many years we collected rounded river stones from Israel and everywhere we visited abroad, using them to create a unique fireplace. In fact, we used many Israeli materials to beautify that apartment through the years. It became both a *beit midrash* (study space) for the exploration of Jewish texts and a shrine in Haifa for chamber music.

The dining room became our family "altar," as we ate lunch together every day. We recreated the "table" of my childhood where we committed ourselves to a life of ethical mitzvot (helping others). Daily, after breakfast, Annette rehearsed with her orchestra or string quartet, I taught at Leo Baeck, and the kids went to kindergarten and later to school. We all gathered around our table at lunch, together with Annette's father (who had made *aliyah* soon after we did), for "show and tell" from our morning experiences, issues of the day, and a conversation on some current event with an ethical message.

Friday night was "entering Shabbat" time. For the first eight years I was rabbi of a congregation, so we went to *t'filah* (religious services) at 5:30 P.M. We were home before 7:00 P.M. in order to sit at the table for our Shabbat meal with all the blessings and songs. Often we had guests, and the atmosphere was always special and spiritual. There was a powerful Jewish and human kindness atmosphere. That dining room table was the key for the six of us to a life filled with value, service, and spirit.

A cornucopia of wonderful family memories was created in that Haifa apartment: at the first sign of spring going out to the *wadi* (ravine) behind our home to find as many tiny wildflowers as possible and then spreading them out at the house to see who collected the most different kinds . . . the birthday parties, each with an original treasure hunt and (long before television) a 16-mm projector screening the same much-loved rented cartoon movie every time . . . the family vacations with ten apple crates on the roof rack of our Peugeot 404 station wagon, each marked for food, camping equipment, boat and swimming gear, clothes, and the OD11 sailboat on the trailer . . . the hike up to the bowling alley followed by a grilled cheese and a milk shake . . . the doll house in Tamar's room and the full almond tree outside Ami and David's room . . . the annual Sukkot congregational party in our sukkah decorated by our kids together with immigrant teens from Leo Baeck . . . the endless stream of visitors and the magical chamber music evenings, with both professional and amateur musicians filling the air with the most glorious classical music.

Ein Hod Artists Village
It was chamber music that gave us the spark to build a home. Annette had created a family string quartet with our children: Annette and Tamar, violin; David, viola; and Ami, cello. During the 1970s when the kids were teenagers, they played together frequently. They were asked to play in Beit Gertrud, the home that Gertrud Krauss, the

renowned dancer and choreographer, had willed to her Ein Hod Artists Village.

As a result of those concerts, Annette and I were invited to make our home in that unique village just south of Haifa. We had lived in our beautiful apartment in Haifa for twenty years, but this was a chance to sink our roots deep into the Israel soil and an opportunity for me to once again create an architectural structure, this time for our family. In 1982 we acquired a one-dunam plot on a steep grade of the Carmel Mountain, overlooking a national forest to the south and the Mediterranean Sea to the west. The whole mountain was bursting with pine, oak, and *katlav* (red-barked strawberry) trees. In order to choose the site, Annette asked me to climb a tall pine to ascertain whether I could see the ocean. "Yes, clear as day," I yelled. "That's where I want the balcony outside our bedroom," Annette answered. And that became the focus for our 300-square meter multi-level mountainside home.

Taking my only Sabbatical during a thirty-seven-year career that academic year of 1983–84, I hired a contractor and several artisans, bought a vehicle for carrying up to a ton of building materials, and in July 1983 began construction. I was fifty years old. Leo Baeck had just given me a "This is Your Life" event, I was in perfect physical condition, and I was energized to realize this "Zionist" statement of planting our Samuels family deep into the earth of our old-new Homeland.

The construction was a joy, though there were many challenges during the process. Ami was a student at Haifa University that year, and he arrived at the site often to work alongside me and our team. The contractor, Ouni Halliliya, was a Muslim Arab from Nazareth. He and three of his sons worked daily. We had Muslims, Christians, Druze, Caucasians, and Jews from everywhere, each with his special skill, contributing to erecting our family dream house. Each afternoon I consulted with Ouni as to the tools and supplies we would need the next day. The next morning I arrived at a supplier as he opened at 7:00 A.M. to load a ton of cement sacks or concrete blocks or steel rods or pipes or tiles or wood planks. I would always get to our construction site before 9:00 A.M., for that was the beginning of the morning break when all of us sat around a fire that heated the spiced Arab coffee. I orchestrated conversations during those half-hour breaks. These are some of the gems.

The men preferred to talk about personal matters rather than national issues. Of course, the most recurring conversation revolved around *food:* olives, olive oil, hummus, tehina, pita, labani (goat cheese), grape leaves, mugaddarah (rice and lentils), zaatar (hyssop), local herbs, and wild plants. The Sephardic Jews and the Arab Muslims, Christians, and Druze, speaking in Hebrew with some Arabic thrown in, were animated as they showed what their wives had put in their lunch boxes. They spoke of their goats when they showed their labani, the grape vines that covered their front porch when trading their stuffed grape leaves. One Bedouin worker brought his wife's chicken, rice, pine nuts, and spicy herbs dish. Together we all picked wild rosemary and wild rose leaves on-site to boil in the *finjan* (pot) to make tea. But mostly we drank coffee, "Arab" coffee with *hel* (cardamom). Each day someone else brought his special coffee grains from home, and his wife was praised for the aroma and the taste of *her* coffee. Food around an open fire, the perfect integrator of ethnic and religious difference among men proud of their family traditions.

Education was a second topic around the finjan. These were not ignorant men. In fact, many were highly skilled and exacting in their professions, in creating space with *Gierung*, the German word they used for "perfect measurement." They had little general education but had absorbed a world of knowledge about life. As we spoke together, they reminded me of Jewish life in Eastern Europe, as in the stories of Sholem Aleichem and Y. L. Peretz and in the Broadway hit, "Fiddler on the Roof." But they wanted more for their children, especially their sons. When they discovered that I was an educator, they asked me to help get their sons into the best technical high schools in Haifa and the Galilee.

Inflation in Israel in 1983 was 400%. A hammer cost some 50,000 lirot. We had endless discussions about the economy but not macroeconomics. Rather, the men complained about the spiraling cost of buying bread, clothes, and school supplies, and running their vehicles. I paid them their wages based on the value of the dollar on that day. In fact, I called my bank each day in order to know how much to pay for tools and supplies. One of the men asked us how a country could survive with that level of galloping inflation. "It can't," I answered, and indeed, three years later the government devalued Israel's currency by 1,000%. Israel not only cut off three digits from our currency but issued new bills called "New Shekels." It took some ten years for our economy to level, but the last twenty years has seen our New Shekel devalue altogether by only 25%.

Shabbat and festivals was another topic of conversation. We never worked on Saturday, and most of the men spent that day with their families. The Muslims often wanted off on Friday as their children were out of school, and the same for Sunday for the Christians. Most of the men were not religious, so our work schedule was not seriously affected. I told the Muslims that if there was a special religious or town event on a Friday, we would not work on that day, but that I needed to know in advance. They never abused that trust. On the other hand, the Jewish workmen were often called for military reserve duty, a sometimes significant factor, for if the plumber or electrician couldn't come, the wall cement could not be poured as planned the next day, and so on. Often, on days like that our whole family would take on a building task for the feeling that all of us had a hand in our *Aliyah al HaKarkah*, our ascent onto the Land.

Construction methods was another serious topic of conversation. Most construction in Israel is concrete frame with hollow block walls. The workers were fascinated with descriptions of American lumber stick framing and with factory-manufactured framed walls. Animated conversation around heating and cooling insulation and methods of ensuring privacy from next room sounds would have provided architects much to learn from these experienced Israeli construction workers.

National issues often provoked heated discussions. Ouni had been a friend of Moshe Dayan. He told us of Dayan's desire that Arabs identify with Israel, feel allegiance to the State, and be model citizens. The other Arabs were silent until I said, "But how can you sing 'HaTikvah,' our national anthem, and salute our flag? Both are Jewish symbols." "We don't," said Faheem from Sachnin. "Your flag is a *tallit* [prayer shawl], and your anthem is about your hope to return to Zion. We don't wear a *tallit*, and we have always been here in Palestine." "Could you feel allegiance if we had a neutral anthem and flag?" I asked. "Yes! But also if our Knesset members could be in the government and represent our interests," answered Haled from Shefaram. Then, we went back to work with our common denominator of building the best we could.

The *Lebanese War* was another subject that came up. Who was responsible for the Sabra and Shatila massacre, Sharon or Begin? Who was the suicide bomber who blew up a bus in Jerusalem, killing six? How could Palestinians continue to live in the territories with a new

Jewish settlement started there every week? The discussions often got heated, but we only had a twenty- to thirty-minute break, allowing us to avert potential conflicts and return to being homebuilders from 9:30 A.M. until everyone but Ouni and I left the building site at 5:00 P.M.

How fortunate we were that my brother, Vic, and his wonderful wife, Bobbi, stood beside us and helped us through the year of construction. Vic loaned us the necessary dollars to ensure there would be no delay in building. He contributed all sixty-four cabinets and closets, lovingly built in his Texas cabinet factory by a talented carpenter who was thrilled that the work of his hands was going to the Holy Land. Vic and Bobbi hosted us in their beautiful home in Houston for three months while we purchased our tiling, carpets, furniture, lighting fixtures, curtains, and other necessities. All of this was stored in Vic's Houston warehouse, together with those cabinets. Then Vic had it all loaded on his dock into a forty-foot container and shipped to the port of Haifa. It is doubtful we could have finished such a project without this tender loving care.

The construction was pure joy for me. A rabbi-educator learning how to use *tools*; the relationship between height and depth for the fifty-two *stairs* in the house and the theory of spiraling stairs; how to create *rounded walls* and *arched windows*; how to weave four kinds of Galilee marble into a mosaic *floor*; how to build four *vaulted roofs*; how to put *a gable* into the roof as a clothes closet and dressing area; how to create *fireplaces* in the living room and in the master bedroom that draw out the smoke and throw out the heat and have the same architectural forms as the window frames; how to *wire* the house for five telephones, for surround-sound, and for intercom; how to hide all *pipes* and *sleeves* in the walls but know how to get to them if needed; how to make a three-floor *laundry chute*; how to treat *wood paneling* so it would never mildew or attract insects; how to insulate *underground walls* from moisture; how to ensure full, no-echo *acoustics* in Annette's fifteen-foot-ceiling music studio, but how to deaden *sound* everywhere else; how to build *retention walls* on the side of the mountain; how to shape the southern *roof overhang* to bring in the warm low-in-the-sky winter sun but give shade from the hot high-in-the-sky summer sun; how to bring in *water*, keep it out, and drain it away from the property; how to *landscape* to fit the Carmel woods; and self-maintenance. Much of this was trial and error and not without many mistakes. Since finishing construction in 1985, I've said that if I ever built a second house, it would be with far fewer errors.

I never will. The experience was hard, physically (I almost cut off my fingers), economically (to borrow money during 400% annual inflation), technically (long before the cell phone), socially (often it was necessary to threaten people to get a task done), and professionally (the master plan for Leo Baeck was put on hold for an entire year).

It was uplifting despite these hardships. If you love architecture as an art, to see the shapes and forms come to life is spiritual. To know that this space is your temple and that you will breathe life into it for years is soul-satisfying. If you love the Land, seeing the trees, bushes, and flowers come to life and color sustains you. If you believe that the Jewish People is reestablishing a covenant for a better world, you are participating in that covenant. To paraphrase the pioneering song "You have built and been built by it," one can believe that you and your creation are a tiny part of a mighty Jewish and human stream.

In fact, our home is above a stream created by millions of years of rain bringing mountain soil down to the sea. It is also just above a natural cave created by that same rain, a cave that housed a family of very early humans some 40,000 years ago. We are therefore in the presence of nature's long, long evolution and one of the earliest human habitations on this planet.

The road up the mountain to Ein Hod also leads to Yemin Orde, an Orthodox Youth Village named for British General Orde Wingate, who courageously trained Israelis in the art of warfare prior to the War of Independence. It is a privilege to live near this pluralistic institution, pioneers in the humane absorption of immigrant youth. They have been led by one of Israel's prime educators, Rabbi Dr. Chaim Peri, to live by the highest ethical standards of Judaism and civil values.

The road continues to the entrance to Nir Etzion, a progressive Orthodox moshav, whose members fled from Kfar Etzion, their unprotectable village near Jerusalem in the War of Independence. Nir Etzion (In Memory of Etzion) is highly successful socially, religiously, and economically.

Further up the road is Ein Chud, a tiny Arab village established by Muchamid Abu el Hisha and his small clan who were homeless following the War of Independence, becoming squatters on their former grazing land. Ein Chud is one of forty Arab villages established since 1948 that, to our shame, were not recognized.

Annette and I have stood by their side now some thirty-five years. Only recently, after more than sixty years, the government and the local municipal council have finally recognized the village. Some of their members have been skilled workers for us, and they and their families have become good friends. I have had the honor of helping some of their children get an adequate education and health care in spite of the severe limitations posed by their life conditions.

If all of us who reside on the landmass called Palestine-Land-of-Israel could live with honor and mutuality as we secular, liberal, and Orthodox Jews and secular and religious Muslim Arabs do on our little piece of the Carmel Mountain, the face of our society would be different and better than it is. And I pray that someday it may be so.

CHAPTER 2
RABBI BOB

PART 3
Beginnings of Reform Judaism

Bar and Bat Mitzvah

I found that boys from non-traditional families were being trained to chant for bar mitzvah by Orthodox teachers. The ceremony would take place in an Orthodox synagogue on a Thursday morning in the presence of the father and other men in the family, without the mother and other female family members invited to participate. The thirteen-year-old adolescent chanted the few verses of the *maftir* (the last section of the weekly Torah reading) and the *haftarah* (the weekly reading from the Prophets), after which he was given a *Mi Shebeirach*, the traditional blessing that each male gets after reading Torah in the synagogue. And that was it. When I discussed this with Dr. Elk, he suggested I train boys and officiate at bar mitzvah ceremonies at his congregation, Beit Yisrael, on Mt. Carmel. It was an opportunity to ascertain how such families would respond to a more comprehensive and existential experience for both the adolescents and their parents.

I inaugurated several reforms: visiting services at three Haifa synagogues (Chasidic, Conservative, Reform); having the ceremony on Shabbat morning; both father and mother blessing their son; and passing the Torah though three generations to the bar mitzvah boy. In addition, the bar mitzvah boy would write and recite an address, including a value for him coming from the Torah reading; receive a *Mi Shebeirach* welcoming the bar mitzvah as a Jewish adult with all the privileges and responsibilities therein; and sing the *Kiddush* and the *Motzi* (blessings over the wine and bread) at a reception for the worshippers following the service in the presence of all male *and* female family members together. All of this was standard for the thousands of b'nei mitzvah in Reform congregations in Western countries, but it was a sensation in Haifa in 1963. Not only were the families thrilled to experience the symbolic change of their son from childhood to adolescence, but the leaders of the congregation were so moved that after the ceremonies for the three boys at which I officiated, Beit Yisrael adopted the practice and continued to do so after becoming an Orthodox institution in the 1970s.

Even more significant and transforming was the introduction of a bat mitzvah ceremony for twelve-year-old girls. Believe it or not, girls entering adolescence had neither a religious service nor a party to symbolize their transition into adult Jewish life. After consulting with Elisheva Egozi, the headmistress of the Leo Baeck Elementary School, I initiated an Erev Shabbat service on the first Shabbat of the Hebrew month in which all sixth-grade girls whose birthday occurred in that month, usually three or four, read from Torah. We used the dining room in the center of the school. Rabbi Porat, Moshe Nativ, and I prepared a monthly creative service, assigning readings and songs, working with the girls in creating and reciting their speeches. This was moving and memorable and revolutionary for Israel in the early 1960s. Those young female Leo Baeck sixth graders and their families loved the experience but were barely aware that they were breaking new ground in the empowerment of Jewish women in Israel. Even today at the bat mitzvah of a young girl, a grandmother will approach me to remind me she was one of the first, way back then in the 1960s.

A Boy Scout World Jamboree

In that summer of 1963, a World Jamboree of the Boy Scouts took place in Marathon, Greece. The United States sent a delegation of eight hundred boys, eighty-three of whom were Jewish. The director of Jewish Scouting in America asked me to serve as chaplain for those Jewish Boy Scouts during the Jamboree, and so in July I made my way to the Plain of Marathon in my Scout chaplain's uniform.

It was to be the only chaplaincy experience of my life. I was rejected by the American Air Force when I was ordained because I had recently had a kidney stone. And in my twenty-three years in the Israeli air force and reserves I was not allowed to be a chaplain because I am a "Reform" rabbi. I loved that Greek experience, as I served as the chaplain for all the nearly 250 Jewish Scouts in the Jamboree. Three experiences there are worth recalling.

First, in the march past, which was done alphabetically by countries, the Israeli delegation of ninety Scouts, including fifteen Arabs, marched near the Scouts of Jordan, Iraq, and Iran. I marched with them, rather than with the Americans, knowing that the Arabs would try to sabotage the Israeli delegation. They threw stones at our Scouts and tried to lower the Israeli flag. The Israeli Scouts, including the Arabs, decided to march with heads high and with dignity and not to respond. We won high honors for that, but emotionally it was not easy.

The second item of interest had to do with our celebration of Shabbat. During the week we created a committee to organize our services. The French-Jewish troop was to prepare the food, and other tasks were divided between the Jewish Scouts from England, Canada, Trinidad, Australia, and Mexico as well as the Americans and the Israelis. I requisitioned a jeep from the American delegation in order to travel the twenty-six Marathon-miles to Athens to meet with the Chief Rabbi there, requesting the loan of a *sefer Torah*, which I promised to return on Sunday morning. The Chief Rabbi responded to my request negatively, stating that if the boys wanted to pray, they should come into Athens to a "real synagogue." I responded by pointing out to the good rabbi that he must expect the entire delegation to run the Marathon twice, both coming to synagogue and returning to base, because he certainly would not want them to ride into Athens on Shabbat morning, and that he would certainly agree with me that any space could be a synagogue if it had two things—ten Jews and a Torah. He was adamant. I left Athens without a Torah.

When I reported this to the head of the American delegation, he was so incensed he picked up his field telephone and called Washington. He reported the problem to the Director of the American Boy Scouts. Ten minutes later the field phone rang. It was Washington, telling us they had spoken to the nearest Jewish chaplain, based in Ankara, Turkey. He would requisition a special plane on Friday to fly up with not only a Torah but everything we'd need for Shabbat worship and celebration. True to his word, on Friday morning Conservative Rabbi Gil Collins descended on the Plain of Marathon in a plane full of Jewish "stuff," including a case of Manischewitz wine, six cases of gefilte fish, and a large briefcase designed for American Jewish chaplains. The front opened to reveal a *sefer Torah* in the center with fifty prayer books neatly stacked in side compartments. In the back of the case *kippot, t'fillin,* and *tallitot.* Underneath, in a sliding drawer, were a battery-operated phonograph and records of cantorial, Israeli, and Shabbat songs.

I don't know how that Shabbat morning service was for the good Chief Rabbi of Athens, twenty-six miles away, but out there on the Plain of Marathon, the souls of those 250 Jewish boys, their chaplain, and a few non-Jewish Scouts and Scoutmasters rose up to Heaven. The absolute acceptance of the First Amendment to the US Constitution by the leaders of the American Boy Scouts ("Congress shall make no law . . . prohibiting the free exercise" of religion), the immediate response by Rabbi Collins, the trilingual prayer service and Torah reading, not to mention the scrumptious food prepared by the French Jewish troop, the gefilte fish, and the fellow feeling of those diverse-culture Jewish boys made for a Shabbat to be remembered for a lifetime.

The third experience had to do with the immediate future of Reform Judaism in Israel. In the spring of that first year, I was approached by a group of German-speaking Israelis who lived in Nahariya, a sea-coast town in the Western Galilee. They, too, wanted to begin a Reform congregation like the destroyed ones they had left behind in Germany. I asked my father-in-law, Rabbi Nathan Colish, if he would help me found this second congregation. He readily agreed. Rabbi Colish had made *aliyah* in our footsteps and was living that first year in a dormitory of the newly opened Solomon Schechter Center for Conservative Judaism in Jerusalem. So there, on the Plain of Marathon, using the American delegation's field-telephone, I called two colleagues in the United States. I asked them for $600 each in order to be able to continue my ongoing work and to begin the congregation to be known as Emet VeShalom (Truth and Peace) in Nahariya. Rabbi Max Nussbaum of Los Angeles and Rabbi Richard Hertz of Detroit immediately responded affirmatively. I had already begun to fundraise for Leo Baeck, but this marked the first time that American Jewish leaders responded to my requests for funding the emergence of Reform congregations in Israel.

Dignified, passive resistance to Arab aggression . . . a spiritual, pluralistic Shabbat experience . . . and successful funding for the beginnings of Israeli Reform Judaism. It was a very successful Jamboree.

Building Congregations: A Strikeout and a Score For the Reform Movement

One week after I arrived in Haifa, I was contacted by Shlomo Maagani, an immigrant from Hungary who had been the organist in the large and distinguished Neolog (Reform) Synagogue in Budapest. It was the largest synagogue building in Europe. Maagani arrived in Israel in 1956 as a result of the failed Hungarian uprising against the Soviet Union. In the six years intervening he had become totally blind and had just received a job as the telephone operator for the Elite Chocolate Factory in Upper Nazareth, a new immigrant development town above Arab Nazareth. Maagani's dream was to once again play an organ in a liberal synagogue in his new town. He had heard about my *aliyah* from Rabbi Unger and called to ask for help. I went to see him and was impressed with his knowledge of the liturgy and his passion for prayer.

Together, we formed what was to be the second Reform congregation in Israel, Congregation Herzl. Mordecai Allon, the founding Mayor of Upper Nazareth, offered us a basement apartment. I found a manual organ for Maagani in Haifa, and our first services were on Rosh HaShanah morning, 1962. I brought the food from Haifa for a *seudat chag* (reception lunch). The service was attended by thirty new immigrants from Transylvania (Hungary and Romania). Many of these people have gone on to live creative lives in Israel, but at the time, they were unemployed and had little knowledge of spoken Hebrew. The congregation that subsequently formed with them and with the B'nei Israel Jews from India gave these new immigrants spiritual satisfaction and a refuge from the strong winds of hardship on this bare mountain in the Galilee.

During that first year of 1962–63, the Herzl Congregation became a focal point for my religious work. I went there every Shabbat and took with me food for the *Seudat Shabbat*. Many of the worshippers came for the meal, and that was fine, as I knew they did not have a proper diet during the week. Through the powerful music of Shlomo Maagani and the friendship with those immigrant congregants, we developed a deep spiritual bond, which was extraordinary. The National Federation of Temple Sisterhoods provided the funds to buy an electronic organ for Mr. Maagani. This instrument had plug-in earphones that could silence the sound in the room, making it possible for him to walk to the synagogue at three in the morning, sit down, and play a Bach fugue or the Lewandowski synagogue music he knew so well.

I became a close friend of Dr. Shmuel Aptiker, a B'nei Israel Indian Jew and a physician at the Afula Hospital who later became chair of the congregation. It was a holy task to bring together these refugees from Eastern Europe and from the Indian subcontinent, these people of difference, in a Judaism based on equality of ethnicity and pluralism. We subsequently found a young man with a beautiful voice, Menachem Kol, who served as our cantor. He later studied at the HUC-JIR School of Sacred Music and has become a respected cantor in the United States.

NFTY has a youth program called Mitzvah Corps that sends Reform Jewish youth to live and work in a community for the summer. I asked Rabbi Cook to send such a group to Upper Nazareth, and he did. We arranged for thirty-five American teenagers to live with immigrant families and build a public park under the direction of the Municipal Department of Landscaping on this mostly treeless and boulder-strewn Galilee mountain. Not one of those American kids complained about the food and the living conditions in those 40-square meter (400-square foot) immigrant apartments. They and their Israeli hosts worked hard all summer, and a beautiful park took shape.

Upper Nazareth had just become a Regional Municipal Council, controlled by the Labor Party. Mayor Mordecai Allon loved the enthusiasm, passion, and industriousness of those kids. I became a friend of this liberal mayor who, as a member of the Labor Party, had absolute control of this new development town. As a result, at the end of the summer he called me in and pleaded with me to come live in Upper Nazareth. He asked me to become either the head of formal or informal education. He told me if I wanted to create the schools and the education curriculum there, he would give me that job, or if I wanted to become the head of the community center, that could become my work.

I had committed to Haifa and to teaching in the Baeck School, so I pleaded with the World Union, the UAHC, HUC-JIR, and a few of my friends in the Reform rabbinate in North America to send a young Hebrew-speaking rabbi to live and work in Upper Nazareth. It was to be a window of opportunity that would quickly close, as Israel's political system produced more and more religious coercion and Orthodox opposition to Reform. A dynamic Reform rabbi or educator would have become an important personality, doing well for himself while developing this new city in Israel. But it was not to be. No one was ready to "step up to the plate." Sadly, it was a missed opportunity, a "lost game" for the Reform Movement. Today Upper Nazareth is an urban city with 35,000 Jews and 8,000 Arabs. In 2015 the city's mayor spoke against Arabs living in his town. It is sobering to think what the city could have become if the roots of liberalism and social justice had been laid back then, over fifty years ago. In my opinion, this was a missed opportunity for the World and American Reform Movements in the socialization of Israel.

Another situation involved the congregation in Nahariya, which consisted almost entirely of *yekkes* (German-speaking Jews). Rabbi Dr. Rolf, an elderly gentleman who had been a liberal rabbi in Germany, Dr. Eliezer Hirshfield, and Meir Shafir became the dominant forces of that congregation. Rabbi Colish and I went there on alternating weeks throughout that first year, and I began going to Upper Nazareth only once every second week.

A telling portrait of two early Reform congregations: the service in Upper Nazareth began when people arrived; the service in Nahariya began exactly on the appointed minute. Worship in Upper Nazareth was loud, boisterous, and often cacophonous; in Nahariya it was orderly and correct. The sermon and Torah commentary in Upper Nazareth were warm and emotional; in Nahariya, intellectual and text-based. The *oneg Shabbat* (reception) in Upper Nazareth was joyful and much appreciated; in Nahariya, it was controlled and formal. A portrait of nascent Reform congregations, showing the culture of different communities in the warp and woof of an integrating Israel, only fifteen years old.

MARAM, the Council of Progressive Rabbis in Israel

Melvin Zeger and I were ordained together in Cincinnati in June 1960. He went to Baltimore, I to Chicago. Both of us wanted to live and work as rabbis in Israel. I was able to do so within two years, he within three. Upon arriving in Israel, Rabbi Zeger changed his name to Moshe Zemer. Rabbi Zemer and I were friends and colleagues for almost half a century.

How pleased we were, therefore, in that September of 1963 to sit together and dream of a flourishing Reform Movement. We decided to form a rabbinic union. We contacted Rabbi Jack Cohen, an active Conservative-Reconstructionist rabbi in Israel. Rabbi Cohen was director of the Hillel Chapter (a student organization) at the Hebrew University in Jerusalem and one of the leaders of Rabbi Mordecai Kaplan's Reconstructionist Movement. The three of us met in Rabbi Zemer's home in Kfar Shmaryahu, searching for a name and a plan for our rabbinic union. Rabbi Cohen suggested *Rabbanim L'maan Hitchadshut Hayahadut*, Rabbis for the Renewal of Judaism. Rabbi Zemer suggested *Meotzet Rabbanim Mitkadmim,* The Council of Progressive Rabbis. Rabbi Cohen and I accepted that name, and so MARAM came to be.

Rabbi Zemer founded a congregation, first in Kfar Shmaryahu, and then in Tel Aviv. His congregation was called Kedem ("looking back and looking forward"). He and his wife, Ilana, nurtured that congregation in the heart of Israel for twenty-five years. Many were the political travails and challenges that Rabbi Zemer had in getting even an inadequate place of worship for his congregants (a basement in a central commercial district of Tel Aviv). But, as history has shown, he was on the right track.

He and I went to visit David Ben-Gurion in his home in the Negev, Kibbutz Sde Boker. Ben-Gurion asked us to tell him of our work in Israel. When we finished, he said, "I like what you do for our People, and I agree with your religious principle of emphasizing ethics over ritual, but you will never get them to come to you in significant numbers until you build a large and impressive synagogue center in North Tel Aviv."

He was right. Rabbi Zemer and his congregation began to petition the Tel Aviv Municipality for such a plot near the Yarkon River in northern Tel Aviv. It was Rabbi Zemer's struggle but was not to be his success. After years of city refusals and court orders, in 1989 the Kedem Congregation of Tel Aviv was finally awarded a plot on B'nei Dan Street. However, Rabbi Richard Hirsch, the International Director of the World Union, decided to close both of Tel Aviv's Reform congregations, Rabbi Zemer's veteran Kedem Congregation and Rabbi Kinneret Shiryon's very successful Ramat Aviv Congregation, in order to form one new congregation with a significant building to be erected on the site. Beit Daniel was created, funded by the Gerry and Ruth

Daniel family. Rabbi Zemer, ending his career as a congregational rabbi in 1990, had fought the good fight and prepared the ground for what was to prove Ben-Gurion correct on a grand scale.

In a larger sense, however, MARAM had already become Rabbi Zemer's spiritual home. He was an expert in Jewish law, especially the responsa literature (questions on Jewish practice asked of leading rabbis through the centuries and their answers). For years, Rabbi Zemer served as chair of MARAM, welcoming younger colleagues as the Movement grew. He became the first *av beit din*, the head of the three-rabbi court of Progressive Rabbis. He taught halachah at HUC-JIR in Jerusalem, emphasizing the truth that it is possible to be faithful to the prophetic demand for justice and compassion in human society while at the same time preserving the framework of Jewish law. He wrote many articles for the national press on current Israeli issues, emphasizing the ethical basis of Jewish law: articles on the Intifada and the exchange of prisoners, and on conversion, marriage, divorce, the status of women, Shabbat, the State's relationship to the foreigner, medicine, burial, and the ultra-Orthodox.

Speaking of Jewish law, conversion was, and continues to be, a key issue in Israel. I had two diametrically opposed experiences related to the process. The first was a positive one in which Doris Andruss appeared one day in 1968 at our Shabbat service. I welcomed her, and she told me she was fifty-five years old, new in Israel, an American Christian, a single divorcee, and searching for her religious identity. I invited her to meet us, and she became a member of our family. She was gracious and kind, loving and thoughtful. I taught her Judaism and in 1975, together with Rabbis Zemer and Elk, converted her. We were close until her death in 2007. We say *Kaddish* for Doris every September.

The second experience was negative. Elsewhere I have written about our work for the absorption of Ethiopian immigrants, but the issue of their conversion to Judaism is a sign of disgrace for Israel. The Chief Rabbinate ordained that most Ethiopian Jews had no record of their mothers' Jewishness. Therefore, they would *all* have to convert, all 100,000 of them. The fact that they had lived in Jewish villages, practiced Judaism, had lived for several years prior to *aliyah* under the auspices of the Jewish Agency, Israel's Ministry of Immigration, and two American organizations for Ethiopian *aliyah*, made no difference to these rabbis, in effect still "living" in seventeenth-century Poland, nor to their political allies, the Israeli government. So as they arrived in waves in Israel, the adults were placed in absorption centers where Orthodox rabbis taught them Ashkenazic Judaism and made them pray every day in their Orthodox religious services where the women were completely separated from the men. Their adolescent children were sent away from their parents to Orthodox youth villages, where they were separated from the other students. It was an act of national religious coercion of the worst kind.

Leo Baeck was ready to welcome as many Ethiopian children and teens as the Ministry would send us, but it did not happen because we are not Orthodox. We pleaded that we, too, are religious and that we, too, can convert. To these authorities, that is worse than being secular. But just consider this. One million Russian speakers arrived in Israel in the 1990s, one-third of them not halachically Jewish. No matter. Live where you want, work where you want, study where you want, and convert *if* you want. To me, this is blatant national racism. If you are white European, the doors are open. If you are a person of color, you will do as we say. Shame.

Marriage was another controversial issue. Miriam, age eighty-four, came to me and pleaded with me to officiate at her marriage with her eighty-two-year-old partner. Why did she come to Rabbi Samuels? She was a childless widow whose husband had died twenty-five years prior. Her husband had a single brother, Daniel, in Australia. This, according to the Book of Deuteronomy, requires the ritual of *yibbum*, in which the childless widow is obligated to marry her dead husband's brother or be released by him. There is a ceremony of release from this obligation called *halitzah*, but it is primitive and humiliating. It also must be done face-to-face between the widow and the departed's brother. Both Miriam and Daniel were not able to travel at their advanced age, which meant the "hands of the Rabbinate" were tied, and Miriam could not remarry in Israel. Rabbi Zemer taught me the evolution of this halachah through the Middle Ages and in modern times, pointed out to me the unanimous resolution of the Central Conference of American Rabbis in 1869 "that the precepts of *yibbum* and *halitzah* have lost all significance, importance, and obligatory force for us." I married them.

Rabbi Zemer subsequently formed the *Machon HaHalachah Bat Z'maneinu*, the Contemporary Halachah Institute. He decided to bring to the attention of the Israeli and Diaspora Reform rabbinate a modern view on contemporary issues where Jewish traditional law was coercive or not in touch with current mores and societal needs of Israelis. In this he was joined by Rabbi Dr. Walter Jacob of Rodef Shalom Congregation in Pittsburgh. Rabbi Jacob was an expert in halachah as well. He was following in the footsteps of his mentor, Rabbi Dr. Solomon Freehof, the acknowledged scholar of Reform Judaism, whose many books on Jewish law often form the accepted path of Reform practice in modern issues of Jewish tradition.

Rabbis Zemer and Jacob recommended that the Institute's board name the *Machon HaHalachah* for Dr. Freehof. The Freehof Institute became an important instrument for progressive rabbis throughout the world to reinterpret Jewish tradition for modern Jewish life. For many years, every conference of the Reform Movement had a Freehof Institute symposium, and subsequent to each conference a booklet was produced on the papers delivered and the issues presented. The issues included such critical topics as Death and Euthanasia, the Fetus and Fertility, Crime and Punishment, the Environment, Aging and the Aged, and Sexual Issues in the Halachah. I was honored to serve as treasurer of the Institute and to support Rabbi Zemer in his historic task.

Rabbi Zemer gathered together many issues about which he had written through the years, producing a book in 1993, *Halachah Sh'fuyah* ("Sane Halachah"). This book, in Hebrew, was a breakthrough in the evolution of a modern interpretation of traditional Jewish law. In 1999 Rabbi Zemer produced an English book, an updated version of the Hebrew, *Evolving Halachah: A Progressive Approach to Traditional Jewish Law*. These two books form a rationale for halachah as an evolving ethical system and deal with real conflicts between life in a modern Jewish State and ossified Jewish law.

This life work of Rabbi Zemer is a landmark in the development of the Israel Movement for Progressive Judaism.

Or Hadash, a New Light Shines on Zion

In retrospect, it was inevitable that a progressive Jewish congregation would be formed in Haifa. The city had all the basic ingredients to make it a success: one-quarter of Haifa's citizens were Muslim and Christian Arabs; there had been Arab mayors; the city was always multicultural and multi-religious with a deep commitment to pluralism and to acceptance of difference. When I arrived, Haifa had many liberal Jews who had immigrated from middle-Europe, several of whom had been members of liberal congregations there for generations. It was not by chance that in 1936 Dr. Elk picked Haifa as a place to live and to found Beit Yisrael, his congregation. Dr. Elk was a graduate of the liberal rabbinical seminary in Breslau and had been a student of Rabbi Dr. Leo Baeck at the *Hochschule für die Wissenschaft des Judentums* (Seminary and School for the Scientific Study of Judaism) in Berlin. He had been the rabbi in the German city of Shtetin on the northern German-Polish border. As a Zionist and an early observer of the rise of Nazism, Dr. Elk decided to immigrate to Haifa in 1935, and some members of his Shtetin congregation followed in his footsteps. He used Beit Yisrael to establish community projects for adults and the elderly, almost exclusively in the German language. The congregation began worshipping in Beit HaKranot in Haifa's Hadar neighborhood, but quickly moved to two locations: Beit HaMoreh on the upper Hadar and on Keller Street near the Central Carmel. As the years progressed, Beit Yisrael became a Liberal Orthodox congregation. As Dr. Elk became more involved in his school, he turned the congregation over to more conservative laymen. When I arrived in Haifa, the congregation was decidedly Orthodox in practice. Dr. Elk asked me to officiate at a bar mitzvah from time to time, as they had no rabbi. By the 1960s Beit Yisrael was no longer a progressive congregation, and Rabbi Elk worshipped there rarely. A group of Orthodox men took the reins, obtained Holocaust funding, and built a beautiful Orthodox synagogue on the grounds of Beit Yisrael.

   Haifa needed a congregation for its religiously pluralistic Jews. The trigger that led me to found such a congregation was a chance evening of chamber music in our home in the spring of 1964. Maurice and Florence Schellekes, a Dutch Jewish couple and Holocaust survivors, were invited to our home by mutual friends for that evening of music. Maurice approached me during the evening and asked me if he could sing some Schubert *lieder*. As soon as he began his first song, I whispered to Annette, "There's my cantor." When he sat down next to me, I thanked him for his inspiring singing, saying, "If you'll be my cantor, I'll be your rabbi. Will you join me in starting a liberal congregation here?" He smiled from ear to ear, replying, "I was a 'hobby' cantor in the liberal congregation in The Hague following the War before we made *aliyah*. It will give me great satisfaction to be your 'hobby' cantor." This started a partnership that lasted for many years and set a beginning frame for Congregation Or Hadash.

I set out to form the congregation. "Stepping up to the plate" here meant I needed five hits: a *sefer Torah*, an *aron hakodesh*, a room for prayer, prayer books, and worshippers.

Dr. Elk had been given a *sefer Torah* by Dr. Baeck when Elk visited him in Berlin to say goodbye in 1935. Elk related to me that Baeck rose from his chair in the *Hochshule* and walked with him to the Oranienburger Strasse Synagogue, a cathedral-like synagogue of eight floors from floor to ceiling. Baeck opened the *aron hakodesh* and handed Elk one of the thirty-odd scrolls there. He said, "Take this with you to Palestine, and with it you will start your congregation." That scroll may be the only one remaining, for the synagogue was torched in 1938 on Kristallnacht and destroyed by Allied bombing in World War II. Dr. Elk had placed this Torah scroll in the *aron hakodesh* in Beit Yisrael on Arlozorov Street in Haifa's Hadar. Since it was no longer needed there, the board of the congregation agreed that Dr. Elk take it in order to establish a new synagogue in Haifa. I had my single (a hit, reaching first base safely).

The story of the *aron hakodesh* is beautiful. During the summer of 1964, ten American high school exchange students arrived on the Eisendrath International Exchange (EIE) Program for an *ulpan* as the first stage of their fall semester study program at Leo Baeck. One of them, Roberta Shapiro, was already a talented artist who was studying art history in high school. Together we designed the doors for an *aron hakodesh*. An Arab friend in Haifa made the box and the doors. The doors were constructed with a deep depression in order to insert a mosaic. During a daily *ulpan* hour we researched the symbols found in the mosaics of Israeli Byzantine synagogues of the third, fourth, and fifth centuries. Each of those ten American exchange students chose a Byzantine mosaic to copy or to recreate in modern mode. This was meant to be a modern parallel to the Ten Commandments, using authentic symbols from Israel's ancient past. Once the compositions were completed, we turned to a noted Haifa ceramicist, Edith Galush. She gladly took on the project, suggesting we create our own ceramics by bringing her multi-colored sands extracted from the Small Crater in Israel's Negev Desert. So, we made a summer field trip to the Negev. It was a project of the spirit, going down to the Negev in early summer to explore the three great craters and to fill our buckets full of blue, green, orange, red, and mostly earth-toned sands. Under Edith's supervision and using her kiln, we made the mosaic tiles from that beautiful colored sand. She taught us how to break them into tiny mosaic squares. For those ten American teenagers, for Edith, and for me, it was a holy task. We completed the doors by the end of August. Now we had runners on first and second base.

The most obvious and central place to rent a room for services for the High Holy Days was Beit Rothschild in Haifa's Central Carmel. This was a building erected by the Rothschild family at the beginning of the twentieth century and had been made into a non-governmental organization with a board of directors to serve as a center for the Mt. Carmel community. It was, in fact, Israel's first community center. I had already come to know the creative director, Dov Malkin, so it was easy for me to approach him. When I asked him for the use of a room to form my liberal congregation on Rosh HaShanah, he looked at me with a stern face and said, "Rabbi Samuels, when we established Beit Rothschild, we determined our programs. We decided there are two forms of communal activity that Beit Rothschild would not offer because they are too political: sport and religion." I was shocked, and responded, "I daresay there isn't a community center in the United States that isn't based primarily on sport. And religion? The residents of the Carmel don't have the right to choose their religious preference?" I lost. Malkin was adamant. So I had to return to Dr. Elk, who once again arranged for us to use the much smaller below-the-street hall of his B'nai B'rith Lodge, also in the Central Carmel. One out, bases loaded.

Rabbi Andre Zaoui, rabbi of Jerusalem's Har-El Congregation, had just published a small *machzor* (prayer book for the High Holy Days). He readily agreed that we could use it in Haifa. We bought 150 copies, thereby solving the fourth of five needs, or so I thought.

Now the question was how to get people to come to the services. I announced at Leo Baeck that all students and their families were welcome to join me and Cantor Schellekes for services on Rosh HaShanah. I put an ad in the local Haifa newspaper and called my friends and the German-Jewish friends of Dr. Elk.

We had another potential source. Every second Friday afternoon for a year, Annette and I had been inviting two students, a boy and a girl, from each of the eight Leo Baeck classes for an Erev Shabbat experience at our home. Each Shabbat Eve it was an eye-opener for those sixteen secular kids. We started with a game of croquet on the lawn behind our apartment. At the exact appropriate moment, we went to the head of the ravine overlooking the Mediterranean for a *Kabbalat Shabbat* service (welcoming the Sabbath), so that the sun would be seen orange as it dipped into the sea, and we rose to recite the *Shema Yisrael*. Then we entered our apartment, sat in a circle on the floor of my study, and discussed the subject, "The Meaning of Shabbat for Secular Israeli Youth." Annette then invited us into the living room where she had prepared *Seudat Shabbat* (Shabbat dinner) for us, with all the appropriate blessings and *z'mirot* (Shabbat songs). We finished at exactly 7:45 P.M. to enable the teenagers to get to the evening meeting of their Scout troop, of which they were *all* members. Perhaps these students might join us for worship in the new congregation.

We had no idea how many people would come. In order to prepare the B'nai B'rith hall, which had only thirty chairs, we hired a truck. Two of my students, Zeev Harari and Mordechai Rotem, who were to become Reform rabbis many years later, helped me bring 150 chairs from Leo Baeck to B'nai B'rith. Everything was in place: A beautiful *aron hakodesh* with an historic *sefer Torah* and a newly printed prayer book in a rented hall. Several dozen people had committed to attend the Erev Rosh HaShanah service. Gil Nativ, a Leo Baeck student who had helped me give content to the student Erev Shabbat program, agreed to partner with me in leading the services, blow the shofar, and read from the Torah.

Maurice and I had rehearsed together and separately during the Hebrew month of Elul, preceding the High Holy Days. I loved those rehearsals. A Dutchman and an American creating worship for *sabras*, a beautiful view of the Haifa Bay and Mt. Hermon from Maurice's apartment on the crest of Mt. Carmel, and a good cup of Dutch coffee. Much of the music was unknown to Maurice, but the Dutch being more orderly than even the Germans, Maurice prepared every note and transliterated all the Hebrew chanting into Roman letters with Dutch pronunciation. As the High Holy Days approached, we were ready.

On Erev Rosh HaShanah over 200 people arrived at the hall. Meanwhile, Cantor Schellekes had found Yoel Goldberg, an amateur organist, who brought an electronic organ to accompany him. We had a home run!

For *Kol Nidrei* (Yom Kippur eve service), there were 300 worshippers, many of whom had to stand. That first High Holy Day worship in Haifa became a grand slam, a home run with the bases loaded.

Before the *Ne'ilah* service (final service for Yom Kippur), I asked the congregation if they would like to have services for Sukkot. An overwhelming number promised they would come. The good news was that the board of the B'nai B'rith Hall agreed we could use the hall for Sukkot. The bad news was that we could never use it after the holiday. On Erev Sukkot, following services, I asked the worshippers if they would like for me to form a congregation. Eleven people spoke, all positively. I then asked for volunteers for the first board of directors of the synagogue. No one volunteered. Herbert Bettelheim suggested that those eleven people automatically become the first board, and so it was to be.

The first meeting of the board took place in the sukkah behind our home, which five new immigrant students at Leo Baeck had decorated. Now we needed a name for the new congregation. I recommended Har HaCarmel, taken from the verse in II Samuel, where Elijah proclaims: *"Send forth and gather the People unto Me on Har HaCarmel"* (Mt. Carmel). Technion Sociology Professor Hanoch Yaakovson recommended a verse from one of the blessings of the Shema: *"May Or Hadash* (a new light) *shine on Zion."* His suggestion carried the day: Or Hadash was born.

The first years of the congregation augured well for Progressive Judaism in Haifa. However, the first year, 1964–65, was difficult. Following Sukkot, we worshipped in five different places in the first two months: a classroom in the Hugim High School near the Central Carmel; a private apartment on Wedgwood St.; the Cafe Pat, a coffee house on Moriah St.; the lobby of a Bed and Breakfast on Sderot Yitzchak St.; the WIZO House on Zivanit St. Each Friday afternoon I loaded the *aron hakodesh* onto the luggage rack of my Peugeot 404 station wagon, the doors, the *ner tamid,* and the *sefer Torah* into the car and spent the half-hour before the service preparing the new space as a synagogue. Rosa Vig, an elderly lady, always helped, as did Elsa Rigler. The membership and Shabbat attendance grew. In 1966 Mayor Abba Khushi offered us the use of a large space in the Herzl Elementary School on the Carmel, and that became our home for a decade.

There was a mini-fight in the congregation seven months after it was founded. In the spring of 1965 I had to fundraise for Leo Baeck, taking my family of five and Cantor Schellekes and his family of three with me. We traveled across the United States in a VW Transporter for three months, April through June 1965, stopping at major centers of Reform Judaism, where the families enjoyed the local scene and I met with rabbinic and lay Reform leaders. Upon our return to Haifa, I found that four members of the congregation (two elderly German rabbis, a lawyer, and a university teacher) had written to Rabbi Shankman, president of the World Union, stating that "not from Cincinnati would come forth the Law." They wanted a more "well-trained" rabbi from Jerusalem. Rabbi Shankman answered they would "have to take Samuels" as "that is all the WU has to offer." Realizing that my leadership was threatened, I immediately set out to put down their rebellion. The Or Hadash membership overwhelmingly backed me, and the four gentlemen were forced to resign.

The word was out that Or Hadash offered a beautiful service, and we began to get both boys and girls who wanted their b'nei mitzvah with us. Many of those twelve- and thirteen-year-olds were to become future leaders of Reform Judaism in Israel. Realizing the potential of secular *sabras* who wanted a beautiful religious service for the High Holy Days, we rented the Shavit Theater, a 1,000-seat movie house on the Carmel for the *yamim noraim* (High Holy Days) and filled it each year from 1966 through 1979.

In another move, Kurt Wohl, an Or Hadash member, became Chairman of the board of the Rothschild Center. He put me on the board, we watched the attendance of the Orthodox members, and at the appropriate time we voted in favor of renting the newly built Cinema, with its 150 seats, to Or Hadash. It was a sweet victory after having been told over a decade before that we could not worship at Beit Rothschild. Or Hadash worshipped in that hall for twenty-five years, until finally building its own building on Hankin Street further up the Carmel.

Throughout the 1960s Abba Khushi looked favorably upon the congregation. When I approached him for a plot for Or Hadash, he took me to the western window of his office, looking out toward an ascending Zionist Blvd. There above the Baha'i shrine on the crest of the Carmel was a magnificent plot, which he immediately offered to Or Hadash: "I want the first building that immigrants see as they approach the coast of *Eretz Yisrael* to be a magnificent synagogue and not a foreign shrine. Build such a building, and you can have that plot." We were unable to raise the capital funds for it, however.

Eventually it was made into a public park with the wonderful children's sculptures of Ursula Malbin, a Swiss artist living in Ein Hod.

The Reform Movement Struggles

During my first years in Haifa, I was generally accepted as a Reform rabbi. However, I did experience several ugly moments of anti-Reform.

Several months after arriving in 1962, I was invited by one of my students to address a meeting of B'nei Akiva, an Orthodox youth group. The subject was "Priest and Prophet." My thesis was that in biblical times the priests were responsible for the practice of tradition and the prophets were voices for change when those traditions were anti-social or led to unethical living. Those sixteen-year-olds listened while relating to biblical times, but when I brought examples of the same phenomenon in our time, there was an explosion of anti-Reform curses and, in effect, they "threw me out." I later learned they had been coached to do so.

Rabbi Dr. Daniel generally left me alone as a teacher of Judaic Studies in the ninth and tenth grades. He was civil when we were together and with my American exchange students. But when I began to train the sixth grade girls for bat mitzvah, and he heard that *females* would read Torah and on *Friday night*, he talked behind my back with the elementary teachers, urging them not to work with me on those "non-Jewish ceremonies." Only because of Dr. Elk's intervention was an intra-institutional crisis averted.

An American Conservative rabbi, Bernie Och, and his wife made *aliyah* to Haifa in the same month that we did. They, too, had been students in Jerusalem in the 1950s, and we had become friends. Together, we were the first couples to drive scooters down to Eilat in 1957.

Bernie became the director of the Hillel Foundation at the Technion. He invited me to participate in a multi-denominational symposium on "The Meaning of Revelation." Rabbi Rabinowitz, the former Chief Orthodox rabbi of South Africa, was to speak on "Revelation at Mt. Sinai, One Truth for all Time"; Rabbi Och on "Revelation: the Written and Oral Torah"; and I on "Progressive Revelation." While the students were congregating, we three rabbis determined the order of the speakers. I recommended that Rabbi Rabinowitz should start, as his position is the classic conception. No, he wanted me to be the first, and we agreed. The three of us were seated behind a large table.

The moderator introduced us and asked me to begin. I stood up, made a comment about how this event showed religious pluralism in Israel, and then was ready to plunge into my thesis. Rabbi Rabinowitz rose from his chair, walked around the table, stood directly in front of me, pulled out a pipe and asked the students if anyone had a light. Shocked, angry, and embarrassed for the Technion's Hillel House, I walked around the table and challenged Rabbi Rabinowitz to explain why he had done this uncouth and anti-social act. He answered me immediately: "Because Reform is not Judaism!" The students were so incensed and became so agitated that the evening meeting was cancelled on the spot. A week later the Hillel students invited me to speak on "Jewish Concepts of Revelation Through the Centuries."

In 1962 I joined The League for the Abolishment of Religious Coercion. It was there that I met Shulamit Aloni.[3] She was fascinated that a rabbi would be a member of that organization and often invited me to join her and speak on why a rabbi would be against religious coercion. Professor Eri Jabotinsky, the son of Ze'ev Jabotinsky, was a member of the Haifa branch of the League. A professor at the Technion, he was a fascinating personality with a rich history of personally saving Jews in Europe. Our backgrounds and political ideologies were very different, but we found common ground in opposition to religious coercion. He was totally secular and had a prejudice against Reform Judaism typical of many secular Israelis.

I once gave a lecture at a meeting of the League on "Democratic Principles in Jewish Texts." He debated with me vigorously, quoting biblical texts about genocide, God's selection of Hebrews over other nations, and killing dissenters within the nation. He believed this was the true nature of Judaism and that Orthodoxy was correct in interpreting our tradition accordingly. As a result, so Dr. Jabotinsky believed, Reform would never take hold in Israel. He was convinced that once we had civil law here we would not need Judaism altogether.

---

3. A lawyer who became a national figure through a radio program advocating for the rights of consumers. In 1970 she was a member of Knesset in the Labor Party, but unhappy that her party would not defend civil rights and civil liberties, she left to found her own party, *Ratz,* which later became *Meretz.* Aloni made that party the defender of democratic principles for Arabs, women, gays and lesbians, Reform Jews, and others. She advocated the separation of religion and state and helped many whose lives were faced with religious coercion. Aloni served as both Minister of Education and Minister of Culture.

I wanted Israel to legislate against any form of religious coercion in order to *reform* Judaism; Jabotinsky wanted it to *rid* Israel of Judaism. We were friends and colleagues in the League, but he opposed Reform Judaism until his death in 1969.

I have already written that at its origin, Or Hadash had a very difficult time renting a room for religious services. During the first months, we worshipped in many venues, often moving from week to week. One of those venues was a small WIZO hall in an apartment house. On the second Shabbat there, a neighbor lowered a speaker down to the window of the hall while we were in the morning service, proceeding to then blast rock music so loud that we had to curtail the service. Some of this was against worship altogether, but some was definitely because we were Reform.

These five examples of ignorance, prejudice, ill will, and even hatred of Reform never weakened my faith in the rightness of our path for non-Orthodox Israeli Jews. But it did sharpen my senses and awareness of the difficulties of our task.

Progressive Judaism Takes Root

By 1965 six Reform congregations had formed in Israel. Har-El Congregation in Jerusalem was already eight years old. Two congregations had formed on the outskirts of Tel Aviv: Rabbi Zemer had founded his congregation in Kfar Shmaryahu in 1963, and in 1964, a group of lay people began a congregation in Kiryat Ono. With my three congregations in Upper Nazareth, Nahariya, and Haifa, we were ready to form a union.

During that first year of Or Hadash, I became friendly with Avraham Meron, the dynamic director of Kfar Galim, a Youth Village at the foot of Mt. Carmel and just south of Haifa. As one of the elementary schools in Haifa, Leo Baeck was sending our students to a section of Kfar Galim called Gan Karmit, whose purpose was to give Haifa's elementary school students a feeling of "working the Land." I wanted my urban congregant families to have such a connection as well. Kfar Galim had 1200 dunams (300 acres) of prime land along a mile of beautiful Mediterranean coast. Avraham was delighted with our suggestion that Or Hadash re-create a ceremony called *K'tzir Ha'Omer* (reaping of the wheat), taken from a tradition of our ancestors as they made their annual spring ascent to Jerusalem. He was enthusiastic about the idea of his village being a center for forging new directions in wedding forms of Jewish tradition with modern Israeli life.

When approached, he welcomed the idea of bringing together leaders of our congregations. My colleague at Leo Baeck, Herbert Bettelheim, had been among the founders of Or Hadash and served as its first chair. In December 1964, he and I sent out a call to form a National Union of Progressive Congregations and Institutions. Gil Nativ helped me prepare the program and arrangements.

On February 26, 1965, representatives of all the congregations arrived at the Kfar Galim Youth Village for the first convention of progressive congregations in Israel. Dr. Elk was the featured speaker. With passion he called for the development of a network of schools to spread the message of "humanistic Judaism, based on the ethics of the prophets of Israel and the values taught by Rabbi Leo Baeck." A national board was founded, and Herbert Bettelheim was chosen chair. The IMPJ, the Israel Movement for Progressive Judaism, was off and running.

The HUC-JIR Israeli Rabbinic Program

Following World War II, the American Jewish community experienced significant growth. The children and grandchildren of the 3.5 million Eastern European Jews who had immigrated to North America in the previous eighty years were receiving a fine civic and general education that led to upward mobility, and the United States offered them religious freedom and many economic opportunities. They moved to cities across America and into middle-class suburbs. New congregations sprang up throughout the country. Those new congregations were mostly Reform and Conservative, and they needed rabbis. When I was ordained in 1960, dozens of such congregations offered me a position. HUC-JIR was training rabbis for those communities.

For those of us keen on developing a modern and liberal Jewish religious movement in Israel, it was clear that a significant number of American-trained Reform rabbis would not take the option of pioneering in our religious and educational work. They were well paid there, had much prestige in their communities, had been trained for that work, and English, not Hebrew, was their mother tongue. If the Reform Movement in Israel was to grow, a program to train native Israelis for the rabbinate was a *sine qua non,* an indispensable and essential action. And we did have an opportunity to do so for two reasons: I had three protégés who might be convinced to study for the rabbinate, and the president of HUC-JIR had pioneered in building the beginning of a significant campus in Jerusalem.

In 1963, Rabbi Dr. Nelson Glueck, HUC-JIR president, dedicated its beautiful Jerusalem campus. Dr. Glueck was a renowned biblical archeologist who, before the 1948 War of Independence, came to Palestine every summer to explore and map ancient sites. He had been the director of the American Schools for Oriental Research (ASOR), which was now on the Jordanian side of Jerusalem and therefore inaccessible to Jews. Each summer in the early years of the State, Dr. Glueck continued his explorations, flying low over Israel, searching for ancient sites. When he had mapped a few new ones, he rented jeeps and set out to explore them. Dr. Glueck would sit cross-legged atop an ancient *tel* (mound) while his assistants and budding archeology students scurried around the site picking up shards of broken pottery. The shards were brought to Dr. Glueck who then arranged them in categories according to culture and date. At the end of the summer he gave a lecture in Tel Aviv and Jerusalem on his finds that season.

He was an impressive figure: tall, thin, deeply tanned, handsome, wearing a white suit. His scholarly but deeply romantic talks about the roots of Jewish life and lore from biblical times were always attended by hundreds of people. Annette and I went to such a lecture at the end of the summer of 1956. Dr. Glueck's listeners were absorbing each word as spiritual sustenance and proof of the historic legitimacy of our Zionist presence in this Jewish Old-New Land.

But Dr. Glueck no longer had a permanent place in Jerusalem to "hang his hat" during his annual summer archeological work. So he decided to build a replacement for the now-on-the-other-side ASOR in the capital of Israel. Dr. Glueck was *persona grata* with the elite of Israel's scholarly and political world, so he approached Prime Minister Ben-Gurion and the Mayor of Jerusalem, Gershon Agron, for a plot of ground. After many years, several frustrating negotiations in the Jerusalem Municipality, and much opposition from the Orthodox parties in the Knesset because of the plan to build a synagogue within the complex, Dr. Glueck received a choice parcel of land on King David Street across the valley from the Tower of David. The HUC-JIR Board of Governors approved the project, Dr. Glueck found the funding, and a new base for biblical archeology was erected.

The building's use for training American Reform leaders was decidedly secondary for archeologist Glueck. The original building was called "The Hebrew Union School for Biblical Archeology." Following the dedication in 1963, I sat with President Glueck in the apartment built on the campus for him. We spoke of the possible use of the facilities for Israeli rabbinic training. I told him of my teaching at Leo Baeck and the mentoring of several of my students. I reminded him that HUC had begun in Cincinnati with only four students in 1875. We could begin with only a few students, but each *sabra* student ordained in Jerusalem would be crucial for Progressive Judaism to take hold in Israel. As we spoke, it was clear that Dr. Glueck's mind was more on finding the missing pieces to some Nabatean pot, and his response was to invite me to bring my EIE high school students to the new campus in order to see a cave there that needed to be investigated. HUC Jerusalem, under the direction of Rabbi Nelson Glueck, was not designed to train leaders for Reform Judaism and especially for Israel.

It would take another seven years before the Board of Governors would agree to accept that first Leo Baeck graduate, Mordechai Wertheim (Rabbi Motti Rotem). Dr. Glueck had not prepared an academic plan. That task fell to his designated successor, Rabbi Dr. Alfred Gottschalk, and especially to the dean of the Jerusalem campus, Professor Ezra Spicehandler.

Dr. Gottschalk had studied at the Cincinnati campus of HUC-JIR in 1955–56. We became close friends there. He and his wife helped us repaint our apartment, and they joined us for watermelon parties on the floor after each painting day. Years later, they sent their son Marc to be my student at Leo Baeck

Following Fred Gottschalk's rabbinic ordination, he was chosen to serve HUC-JIR as the dean of its quickly developing Los Angeles center. Rabbi Gottschalk very successfully built a campus near the University of Southern California and developed a combined academic program with that great center of learning, inaugurating programs of study for the training of rabbis, cantors, educators, and community service workers. He was chosen for the presidency upon Dr. Glueck's death in 1971. As he prepared for his presidency, he found himself at a crossroads for the training of Jewish leadership: the ordination of women, the first year of training for the American rabbinate in Israel, and the ordination of native-born Israelis in Jerusalem.

Sally Priesand had been a long-time student for the rabbinate. Dr. Glueck had encouraged her, but it was to be Rabbi Gottschalk's courageous leadership in the first year of his presidency to ordain her as the first woman rabbi in North America, a pioneering act that has had a profound effect on rabbinic leadership in America and subsequently in Israel and throughout the Jewish world.

Similarly, he became the leader of the effort to have all HUC-JIR rabbinic students spend their first year studying at HUC Jerusalem, thus turning that campus from an archeological center into an Israeli institution for the training of Reform Jewish leadership.

For me, the most important contribution of Rabbi Gottschalk was his leadership in the training of *Israelis* in Israel for the Reform rabbinate. This was to be the key for the continuing development of Reform Judaism in Israel. Previously, in 1964, Israelis Tovia Ben Horin, whose father founded Har-El, and Shmuel Kehati, a Yemenite, had been sent to the United States to study and receive ordination there. But the studies at the American campuses were too rudimentary for graduates of Israeli high schools and universities. *Sabras* could study rabbinics in more depth than what was offered in Cincinnati. And it was inappropriate for native Hebrew speakers to pursue their rabbinic studies in America. The temptation to remain there because of economics and community status was too great. Only Tovia returned to Israel to work in the Movement. Moreover, it was impossible to recruit Israeli men after army service and university training, now at least twenty-four years old and without any prior Reform training, to continue their education at an American rabbinical seminary.

Three of my early Leo Baeck students had now become protégés, working with me in the 1960s as senior high school students, while serving in the IDF, and then as they began their academic studies in one of Israel's universities. Another young Israeli, Uri Regev, a protégé of Rabbi Zemer in Tel Aviv, had also been an EIE student in the United States and had shown an interest in the Reform rabbinate. They all took roles in those first years of the Israel Movement for Progressive Judaism. They all began rabbinic studies at HUC-JIR in Jerusalem in 1970 and 1971. Mordechai (Motti) Rotem, Zeev Harari, and Gil Nativ combined their M.A. studies at the Hebrew University or Haifa University with a truncated program at HUC-JIR.

Professor Spicehandler, who had taught me Modern Hebrew Literature in Cincinnati and had been a mentor in my developing Zionism, was the dean of the HUC-JIR Jerusalem campus from 1966 to 1980. We had became close friends in Cincinnati and our friendship grew in those first years of his being dean of the Jerusalem campus. He was the most Zionist of all American Reform rabbis, and an expert in Hebrew literature and in the Israeli Labor Movement. Each time he came to Haifa, he would visit Leo Baeck and/or Or Hadash, and each time we talked about opening that rabbinic track in Jerusalem for those four pioneering *sabras*. For several years, 1966–70, I also met with Rabbis Glueck and Gottschalk to encourage them to recruit and accept Motti, Zeev, Gil, and Uri. I even prepared an outline for a four-year curriculum based on biblical, rabbinic, medieval, and modern themes and texts. It was never accepted, but it did put the issue on the table.

With the backing of Drs. Glueck and Gottschalk, in the fall of 1970 Rabbi Spicehandler quietly accepted Motti Rotem to be his personal student while Motti was working on his M.A. at the Hebrew University, and with a whisper the Israel Rabbinic Program at HUC-JIR Jerusalem began. Ezra taught Motti "The History of Reform Judaism." Motti was followed by Zeev and Gil the following year and then by Uri.

Rabbi Spicehandler was joined on the faculty by Rabbi Moshe Haim Weiler, who had come to Israel on pension from his pioneering of Reform Judaism in South Africa, and by Professor Zeev Falk. Together, they changed the direction of that Jerusalem campus. Motti became the director of the Israel Movement even before his ordination, and Uri took early leadership at HUC-JIR Jerusalem. It had been a time of *"Et La'asot L'Adonai,"* a time to "step up to the plate" to do God's work in Israel. By 2015, around one hundred rabbis had been ordained in Jerusalem, most to serve as leaders of Israeli Reform Judaism, some to lead in the former Soviet Union, and some in South America. Several other leadership programs have subsequently been established.

Since then, the Jerusalem Center on King David Street has been transformed, as a result of the joint efforts of both the World Union and HUC-JIR. Moshe Safdie was awarded the architect's contract to build additional academic, administrative, and living facilities. The World Union and the IMPJ, under the dynamic leadership of Rabbi Richard Hirsch, now have a large hostel and convention center on the campus. The expansion of the campus facilities is the product of the outstanding leadership of Rabbi Gottschalk and of philanthropist Richard Scheuer, who in those years chaired the HUC-JIR Board of

Governors. That campus has also seen the ordination of many women, including its present dean, pioneering woman ordainee, Naamah Kelman-Ezrachi. In fact, all three leaders of HUC-JIR Jerusalem are graduates of the Israel Rabbinic Program: Rabbi Michael Marmur, Provost; Rabbi Kelman-Ezrachi, Dean of the Jerusalem Campus; and Rabbi Ofek Meir, Director of the Israel Rabbinic Program.

The archeological school was subsequently named for Nelson Glueck and has pioneered work in archeology in Israel, especially the multi-year dig at Tel Dan. But it is the Israel Rabbinic School that has contributed so significantly to the leadership of liberal Jews in Israel and in the former Soviet Union.

In 1973, Rabbi Hirsch made *aliyah* to Jerusalem. He had been one of the leaders of the UAHC (now URJ) and was the founding director of the Reform Movement's Religious Action Center in Washington, D.C. Rabbi Hirsch is a life-long Zionist, a dynamic organizer, and a powerful speaker and writer on both Progressive Judaism and Zionism. He came to Israel as the international director of the World Union, convinced their directors to make Jerusalem its center, and inspired the Reform Movement to reappraise its approach to the State of Israel and the Zionist enterprise. He led the Movement in joining the World Zionist Organization and the Jewish Agency and has had many leadership roles in the re-creation of Jewish life in the former Soviet Union. Rabbi Hirsch was the most active ideological and political Zionist in the American Reform rabbinate while still Director of the Religious Action Center in Washington. Even before his *aliyah*, he joined in urging Presidents Glueck and Gottschalk to convince the HUC Board of Governors to agree to both the Israel Rabbinic Program and the First Year in Israel American Rabbinic Program.

The American Reform rabbinate has been enormously enhanced by the augmented Hebrew capacity of HUC-JIR students because of that first year in Jerusalem. The fledgling Movement of Progressive Judaism in the former Soviet Union has seen several of its sons and daughters ordained as rabbis in the HUC Israel Rabbinic Program. Today, these rabbis give leadership to communities in Eastern Europe and to the large Russian-speaking population of Israel. I consider it a privilege and the fulfillment of one of my dreams that I have had an opportunity to be a part of that powerful leadership institution. I currently serve on the HUC-JIR Board of Overseers of the Jerusalem campus, which awarded me an honorary Doctor of Humane Letters during the year of my retirement in 1999 with this citation:

Beloved Director of the Leo Baeck Education Center in Haifa,
Whose vision of a Progressive Israel has inspired dreams and created realities,
Whose commitment to education in the spirit of Judaism and Emancipation has helped mold generations of students,
Whose passionate advocacy of social justice, immigration absorption and understanding between peoples has widened horizons and bridged divides,
Whose institutional genius and indomitable spirit have made him a true pioneer of Progressive Judaism in Israel.

I am grateful for the recognition. At the same time, I am profoundly disappointed that the HUC-JIR has not, as yet, developed a significant education department, despite many proposals. If Reform Judaism is to sink deep roots in Israel, it must have its own educational system. Such a department would have three goals: (1) to offer retraining of Israeli school principals and teachers, emphasizing pedagogical methods for teaching the link between Jewish ethics and Israeli democracy; (2) training new teachers, guidance counselors, and educational staff in liberal values, and, (3) developing a large network of poets and song leaders, trained in implanting in the hearts of secular Israelis the spiritual depth of Israeli poetry that links our Jewishness with our democracy. Over a period of two generations, together with the opening of our own network of schools, this breadth of training could profoundly change Israelis' conception of our identities both as Jews and as citizens. Perhaps the world of Progressive Jews would help us to fund such a department and network.

Those who capture the minds and spirits of each new generation mold civilization's future. Religion in Israel is coercive and political. It is either accepted as Orthodox, or rejected and even abhorred. Chasidism has its "song." The hilltop settlers have their "song." HUC has to produce those whose lives, words, and melodies give Israel's next secular generation its "song." Reform is religious, but without critical influence and political power. Reform Judaism as a religious alternative is limping along in the State of Israel. If we are ever to make a breakthrough as a molder of a generation, it will only be through example, education, and our authentic, spiritual "song."

Full Gas in Neutral

From 1965, following the Kfar Galim inaugural conference, until 1985, my senior staff at Leo Baeck and I dedicated perhaps a quarter of our time to developing the religious and social justice foundations for the Israel Movement. I was a member of the Va'ad Ha'Artzi, the National Board, and very active in MARAM. I was part of the rabbinic team that created the first prayer book for the Movement. Eventually, working alongside me were several Leo Baeck graduates: Itzik Cohen, Meron Tal, and Benjy Golan. Meron, Leo Baeck's Director for Finance, became the chairman of the Movement's Social Action Committee. Benjy, Leo Baeck's Administrative Director, headed the Committee for the Movement's administration. Itzik, the first Director of our Community Center, was the head of the Youth Committee. I authorized each rabbi at Leo Baeck to become active and spend a considerable part of his or her professional work in building the Movement.

The first three students in the Israel Rabbinic Program in Jerusalem were graduates of Leo Baeck. The first youth group of the Movement was at Leo Baeck and Or Hadash. Several of the first *garin* (nucleus) for Kibbutz Yahel, the first Reform kibbutz in Israel, founded in 1978, were Leo Baeck graduates. In spite of this massive effort, the Movement was not growing and not progressing to a degree that justified that amount of energy. Meron said to me one day, "I feel that our work in the Movement is full gas in neutral." I took a long look at where Leo Baeck could go if all that energy was invested in it and where the Movement was going, concluding that we should shift gears. The absence of our leadership in the IMPJ would be felt much less than in the developing of the school and the community center at home. As soon as we concentrated the power of our leadership inward, Leo Baeck skyrocketed.

This is the subject of the next chapter.

CHAPTER 3
BOLD THRUST IN EDUCATION

PART 1
The Challenge

The Gap Between the Facilities and the Vision

The fact was that in Israel's early stages of development, the Leo Baeck School succeeded even under very difficult circumstances. Prior to my arrival in 1962, the Leo Baeck Board had rented that old Arab house at 47 Hillel Street. I'll never forget Mr. Sheafer teaching music while sitting up on the counter of a kitchen sink. Yet such a converted apartment could never meet the growing population and changing educational needs of Israel. I had a vision of a different kind of educational system altogether, and we needed a major campus to make that happen. Such an undertaking would require the cooperation and the power of world Jewry, the Reform Movement, the Israeli educational system, including the Ministry of Education and the Haifa Municipality. I vowed to attempt to realize that vision and raise the funds necessary to build a campus with the breadth to match the vision.

It happened. How?

Grappling With Power

In my first year Dr. Elk sent me out to the *ma'abarot* to recruit Sephardic students. Although Sephardic Jews were no longer considered immigrants, their economic situation and cultural norms did allow them to take advantage of the education available at schools like Leo Baeck. For this purpose, the UJA's Israel Education Fund (IEF) was founded, and Leo Baeck responded with energy and belief that it could make the difference in the lives of adolescents of Middle Eastern and North African backgrounds. I spent twenty-five years of my professional life learning the needs of this population and responding with programs. The Sephardic population definitely had a lower expectation of getting a quality education that would give them the tools for success in an industrial and post-industrial urban-economic society.

In 1965, we heard that the Ministry of Education was to enact an education reform that would bring Sephardic children into secondary school, as the old system was creating a "second Israel." Eight-year elementary schools (free and compulsory) were for children ages six to fourteen. High schools, ninth through twelfth grade, were tuition-based. Students could be accepted only if they passed the *Sekker* national examination, which was given to all eighth graders. This examination favored Ashkenazic children, most of whose parents had at least a high school education, and, even if they were poor, were motivated to see that their children received secondary school matriculation. A high percentage of Sephardic families, on the other hand, were patriarchal. The parents generally had little formal education, had multiple children, were in desperate financial condition, and lived in very crowded quarters. As a result, they wanted their children to leave school at age fourteen in order to earn some income for the family or care for their many younger siblings.

Israel was heading for a social disaster. An education reform was desperately needed in order to assure that Sephardic children would have access to upward mobility. The government did two things. They passed a law changing the school system from an eight-year elementary (free), four-year secondary (tuition-based) system to a six-year elementary (free), three-year junior high (free), three-year senior high (tuition-based). Zoning was passed, so that Sephardic and Ashkenazic children would be integrated in junior high. During those three years, an in-house counseling program was to track each student's progress in order to get them into a senior high school academic or technical program that would lead to partial or full matriculation. The government planned to build sixty-four new six-year high schools throughout the country, and the worldwide United Israel Appeal (UIA) was asked to create a special campaign to raise large sums for the construction of these schools. This was Leo Baeck's chance to survive and flourish.

When I learned of this reform-to-be, I turned to our Leo Baeck Board. They accepted my thesis that we were at a crossroads. We did not have the luxury of deciding whether to stay small or become a major school. Under the new reform, all small private high schools would dry up. With the new national plan to be implemented five or six years hence, we knew the elementary school would survive if we continued with our present structure. But our high school would go under without a junior high. Dr. Elk, who was already sixty-six years old, was not in a frame of mind to build a totally new Leo Baeck Secondary School. He was also skeptical that we could succeed in getting a plot from the municipality and raise the necessary funds for construction. I promised the board that I would take responsibility for negotiating with the Ministry of Education and the Haifa Municipality. Dr. Hanan Brin, Professor of Education at Haifa University, had recently joined the board, and he backed my recommendation. Dr. Elk agreed to be neutral. The board reluctantly agreed and gave me the authority to attempt to include the Baeck School in the education reform.

After several months of pressing the Education Ministry, a meeting with the Minister of Education, Zalman Aranne, was finally arranged. Also attending the meeting was the head of the new division set up for this reform, Eliezer Shmueli, who subsequently became Director General of the Education Ministry. I told them about Leo Baeck, the man, and Leo Baeck, the institution. We had prepared a statement of the four goals of the school, including the integration of children from Arab countries. They turned us down on the spot. Shmueli was adamant that we would not be able to integrate Sephardic teens into our structure in Haifa, but I was not convinced about his motivation. My three years in Israel had already given me rich experience to validate my Reform paranoia.

I was sure this was a do-or-die issue for Dr. Elk's dream and mine. I now needed to go to my potential source of power, the fundraisers in America. My handle to get to the top was the Director General of the United Jewish Appeal (UJA) in New York. *He was a Reform rabbi.* Prior to World War II, Rabbi Herbert Friedman had served in a large congregation in Denver where, contrary to the prevailing ideology of most of his congregants, he advocated for Zionism and the establishment of a Jewish State. As a soldier in Europe during and following the war, Rabbi Friedman dedicated himself to the rescue of refugees from the camps and forests of Europe. He became a world leader in rescuing Jews, getting them to Palestine, and enhancing their Jewish life.

Subsequently, as Director General of the UJA, his energy and charisma inspired Jews of wealth throughout North America to support and finance the young Jewish State. Under his leadership, the UJA became one of the largest and most powerful fundraising agencies in the world. The story of the role of the UJA in the establishment and underpinning of the Jewish State is one of honor for the Jewish People, and Rabbi Friedman led that surge. I knew of Rabbi Friedman's work but had never met him. I determined that he would be the key to get us under the umbrella of the Israel Education Fund, the large gifts fund established by the UJA and run by the Jewish Agency with a master plan for the massive construction of the new schools in Israel.

After being refused an appointment with Rabbi Friedman in New York, I asked Chaim Vinitzky, the Israel Director of the UJA, to do me a favor. I needed to know the day and time that Rabbi Friedman would next arrive in Israel so I could place myself in front of him to gain his approval for including Leo Baeck in the project. Mr. Vinitzky knew that this was a "do-or-die" moment for a school like ours, and therefore agreed to give me the information under one condition: I was not to reveal my source for twenty years or until Mr. Vinitzky's death. So on April 5, 1965, I was standing in the doorway that led from the plane tarmac into the reception room at the Israel Airport. I stood in the doorway as Rabbi Friedman, wearing a large cowboy hat, stepped down from his private plane with his retinue. When he reached the door, I said, "Rabbi Friedman, I am Rabbi Samuels, a Reform rabbi living in Israel. I must talk with you about the Reform Movement's school in Haifa." Totally unimpressed, he said, "I don't have time to talk to you now. You can make an appointment." I said, "Rabbi Friedman, this is do-or-die for the Reform Movement in Israel. If you don't give me three minutes, you'll have to knock me down to get through this door." He looked at me incredulously, thought for a second, seemed to like my chutzpah, and said, "Come to the side here. You have two minutes." I said, "I don't need two minutes. Rabbi Friedman, you have initiated a special campaign to finance the construction of sixty-four high schools for the poor Sephardic population. There is only one school in Israel that teaches Progressive Judaism. The Ministry of Education has refused to put this school in the program. Tell them to build this school, and I guarantee we will integrate Sephardic Jews and bring them to matriculation. Here's my card." He understood immediately and agreed on the spot. It was a pivotal moment in the life of the school, the IMPJ, and, in a small way, in the history of

Israel. Two weeks later, I received an envelope from Rabbi Friedman with this handwritten note: "It's a done deal."

I was now able to negotiate with the Haifa Municipality for an appropriate plot. An appointment was made with Mayor Abba Khushi. Max Kargman, a devoted friend of Leo Baeck from Boston, accompanied me to the meeting with the mayor. Max was a successful developer, had a Ph.D. from the Harvard School of Education, and was a lawyer and potential donor. After the pleasantries, this is the way the conversation went with the mayor.

"Mr. Mayor," I said, "Leo Baeck is going to build a major school in your city. We have the backing of the Education Minister and the UJA, but we need a suitable plot. Will you provide us with one?"

Abba Khushi looked at me and then turned to Max: "Mr. Kargman, how much will you give me for a 'suitable plot'?"

Max answered him instantly and forcefully, "One dollar!" he replied.

The mayor looked at him with a twinkle in his eye and said, "Sold!"

He then pressed a button under his desk, and the City Engineer appeared instantly. Abba Khushi said, "We're going to give a plot of ground for the building of a large Leo Baeck School. What property of ours can we give them?"

The engineer replied, "If the gentlemen will come into my office, I will show them a map of the city, and any plot we have zoned for public building is theirs."

We were instantly offered four plots: one in downtown Haifa, two high on the Carmel, and one on the French Carmel, halfway between the sea and the Central Carmel. Off we went with an assistant engineer to ascertain which plot was most suitable. At each site I asked, "Where do the Sephardic children live near this neighborhood?" In the city, the answer was: "Almost all of the children here are Sephardic." On the Carmel, the answer was "Very far away." On the French Carmel, the answer was, "Right down the hill, near the sea." "And who lives above us on the mountain?" I asked. "Officers in the Navy and middle-class Ashkenazic families." I immediately said, "This is what we want. I would like to visit this site with the mayor."

The following week, Abba Khushi and I stood on the balcony of one of the multiple family homes on Edmund Fleg Street. We looked out over an almost unspoiled mountain leading down to the sea. Only at the bottom were there large blocks of public housing, with apartments of forty-five square meters (450 square feet,) constructed for the poor and especially for those who had lived in and protested against Haifa's Wadi Salib, a slum area of former Arab homes that was as stultifying for our new immigrants as it had been for the Arabs before them. So the government had built *shikunim*, public housing, primarily small apartments for large Sephardic families. One such area was in Western Haifa with neighborhoods called Kiryat Sprinzak (named for the first speaker of the Knesset), Ein HaYam ("spring leading to the sea"), and Shaar HaAliyah ("gate of immigration").

I saw the plot of twenty dunams (five acres) on the side of a hill going down toward the sea. It was on the crest with views of an open *wadi* on both sides, halfway between those Sephardic Jews living in the *shikunim* and the Ashkenazic Jews who filled the elementary schools above this plot. I looked to the right of this plot and saw a small building. I asked the mayor what it was. "That is Municipal School D, our pedagogic high school for 200 high school girls." "Can we have it for our junior high?" I asked. "If you will take in those girls and their teachers." "Done, if our board agrees," I responded.

We now had permission to become part of the education reform, the covenant with the UJA to raise the funds necessary, and the possibility of a great campus on a plot offered by the municipality. Through the Jewish Agency, we let a bid for an architect. I prepared a program with what we thought would be the maximum number of students and the kind of buildings that would lead to openness, sharing, and community building. The Education Ministry approved the plan, which we then presented to three architectural firms. What I asked for was something like a stepped pyramid as built by the Mayans and the Aztecs in Central America. In the summer of 1961, Annette and I had traveled to Mexico with my parents. I was fascinated by the architecture of the Tenochtitlan Aztecs. They had created stepped pyramids that allowed for a large area in the center where they buried their kings. I asked the architects to design a central building so that when teachers and students left their classrooms, they would all move into a large open space suggesting equality and pluralism. The Tel Aviv firm of Nadler, Nadler, Bixon and Gil created a design so successful that it eventually won many architectural prizes. Moshe Gil was the lead architect and became a creative partner with us in the development of the campus for almost thirty years.

CHAPTER 3
BOLD THRUST IN EDUCATION

PART 2
Raising $1 Million and More

Competing for Dollars

Rabbi Friedman wanted the active participation of the American Reform Movement in this huge campaign for education in Israel, so he asked me to take responsibility for the fundraising for the new Leo Baeck Center. He expected me to open the doors of Reform congregations, their rabbis, and their wealthy lay members for the *entire* campaign. I was the only Israeli asked to raise the funds for the construction of his school. I took on the task reluctantly, as the Movement was still somewhere between anti-Zionist and non-Zionist. But if Leo Baeck was to survive, I had to accept Rabbi Friedman's challenge.

For the next two years I went to New York every four months for ten days in order to raise the $1.1 million needed for the first stage of our new Center. I worked in the Israel Education Fund offices under the direction of Ralph Goldman, one of the giants of Jewish philanthropy in the twentieth century. I went through the lists of wealthy Reform Jews in North America. When my list had the names of ten potential donors, I went up to the office of Rabbi Friedman who, while attending to some other urgent matter, would say "yes" or "no" for each donor whose name I read out to him. He knew them all and whether they had paid their annual UJA pledge. If "yes," he counseled me how to approach the person and who should accompany me.

As for the Reform Movement, the leaders were concerned for their own fundraising efforts. My employer, the World Union, was not a player in this ballpark. Rabbi Maurice Eisendrath, the leader of the UAHC, was always encouraging but could not help me fundraise because of the financial constraints of his organization. Dr. Nelson Glueck, who headed HUC-JIR, was uncomfortable with an Israeli organization competing in fundraising with its new Center in Jerusalem. Rabbi Jacob Weinstein, president of the CCAR and an esteemed and valued older colleague when I served in Chicago, was encouraging but not ready to recommend such a large campaign to his membership. I was essentially on my own with the leadership of the American Reform Movement

Rabbi Friedman was profoundly disappointed. We met separately with both Rabbi Eisendrath and Rabbi Weinstein. Rabbi Friedman challenged each of them to work together with the UJA on this huge project, suggesting to them that the Reform Movement would benefit financially in the long run if their wealthy members know that Reform's leadership was helping to build Israel's educational infrastructure, but to no avail. Rabbi Eisendrath was ready to help me, but not to expose the entire American Reform Movement to the Israel Education Fund. I saw this as another missed opportunity for the Reform Movement to influence Israeli society by becoming a major player in the developing educational policies and programs of a young and dynamic Israel.

Nonetheless, Rabbi Friedman backed my efforts, and I was making headway. By the summer of 1968, we had commitments from five Reform families for the $850,000 needed to begin construction. With all permits in hand and signed contracts with the architects and the contractor, we began construction in 1968 under the auspices of the Engineering Department of the Jewish Agency.

Eliezer Shmueli was less than happy that Minister Aranne had accepted the demand of Rabbi Friedman that the Leo Baeck School be included. He demanded that in addition to our center on the French Carmel, I take responsibility for raising the funds for two additional high schools to be built in Haifa and in Tirat HaCarmel, an immigrant suburban township of Haifa. It was very tempting, as Leo Baeck would have administered the three campuses as one school, and such opportunities occur rarely. I did report this to the WUPJ and the UAHC, recommending once again that the official Reform Movement take on this large project and send us a second rabbi or an educator. Rabbi Jacob Shankman, WUPJ President, and Rabbi William Rosenthal, Executive Director, felt the project was too large for their organization. Rabbi Eisendrath rejected the proposal. When I reported this to Eliezer Shmueli, he had some inappropriate remarks about the Reform Movement, but, sad to say, it was a correct evaluation of American Reform's role in the upbuilding of Israel.

Rabbi Friedman interjected on my behalf, promising Shmueli he would personally find the funding for those additional campuses. That angered Shmueli even more, and he put stumbling blocks in my path for several years. However, at the dedication of our Klorfein Auditorium in 1973, Shmueli, now Director General of the Education Ministry, gave us the ultimate compliment. He acknowledged he had been against our project but was now convinced we had already done more to integrate Sephardic and Ashkenazic students and to lift the level of the former than any other of the dozens of schools built for this purpose.

From 1966 to 1970 I made biweekly or monthly visits to Tel Aviv to the offices of Eliezer Shavit, the Israeli Director of the IEF, to work on getting the many necessary permits and contracts, and ensure that the buildings would be constructed as necessary for us.

The Jewish Agency requested bids. The Histadrut's Solel Boneh, Hachsharat Hayishuv, and Dori, all large construction firms, submitted bids. A small company in Haifa, Lebowitz-Levin, also submitted a bid, which was 20% lower than those of the large firms. I recommended that we not take this bid, as I believed they would not be able to build it for that amount. But the other members of the selection committee were adamant that the firm had finished several buildings on schedule and on budget, and therefore they were giving the contract to the lowest bidder. It turned out to be a mistake.

The company had miscalculated the actual costs and went bankrupt while in construction. It was a sad day for all of us, as we had grown to like and to respect the contractor, and it meant an additional delay in construction. The Haifa Municipality had determined to be the first city in Israel to implement the country-wide reform of six-year high schools, and it was to begin in September of 1970. In June of that year, there was still no roof on the main school building, no auditorium, no synagogue, no library, no sports facilities, and no contractor. We did manage to offer the contractor the money set aside for our auditorium, so that, working feverishly throughout July and August, he could set the roof and construct the interior. It was to take us four more years before we could complete the auditorium and the shell of the synagogue and library.

"All My Money Will Go for Your Children in Israel"

Where did the money for construction come from? It was my one opportunity in fundraising to be with the "big boys." In those first years of the late 1960s I knew that on my own, if I reached out to a wealthy Reform Jewish individual or foundation for a contribution for my school and made a fine presentation, I would receive something. But it never exceeded $10,000 and usually was in the hundreds. Now, in 1966, coming in the name of the UJA, those same Jews would respond with several more digits.

I moved from the bush league to the majors. I was to be, for the first and only time, in the playoffs. The minimum we could ask for and receive was $100,000. I stepped up to the plate with the future of my work in Israel dependent on my getting some hits and RBIs (runs batted in). Never in my life had more been riding on my skill at the plate. My partners were there; my strategy was in place. I dug in at the batter's box and the umpire called out, "Play ball!" I swung at a fast ball over the middle of the plate, the ball sailed toward the outfield, and as I ran toward first, I looked up as it cleared the center field fence. Home run!

That first hit, that home run, was Caroline Greenfield. Caroline was eighty-five when we met in 1966. A single woman who lived in Manhattan, Caroline had inherited enough money from her Macon, Georgia, parents to live comfortably for the rest of her life. She was known to the UJA professionals, though she was not a regular contributor to their campaigns. She had told me in our first conversation that with no children of her own, she was interested in investing in the future of Israel's children.

I called her and made an appointment to meet her in the NFTY offices at 838 Fifth Avenue, the UAHC "House of Living Judaism," as it was called. Sitting around the table with me were Rabbi Samuel Cook, Director of NFTY, who for years had been the spark for Reform's support of the Baeck School; Shimon Chasdi, the Director of the EIE Program with Leo Baeck; and Ira Levine, the representative of the IEF. Caroline listened intently to our presentation. I gave her a few vignettes of Leo Baeck's students from all ethnic and social backgrounds. Sam told her of his thrill to be able to partner with Dr. Elk, who was pioneering progressive education in Israel. Shimon spoke of a new Zionism where American and Israeli Jewish youth were to repair a broken world together. Throughout the presentation, Ira looked out for Caroline's comfort. She asked a few questions about what we planned to build. I pulled out my own sketches of an educational center in which teenagers would learn, and through which the community would be enriched.

When she told us this was to be the gift of her lifetime, I asked if she wanted to memorialize her parents by naming the school building. She began to cry, and so did we. This became a defining moment in her long life. She asked the cost of that building. Without a professional estimate in hand, I decided to ask her for $350,000, a third of the project's total cost. That was a very sizable sum in 1966. She cried once again and said she would do that. Ira thanked her in the name of the Jewish People and promised to arrange all the details.

This highly emotional and substantial gift set us on a successful path. Rabbi Cook felt for the first time he could rest assured that Dr. Elk's and his dream would survive. Rabbi Friedman was very pleased, as it was at the time the largest donation to the IEF. Rabbi Eisendrath was amazed.

The World Union's volunteer legal counsel, Judge Emil Baar, represented both the World Union and the Leo Baeck board in the contract with Caroline and the IEF. It was the first of several important tasks that Judge Baar undertook for Leo Baeck, and he did it with all his heart. In the end, Caroline wanted us to have her entire estate. After giving us $350,000, she had just over $250,000 left. The interest on this was enough for her annual expenses.

We invited Caroline to attend the groundbreaking ceremony in June 1968. It was her first and only visit to Israel. Ira accompanied her from New York, and high-ranking Israeli officials were in attendance. Rabbis Friedman and Eisendrath attended, embracing Caroline and speaking of this as a historic event for Israel and for the Reform Movement. Caroline said it was the most significant event in her life. All of us fell in love with this cultured and sensitive woman.

For several years following, I invited her to lunch each time I came to New York in order to give her *nachat* (satisfaction) from the beauty of life at Leo Baeck and the progress of construction. She always met me at her favorite deli on the corner of Sixth Avenue and Fifty-Seventh Street. One year I called her, but she said she could not meet me as she was ill. "Caroline," I said, "I can't be in New York and not see you. I will come up to your apartment." She argued with me, but I insisted. It was a fortuitous decision, as upon entering her apartment hotel, which was near Carnegie Hall, I found a criminally neglected abode with many questionable characters loitering in the lobby. Caroline Greenfield, the largest benefactor to the building of Reform Judaism's Israeli educational flagship, was living in a dump.

I pleaded with her to come to live with us in the B'nai B'rith Senior Citizens Home in Haifa, where she would have hundreds of appreciative and loving children and community. "No, all my money will go for your children in Israel!" she insisted. Now it was time for Judge Baar's second mitzvah for us. We met together with Caroline's nephew, Rabbi Abram Goodman, and formed a conservatorship as agents for Caroline, now ninety years old. Judge Baar, Rabbi Goodman, and I invested her money by entering her into a beautiful facility on Long Island where she lived comfortably until her death at the age of 104.

In 1984 Leo Baeck received the residue of Caroline's estate, almost $250,000. The Julia and David Greenfield School Building in Haifa is her Georgia parents' lasting legacy, and the many teenagers who have received Caroline Greenfield Scholarships are her immortality. It is one of the inspirational spiritual tales of twentieth century Jewish life.

Giants of Industry

Maurice Saltzman, Women's Clothing
We received $100,000 from Maurice Saltzman, who had grown up in the Cleveland Jewish Orphanage. As an adult, he founded Bobbie Brooks, a major clothing line for women. He made a fortune and gave away a fortune. Subsequent to that initial gift, I went to see him once a year. He always gave me five minutes. I would fly into Cleveland, rent a car at the airport, and arrive at his factory fifteen minutes before our scheduled meeting. His secretary would usher me into Maurice's office. At the exact moment of our scheduled meeting, he would dash into the room and say, "I'm glad to see you, Bob. How can I help you this time?" I knew the routine. No small talk. I told him what we needed, handing him a written request. He always said yes, apologized for being busy, and ran out of the office. I then got back into my car and drove to my next appointment or back to the airport to fly to the next city.

Robert Wishnick, Industrial Chemicals
And so it was with Robert Wishnick, the founder and president of Witco, a major chemical firm with offices in Manhattan. Mr. Wishnick was a kind man, a passionate Reform Jew, and a gentleman. He had given the World Union the funds to purchase a beautiful home in Rehavia to house Jerusalem's Har-El Synagogue and, with the approval

of his rabbi, Jacob Shankman, a World Union leader, Mr. Wishnick gave us $100,000. In subsequent years, I would meet with him in his Manhattan office. He never turned me down.

Jac Lehrman, Supermarkets
Jac Lehrman lived in Washington, D.C. and was a member of Washington Hebrew Congregation. He owned 200 supermarkets in and around Washington. I culled his name from the lists of potential Reform Jewish donors. Mr. Lehrman agreed to meet, and an appointment was made. Rabbi Eisendrath accompanied me to Mr. Lerhman's palatial home, and we were joined by the chair of the Washington Federation of the UJA. Jac Lehrman had a huge presence. He sat down in his favorite easy chair and asked, "How can I help you?" I gave him the story of Leo Baeck, the state of education in Israel, and then asked him to become a $100,000 donor to the IEF. Rabbi Eisendrath seconded the request and asked him as a personal friend to make the gift.

Mr. Lehrman said, "Sometimes, when traveling for my business, I go to Boston. And whenever there, I make a point of entering the Harvard Yard with its statue of John Harvard. Standing under the statue, I ask myself, 'What did that man give to get all that immortality?'" I understood the question immediately and replied, "The price of immortality at Leo Baeck is $350,000. Caroline Greenfield has given us that amount to name the school building for her parents. Give us a similar grant, and we will name the community center for your family." "*That* interests me," he said. "I will speak to my wife, Charlotte, and you will hear from us."

One month later I received a call from the Israel office of the UJA. Jac and Charlotte Lehrman were coming on the UJA's Presidents' Mission, and they were extending an invitation to Annette and me to be their guests at the closing ceremony at the Tel Aviv Hilton. The invitation included spending the night in their suite, with breakfast on their balcony in the morning. We had a lovely evening as the guests of the Lehrmans at the Mission's closing ceremony, featuring Abba Eban. The next morning on the terrace of their suite over breakfast, Mr. Lehrman said, "Charlotte and I have decided to make the gift of immortality at your school." Thrilled, I thanked him profusely and asked him to go downstairs with me to meet with Eliezer Shavit of the Jewish Agency in order to arrange the contract. Mr. Lehrman said, "I'll give you $200,000 this year and the remainder next year." The $200,000 arrived quickly, enabling us to continue construction of the auditorium, the synagogue, the library, and the teachers' room.

The following year, I did not hear from Mr. Lehrman or from the UJA. We were in the midst of construction. When I queried them about the $150,000 the Lehrmans still owed for the naming gift, I received vague responses. It turned out that the UJA had made a personal appeal to Mr. Lehrman for an addition to his regular campaign gift, and when he said he had a commitment of $150,000 to Leo Baeck, was told this amount was needed for an emergency project and that Leo Baeck could wait until the following year. Mr. Lehrman agreed, but we were not informed.

Three months later, Mr Lehrman contracted cancer of the liver. He died three months later, without leaving the $150,000 commitment in his will. No one was ready to fund it, and we never received the money. So it is when you are low man on the totem pole.

Walter Haas and Dan Koshland, Levi Jeans
One of the bright lights of my fundraising came as a result of being introduced to two of the owners of Levi Strauss, the Levis blue jeans families of San Francisco. Walter Haas and Dan Koshland were in their seventies when I met them in 1967. They had already been primed by Rabbi Friedman and expected me to ask for the UJA minimum $100,000 gift.

Levi Strauss was a Jew who went west to San Francisco following the Gold Rush of 1849. Most of those who rushed out there thought gold was the true wealth to be found in the California streams and rivers. But Levi Strauss knew there was another form of gold, in the form of money those thousands of prospectors had and would pay for durable trousers. He discovered that denim could take the heavy beating of rock panning. Blue jeans became an instant success, and Levi Strauss and his family turned those denims into an enormous business. Strauss never married but turned his business over to a relative whose three granddaughters inherited it. One married Dan Koshland, one married Walter Haas, and one married Philip Lilienthal.

When I was ushered into the simple factory offices of Levi Strauss, Haas and Koshland told me that Lilienthal had just died, and they would like something in the new building to be named for him. I suggested the Science Center, and they agreed.

In each of the subsequent eight years, I made a pilgrimage to Battery Street in downtown San Francisco with a request for further development of the Philip Lilienthal Science Center. Mr. Koshland and Mr. Haas always greeted me warmly, listened to my report on Leo Baeck, and their project specifically, and then agreed to give the furnishings, equipment, and annual scholarships for the study of science in the Lilienthal Center. This continued until 1975, when Dan Koshland, then in his eighties, told me he and Walter had decided use their remaining time to contribute to the San Francisco Foundation, to give back to the city that had made their achievements possible.

Max Kargman, Real Estate Development
Rabbi Friedman had been disappointed with the leadership of the UAHC, which had not helped the UJA raise the hundreds of millions required for the economic and social infrastructure Israel needed. He urged me to try to convince Rabbi Eisendrath that one of the $100,000 gifts would come from the UAHC. Rabbi Eisendrath was reluctant to take on that responsibility, though he was very supportive of me and my work. It was a catch-22. On the one hand, Rabbi Friedman made the Union's commitment a *sine qua non* for allowing me to use the offices of the UJA to raise the $1.1 million necessary for our new Center, but on the other hand, I could not count on the Union to make the first $100,000 pledge, and it never did.

Max Kargman, who had initially helped me get the plot of ground in Haifa, pledged $100,000. He gave $50,000, promising to give $10,000 a year for five years. Those five years stretched into twenty-five. We treated this pledge as if it fulfilled the UAHC commitment, even though Mr. Kargman would likely have contributed in any event. With his Harvard Ph.D. in Education, he was the only donor who understood the unique educational path of Leo Baeck. I would meet him every year in Boston. His contribution was not just his $100,000, but also his perception of our attempt to produce the finest and most humane high school graduates in Israel. The gift was in his and his wife Marie's names. Toward the end of his life, they made a trip to Israel, and upon seeing Leo Baeck and the plaque with their names as founders, Marie also became both a personal and an institutional friend.

Jerome Klorfein
Another gift through the UJA came in a most unusual way. Jerome Klorfein had inherited Manhattan real estate from his father. A graduate of New York University, he lived in Rockville Centre, where he and his wife were members of a Reform congregation. Despite not being Jewish, his wife was very active in the congregation and in Hadassah. But when she died, the rabbi of the congregation refused to officiate at the funeral. Klorfein was incensed and called his close friend, Rabbi Friedman. Mr. Klorfein was a regular $75,000 annual donor to the UJA campaign in New York. When he told Rabbi Friedman of his dilemma, he immediately agreed to officiate at the funeral. By chance, I had visited Rabbi Friedman in his office that day, and we had gone through a list of possible Reform donors. So when at the end of the funeral, Mr. Klorfein and Rabbi Friedman were walking together back to their cars, and Mr. Klorfein asked, "Rabbi, what can I do for you?" Friedman responded, "I want $100,000 for the Leo Baeck School in Haifa. Rabbi Samuels, who works there, is in New York. If you agree, invite him to lunch at the NYU Club, and he will tell you about the school."

And so it was. Jerome Klorfein needed a friend, and I became his proxy rabbi. He conferred with me on many matters, from business to family. We decided to name something in his and his mother's names. We still needed to build an auditorium and a gymnasium. He chose the auditorium as he was a major contributor to the American Israel Cultural Foundation, which gave scholarships to promising young Israeli musicians and artists. The AICF encouraged him to fund a cultural hall in Israel. And so it was that we built the Rose and Jerome Klorfein Auditorium, a beautiful hall with 700 seats, which has allowed Leo Baeck and our community many experiences of creativity through the years.

When the great violinist, Isaac Stern, told Mr. Klorfein that he was going to Israel the following month, he said, "I want you to visit my auditorium." Isaac Stern promised he would not only visit but would check the acoustics. Sure enough, Isaac Stern actually appeared at Leo Baeck one day. He bounded down the stairs and bounced onto the stage of the auditorium. He clapped his hands loudly twice, exclaimed, "Good acoustics!" and ran back to his limousine. As a result, Mr. Klorfein made additional gifts for the 700 seats, the carpet, the lighting, and the stage curtains. For a number of years, the director of the AICF arranged an annual concert with Israeli teens, many of whom were to become world class performers, including Yefim Bronfman, and the three Tzori children, Hillel, Nitai, and Carmel.

Several years later, Mr. Klorfein promised me that Leo Baeck would receive one quarter of his estate, and so it did. He left us property worth $850,000. Jerome Klorfein is permanently memorialized here in Israel. Now, forty years later with a much enlarged student body, Leo Baeck needs to expand and upgrade its Rose and Jerome Klorfein Auditorium.

Another Attempt at Entrepreneurial Funding

In the 1980s I played first base on the "Triple T" softball team. Hal Gutterman played on my team, and we became friendly. He sent one of his children to study at Leo Baeck. Hal was an executive at Elscint, one of Israel's pioneer medical imaging companies. Over a beer one day he told me of his contacts with McDonnell Douglas (MD), the American aerospace company in St. Louis. MD sold millions of dollars of aerospace products to Israel annually, and Israel was able to pay through "offset," whereby MD was paid by American companies that bought goods and services from Israel. The Israeli companies were then paid in local currency by the government who owed MD. This saved Israel from having to pay in dollars, then a very expensive commodity for an Israel with few foreign reserves and an economy crippled by high inflation.

Israel was at the genesis of what would become its high-tech revolution. The Technion was producing computer knowledgeable graduates, but the computer industry was in its infancy in Israel, and there were too few jobs for those graduates. Hal told me MD had a subsidiary company called McAuto (McDonnell Douglas Automatic Services), which was creating healthcare software for hospitals, medical clinics, doctors' offices, and laboratories. I believed that Haifa had the infrastructure necessary to produce some of that software as a subcontractor for McAuto. We would be able to receive payment for our work in shekels through offset. I convinced Leo Baeck's financially conservative Board to let me attempt to establish a Community Development Corporation (CDC), an entity designed to produce income for communities by establishing businesses.

So off I went to St Louis in search of a contract with McAuto. I was received warmly and asked to prepare a business plan with the promise that if they felt we could indeed produce the product more cheaply, they would work with us. McAuto was ready to pay us $35 an hour per programmer at 2,000 hours a year (a forty-hour week for fifty weeks). Back in Haifa, we resurrected Carmel Development Industries (CDI), set up a team consisting of a lawyer, an accountant, and a computer expert (all pro-bono), which concluded that we could hire ten programmers, one of whom would head the team. That would give us an annual income of $700,000. We needed to find ten computer programmers, access to a main-frame computer in Haifa, and negotiate with the Israeli government for offset.

We received more than a hundred responses to our ad for programmers. Most were young graduates of the Technion, highly trained with few job opportunities. We selected our ten, including a general manager (GM). We found office space in a building with access to an IBM main-frame computer. The business plan called for a $200,000 (or in a worst-case scenario, $150,000) net profit. The annual deficit of Leo Baeck in those years amounted to no more than $50,000. We registered CDI and sent our GM to St Louis to learn McAuto's medical software business and receive our 20,000 annual hours of subcontracted work.

The contract we drew up for our programmers included a condition that if they left us to create a computer-based start-up, CDI would have the option of owning 33.3% of that company. I predicted that Israel, which had moved from an agricultural to an industrial economy, was on the threshold of a new economy based on the knowledge, intuition, and entrepreneurialism of these computer-trained Israelis. High economic yield from a knowledge-based company could go into Israel's social development as well as accrue to the personal finances of the owners. I had fantasies of CDI becoming a multi-million-dollar company that would divide its profits between continuing R&D and expanding Leo Baeck's educational values throughout Israel, together with providing the Israel Movement for Progressive Judaism (IMPJ) with the finances for it to become a major player in the socialization of Israel.

But it was not to be. At the last minute McAuto turned us down. MD was downsizing, so they, too, had to downsize. It was a huge disappointment for me, and in retrospect, the most significant failure of my career. Had McAuto given us five years, I believe we could have morphed into a major player in the high-tech world, and we would have been on the ground floor of the financial revolution that drove Israel's 1990s economy toward solvency and significant growth.

CDI would have become an eye-opening CDC. We would not have needed hard-to-get funding from fundraising, the Zionist Movement, or government grants. We would have turned the profits from business into significant funding for education, community building, and spirituality for Israelis. I believe that it could have changed the perception of Reform Judaism in the eyes of secular Israelis, made those with political power take us seriously, and thereby been a game-changer for Leo Baeck, for the Movement, and for Israel itself.

There was one more attempt at entrepreneurial funding. Kibbutz Yahel was founded in 1977 by leaders of TAKAM, the Kibbutz Movement of the Labor Party, together with the Youth Division of the American Reform Movement. This is a story in itself, as it was the first serious venture of a wing of American Reform to place itself on the Land in Israel. Yahel is in the Arava, the dry desert north of Eilat. It based its economy on agriculture: dates, vegetables, onions, which they marketed in Europe in the winter. However, agriculture alone cannot sustain the kibbutz economy. Therefore, they built guest houses and a Negev tourism industry, funded through contributions from both American Reform Jews and the Israeli Tourism Ministry.

The intimate connection between Yahel and the American Reform Movement led to a potentially large industry for the kibbutz. In the 1970s, research on the effects of UV radiation on the skin had proven that sun tanning was dangerous, potentially causing melanoma. In 1978 the US Food and Drug Administration determined that sun lotions must be labeled with the warning, "Sun tanning may be dangerous for the skin." This would lead to a multi-billion-dollar industry in sunblock lotions and creams. A group of Reform Jewish investors in Cleveland, Ohio, realizing the potential in this budding sunblock revolution, proposed to Yahel that they produce a product called *Mediterranean Sun Block*. They commissioned a $50,000 market research study to ascertain whether *Mediterranean Sun Block* could get 1% of the rapidly developing American market, the results of which were positive. Thus the proposal to Kibbutz Yahel.

The members of the kibbutz, all in their twenties, were pioneering in every sense except in an understanding of economic solvency and growth. At their weekly Saturday night assembly of members, the business proposal was presented and voted down. Those youngsters did not want to get into an industrial business. Their American business friends were profoundly disappointed, and they dropped the idea.

Six months later in New York, Rabbi Stephen Schafer, who together with Israeli Rabbis Hank Skirball and Allan Levine and Israeli youth emissary Dr. Michael Langer had been the chief engine that produced Yahel, told me the story. Realizing the potential in another emerging industry, I contacted the Cleveland investors who had headed the proposal and the research, made an appointment for the next day, and flew to Cleveland to meet with two colleagues at the Cleveland airport. They showed me the results of their research, including the agreement of a Reform Jew who owned 2,000 drugstores in North America to stock *Mediterranean Sun Block* in his stores. But they also told me they had missed the initial stage of what was to become a booming industry. They felt that they could no longer guarantee the market percentage necessary to make the business profitable. Once again, a golden opportunity for CDI was frustratingly aborted.

In the 1990s the continuing development of Leo Baeck, the opening of many community outreach projects throughout Haifa, and our work in the integration of the huge Ethiopian and Russian immigration prevented further pursuit of CDI as a Community Development Corporation. By the end of the 1990s I was passing the baton to my successor, and the concept has remained only a dream. As both Leo Baeck and the IMPJ have expanded in the last twenty-five years, we are still frustrated by the lack of finances for our message of merging of the values of democracy and Jewish spirituality to launch us as significant players in Israeli society.

CHAPTER 3
BOLD THRUST IN EDUCATION

PART 3
The Leo Baeck Education Center

Committing to a Life in Israel

The year 1970 was a stellar one for Leo Baeck and for me. Annette and I loved our life in Haifa, our children were growing beautifully, and we had purchased an apartment with a three-acre open park behind us. We had determined that our life in Israel was what we wanted, and we would make our family permanent here.

It had not been easy. In 1966 Israel was in both an economic recession and an ideological crisis, and we wavered. I was offered two major positions in the United States. One was to become the senior rabbi at NSCI upon Rabbi Siskin's retirement. This is one of the great congregations of North America, a synagogue with 1,800 families and 2,000 children in its religious school. Located along Chicago's beautiful North Shore, the world class physical facilities, designed by the great Japanese-American architect Minoru Yamasaki, are located on the former Lady Esther estate (of cosmetics fame), occupying twenty acres on a cliff above Lake Michigan. The search committee had sent a delegation to Haifa to offer me the job. It was most tempting. Had we decided to return to the States, this would have been a launching pad for a career that allowed leadership roles within the Reform Movement and in the wider American society.

I was also sought out by Shlomo Bardin, the creative founder of Brandeis Camp Institute (BCI) in the Simi Valley near Los Angeles. He had met with me in Haifa, saw my work at Leo Baeck and Or Hadash, and invited me to come in February of 1967 as scholar-in-residence for what he called "The House of the Book," a weekend for adults to experience and learn Judaism. As a result of that weekend, he invited me to teach for the entire summer at their Institute for college students and to direct Camp Alonim, the large children's camp on the 2,000-acre campus of BCI. My family joined me that summer, leaving Israel a week after the termination of the Six-Day War. Toward the end of the camp session, I was invited to meet with the board. They offered me a most generous contract, including a guarantee that if they were pleased with my work, I would succeed Shlomo when he retired. The list of board members included many of the movers and shakers of the Jewish community in Los Angeles and Hollywood.

The Six-Day War was one of the critical turning points in the history of modern Israel. In effect, it showed the world, the Arab nations, and us that Israel was to be permanently established in the Middle East. It was a triumphant time. Annette and I decided that in spite of the promise that awaited us back "home" in America, our real home was in Israel. It was a gutsy decision to turn down both NSCI and BCI, either of which would have been a major stage for exercising creative spiritual leadership.

It was certainly a bad economic decision, as either of those institutions would have provided us with a fine upper middle-class life and lifetime financial security. At the time, Leo Baeck was struggling with its budget, and the World Union was unresponsive to raising my salary to a level that would allow us to live with dignity. Annette is the heroine here, as she was perfectly content to live a simple economic life for her and our household. Such a decision would never have been successful without our partnership. We had saved some money from our two years in Glencoe in the early sixties. This and Annette's father's gift to us of two-thirds of the cost of our apartment made it possible for us to own a home without a mortgage but with all the basic appliances and appurtenances a family needs to raise children. We had a happy and fruitful family life.

We never had the funds for travel and for family vacations, but we were able to take them by my bartering my services as rabbi for the Pesach Seder in a kibbutz guesthouse or hotel for a vacation for the family. Over the years in the sixties and seventies, I offered my services to the Kayit Veshayit guest house at Kibbutz Sdot Yam, the Caesarea Hotel under the management of Club Med, the Kibbutz Beit Oren guest house, and the Hotel Kinneret in Tiberias. In 1974, when I succeeded Dr. Elk as general manager of Leo Baeck, I received an adequate income that covered our annual expenses.

The three senior World Union rabbis, however, received salaries that could not be considered adequate. One even felt he had to leave the country for better opportunities. It is sad that the decision-makers did not have the vision and the drive to fund opportunities to advance the Reform Movement in Israel.

The Reform Movement Wakes Up

In those first years of my leadership of Leo Baeck, we struggled to get a critical mass of students in the senior high school. As noted in the earlier part of this chapter, Haifa had been the first city in Israel to establish education reform. The system changed from eight years of free, compulsory state elementary education and four years of private high school to a free six-year elementary and three-year junior high education and a tuition-based three-year senior high.

The new system was made into law in 1966 but not instituted until the fall of 1970. Haifa took the pioneering step in being the first municipality to change the system, to develop junior high schools throughout the city, and to map the city so that the graduates of elementary schools were by law mapped into specific junior highs. The problem with Haifa's solution, however, was that most of the schools were academic and some of the schools were vocational, but none of them were comprehensive schools where all students could progress according to their interests and achievement level. Since we took seriously the national challenge of bringing the children of Sephardic families to the high school, giving them the tools to succeed in a rapidly developing urban, technological environment, it was necessary to have both academic and vocational tracks. Given that Haifa had one high-level vocational high school, Bosmat, the Haifa Municipality said, "No comprehensive high schools. We have enough of an infrastructure for vocational tracks in the schools that already exist."

Since one-third of the students coming into our junior high were from a deprived neighborhood, and they came into high school with an academic background decidedly inferior to that of our other students, it was imperative to develop vocational programs in the senior high in order for them to be able to continue to study with us through the twelfth grade. Time and again I approached the Ministry of Education and the Haifa Municipality to support and to finance vocational studies such as electronics, auto mechanics, woodworking, drafting, and philatelic studies, to no avail. In those first years, therefore, the percentage of ninth-grade graduates from the junior high that entered the tenth grade was small, and the achievement level of the graduates was not as high as we needed.

Our staff was dedicated to those children as if they were to become leaders in the next generation. Most of them achieved at a higher level than we believed possible when they entered our tenth grade. The entire teaching body was dedicated to challenging those teenagers to reach beyond themselves.

One of the classes each year was called *Kitat Gemer*. The students in this class were expected to be able to complete only partial matriculation. But we trained the staff in methods to inspire the students to believe in themselves and work hard, and 90% of them achieved full matriculation. Our senior teaching staff, headed by the gifted Tzeira Trifon, worked wonders. They were to become the pioneers that paved the way for the future development of the senior high.

As noted in a previous chapter, it was during this period that Rabbi Richard Hirsch began his leadership of the World Union by bringing the international headquarters to Jerusalem and by raising the Zionist profile in the Reform Movement. A few of the American Reform rabbis were dedicated Zionists. Together with them we sought a dialogue with some of the ideological leaders of the Kibbutz Movement. We saw those two diametrically opposed movements as coming out of the same nineteenth-century emancipation of the Jew, each seeking a new way for Jewishness over one hundred years ago. Reform Judaism had been a Diaspora movement, accepting the principles of equality among peoples and of the need to form anew the *religion* and traditions of Judaism in order to make them relevant and in confluence with the values of the Emancipation and the American and French revolutions. The kibbutz movement was born out of the same revolution, but it looked at the *nationalist* side of Jewishness, determining to create a new Jew free of the burdens of tradition and headed toward a new, national renaissance. A.D. Gordon and Berl Katznelson were the secular "rabbis" who taught the ideology of simple agrarian rural life, when the Jew puts his hands in his own soil and "builds a nation and is built by it." Reform felt it could stop anti-Semitism by becoming devoted citizens of the countries of the West, which were moving inexorably toward more and more freedom for the individual and freedom to change ritual observance. The kibbutzim became a haven of self-help, away from the ever-present demons of anti-Semitism in the European countries from which these pioneers came. In their attempt to develop a new Jewish zeitgeist, the reformers had shucked Zion, and the kibbutzniks had shucked religion.

In the early 1970s, it was now time to seek common ground. We brought together ideological leaders of the Kibbutz Movement and Reform Judaism. The leaders of the kibbutzim came mostly from Oranim, a Kibbutz Movement academic college near Haifa. They were led by ideologists like Moshe Kerem from Kibbutz Gesher HaZiv and Muki Tzur from Kibbutz Ein Gev. The leaders of the Reform Movement came mostly from the United States: Rabbi David Polish of Chicago's Temple Beth Emet, Rabbi Roland Gittelsohn of Boston's Temple Israel, Rabbi Stephen Schafer, Director of NFTY. The first meeting took place at Leo Baeck in 1975, and subsequent meetings took place at Oranim College. These conversations became known as the Oranim Process.

Moshe Kerem spoke of the common denominator between a religious and an agricultural response to emancipation. Both are secular, as they break with the belief in a supernatural God. A kibbutz in the Labor Movement could have a room for prayer where members seek self-realization, but it would not be a synagogue where the fate of the kibbutz would depend on petitions to God. Muki Tzur asked the Reform leaders if they could replace their commitment to prayer with the acceptance of the will of the majority of the kibbutz members to reject a religious way of life no matter how liberal it might be. Rabbi Polish, courageously speaking in Hebrew, said that the trauma of the Holocaust had seared the conscience of American Jews, resulting in a shift in ideology in the Reform Movement toward the strengthening of Jewish life in Israel. Rabbi Gittelsohn responded to Moshe Kerem, stating he agreed that our common denominator was the emancipation of Jews from the ghettos. However, breaking from a supernatural God did not mean that modern life had to reject a Supreme Source of both nature and human nature. Such a belief should be pursued in Israel as in America, and a wedding of educated young Jews from the free world living with Israeli youth would change religious perceptions in Israel.

I interjected a new conception of Zionism, summarizing my experience teaching the American high school exchange students at Leo Baeck. All of us have rejected *messianism*, I said, being ready to build

Jewish life in Zion and not wait for God to send us a Savior. Herzl gave us *political* Zionism; Ahad HaAm taught us *cultural* Zionism; A. D. Gordon gave us *labor* Zionism. It was now time for *exchange* Zionism, where the new religious experience of North American Jewry meets the modern Jewish world in Israel in search of a new Jewish way of life. Rabbi Schafer promised North American Reform youth who would come to settle in a kibbutz based on both agriculture and a renewal of Jewish life.

The crucial outcome of these meetings was to be the formation of a kibbutz based on both the social equality of the secular kibbutz movement and the spiritual principles of Reform Judaism. The first of these kibbutzim, founded in the Arava, was Kibbutz Yahel, established in 1978. Several of the first Israelis to go to Kibbutz Yahel were graduates of Leo Baeck. Rabbi Allan Levine brought graduates of the Ben Shemen Youth Village. Rabbi Schafer brought Dr. Michael Langer as a *shaliach* (emissary) to America to form a Reform youth nucleus for the kibbutz. Both of these groups were trained and brought together in a very meaningful ceremony when Kibbutz Yahel was inaugurated. Yahel planted fields and built a synagogue center. A second "Reform" kibbutz, Lotan, followed in the Arava. Lotan has emphasized the relationship between nature and Judaism. These young kibbutzniks are pioneering a new way of life, adding a chapter to the history of Reform Judaism and Israel.

It was in these years that the Israel Rabbinic program at HUC-JIR was founded (see previous chapter). The first students were Zeev Harari, Mordechai (Motti) Rotem, and Gil Nativ, all graduates of Leo Baeck who had worked with me through the years both at Leo Baeck and in Or Hadash. They were to be followed by David Maredich and Meir Azari. These young pioneers, who both went down to the Arava to free the soil and themselves, and who studied for the rabbinate to free Judaism and themselves, came out of the crucible of the youth group and the environment of liberalism we created at Leo Baeck.

Our New Campus

In the summer of 1970, as a citizen of Israel and the successful entrepreneur of the new Leo Baeck School Campus on Haifa's French Carmel, it was a great satisfaction to welcome the delegates to the first Israel Convention of the CCAR. We gathered in the internal courtyard of the new stepped pyramid building, the roof of which was still not completed. Rabbi Roland Gittelsohn, then president of the CCAR, a strong Zionist and long time supporter of both Leo Baeck and Congregation Or Hadash, said the following:

> *We American Reform rabbis have watched with great pride the pioneering work of Rabbis Elk and Samuels. I personally have lectured in the school and in the congregation. We are sending our best young people on the Exchange Program and welcoming Leo Baeck's students in our communities. Under great pressure from Israel's political and religious leadership, but with unswerving dedication to their principles, these Reform rabbis are blazing a trail toward a movement based on our highest spiritual conceptions. We salute you and will continue to support you.*

Two months later, on the first of September, 1970, we greeted our first students in the new junior high school. It was housed in the building of the former Ironi Daled school, whose 200 students were integrated into the new senior high school in the magnificent facilities we had worked so hard to build. Dr. Elk was still headmaster and was somewhat bewildered by the size of both the student body and the campus. He was to remain headmaster for four more years, until the age of seventy-five. My work in those years was to create the spiritual content, identify and work with strategic partners, unite the staff around the concept of the school, and fundraise for both the continuation of construction and the annual budget.

There were many challenges. First among them was the wide disparity in learning skills and acquired knowledge of the entering seventh-grade students. Our national task was to integrate students from different ethnic groups and socioeconomic backgrounds. Our junior high was zoned from four elementary schools: the Leo Baeck Elementary School on the Hadar (a different section of Haifa), coming from both lower- and middle-class families; the Tchernichovsky School on the French Carmel, coming from established middle-class families; the Ramot School in Ramat Shaul, coming from lower middle-class families, and the Sprinzak School in Kiryat Sprinzak, one of Haifa's poorest neighborhoods.

Our first task was to integrate this very heterogeneous population of twelve- and thirteen-year-olds into a healthy social environment while providing a challenging intellectual experience for students with such a wide gap in acquired learning skills. We experimented with homogeneous classes in order to teach on the same level, but this led to little social integration between Ashkenazic and Sephardic students, and the learning gaps only widened. The Sephardic kids from Sprinzak were at a decidedly lower reading level. We moved to heterogeneous classes. There was more social mixing, but with forty students in a class and at least three different levels of learning skills, the teachers became very frustrated. They had to beam their lessons toward the thirty students in the center and ward off the discipline problems from both the less and the better prepared students, who quickly became bored.

We experimented with various pedagogic programs, the largest of which was the long school day with special classes and tutoring in the afternoons. But it became increasingly clear that we needed a long-term solution, starting with the children from lower socio-economic families in the two less demanding schools, raising their learning level from the first grade. The two keys were the level of reading proficiency and math perception at the end of the first grade. This would determine whether we could bridge the continuing learning proficiency throughout elementary school and thereby lower the gap between disadvantaged and advantaged students entering the seventh grade.

It was our connection with our American partner donors that helped us make a major breakthrough. Houstonian Hershel Rich, a wealthy engineer and a long-time friend and supporter, was involved in a reading project stemming from the same socio-economic issues in Houston that we were experiencing in Haifa.

I had studied programmed reading at Northwestern University in the early 1960s while living in Chicago and was familiar with the theories of psychologist B.F. Skinner. In 1961, Northwestern researchers were experimenting with the use of mechanical devices for teaching his theory of positive reinforcement. In the early 1970s Houston had used new research in psychology at Indiana University to determine the effect of positive reinforcement on the reading level of the city's black and Hispanic first graders. Reports were promising.

We asked to become a part of the experiment, and Hershel was ready to fund it. After getting the approval of the principal of the Sprinzak School and her supervisor, we sent one of our teachers to Indiana to learn about it. She produced first-grade readers in Hebrew based on the psychology of positive reinforcement. The books were designed with a page on the left for the reader and a page on the right for the tutor, with instructions to respond to the reader *only* in positive language.

The results of the experiment were good, but not enough to ensure a high reading comprehension level. The first tutors were teachers, then volunteer adults, then seventh-grade highly skilled readers.

The breakthrough came when we experimented with seventh-grade graduates of the Sprinzak School who were far below a seventh-grade reading level themselves. Part of the experiment, which included a control group, was to determine if by tutoring six-year-olds from their same environment, the seventh graders themselves would advance significantly in their own reading levels. The results were dramatic. The tutors shot up in both reading comprehension and in their own feeling of self-worth over their contemporaries in the control group. The six-year-olds also responded positively, as these thirteen-year-olds from their neighborhood became their heroes and goal setters. (The program lasted for several years until Ruth Miller, the junior high principal, decided to end it.)

The junior high was a public school, whereas the senior high was private under the auspices of the Leo Baeck board of directors. This meant there were constant conflicts between our board on the one hand and the Ministry of Education supervisors and the Haifa Municipality's Department of Education on the other.

I was determined the school would have a liberal and religious orientation. There were liberal schools in Israel and there were religious schools in Israel, but no school that combined the two. We were free to develop the modes we wanted in the senior high, but not in the junior high. The first principal of the junior high, Yair Magen, became a personal friend. He did want to see the integration of both schools, but the Municipality wanted to ensure that the junior high would be considered its school. The only connection was that Dr. Elk was the overall headmaster and that the graduates of the ninth grade, being zoned on the French Carmel, were to be accepted by the senior high. We knew that the future of the school depended on our finding the right balance between students with excellent achievement and weaker students who would need much enrichment.

In those years, parents wanted their children to receive a technological education. Haifa had many such schools, the flagship of which was Bosmat, as noted earlier. In its heyday in the 1970s, the school had sixteen parallel classes in a grade. In those first years, not only the parents of our junior high exceptional students wanted their children to go to Bosmat, but even our junior high teachers recommended they do so.

Bosmat had been founded in 1933 by a group of educators who saw the school as preparing excellent students to continue learning science and engineering in the Technion, which was housed next door on Haifa's Hadar. By 1970 it was considered the primary preparatory educational institution for math and science. But over the years, as Israel began to develop a technological base, there was a need for students less talented in the sciences to be trained for jobs in industry, such as auto mechanics, on-line factory mechanics, and mechanics in support of the military. As the need for such employment grew, so did the number of classes in Bosmat. As we began our six-year high school in 1970, parents of our ninth graders had a fine alternative to our senior high.

The Leo Baeck Senior High School struggled to get a critical mass of students who would attain a high achievement level in the physical sciences, the social sciences, and the humanities. We had to prove we could match the Reali School and Bosmat in teaching science and convince students and their parents that a liberal arts education would be far more valuable to them in the future.

Our teachers had endless meetings on the relative importance of mathematics and history, physics and Bible, chemistry and Judaic Studies, biology and sociology, English and music, Arabic and theater. A hierarchy of importance was "in the air." The brighter the students, the more they were expected to study math and physics. The second level of achievement was for chemistry and biology, and it went down from there. The humanities and Hebrew literature were seen as subjects "for girls" and not for the highest achievers (assumed to be boys). It was saddening, but a fact. By 1974 the critical question was whether a senior high committed to the liberal arts could survive this kind of atmosphere. We had only two parallel classes in a grade, and the level was definitely considered subpar. We had to brand Leo Baeck as *the* alternative to a technological education, at every level.

The Yom Kippur War Alters Our Paths

We had built an underpinning for a nascent youth movement for Reform Judaism in Israel. Leo Baeck had a wonderful and powerful group of its students and their friends from other schools that molded together into a dynamic and spiritual *chavurah to* renew themselves in the spirit of Progressive Judaism. One of the leaders of this group was Itzik Cohen, who as an adolescent had come to Leo Baeck from Tirat HaCarmel, an immigrant community just outside of Haifa. Itzik, born into an Egyptian Jewish family, was extremely talented and motivated. As a teenager he became a member of this group, and as a young adult, became its leader.

All of these young people went into the Israel Defense Forces (IDF) upon graduation. They got together whenever they could. One such gathering was on the second day of Rosh HaShanah, 1973, when they took a hike together. Then came the Yom Kippur War. One of them, Itzik Breitner, was killed in the War. His friends decided to memorialize him the following year by revisiting the hike they had taken the year before on the second day of Rosh HaShanah. It is that day that the *Akedat Yitzchak*, the binding of Isaac, is read in the synagogue. Together with the Leo Baeck graduate who had become their leader, Rabbi Gil Nativ, they took a *sefer Torah* with them and read about the original Isaac and spoke about our Isaac. Then they blew the shofar. The experience was so powerful that year, and the memory so fresh and vivid, the group decided that every Rosh HaShanah, on the second day, they would hike somewhere else in Israel and memorialize their lost friend. Dorit Menashe, who had been the first bat mitzvah at Or Hadash, agreed to arrange all the logistics. Aviva Shafer, a Baeck graduate affectionately called "Habibti," agreed to write a poem about Itzish, as they called him, and about "the situation." The Breitner family donated a *sefer Torah* that had been in their family for several generations, brought to Israel from Bulgaria. This Torah was put into the *aron hakodesh* in Ohel Avraham and is read every Rosh HaShanah.

The annual hike has become a sacred tradition. It still continues, as I write, forty years later. The children of those friends of Itzish have now finished their military service, married, and have children of their own. Each year on Rosh HaShanah four generations of Israelis rededicate themselves to a liberal, Jewish life of the spirit in our country. There is nothing more holy than to be in the midst of nature somewhere in Israel, from the Golan Heights to the Negev, and to be called up to the Torah, all the women together, all the men together, all the children together, all the teenagers together, all the soldiers together, as we reread Abraham's readiness to sacrifice his son. It is a powerful message for us Israelis who still live in the trauma of conflict and war to be reminded that God does not desire the sacrifice of Abraham's children, even today.

The Yom Kippur War of October 1973 was the shock of an earthquake for Israel. The proud days of the late sixties, when our 1967 Six-Day War victory had given us an arrogance of invincibility, was brought to a shocking end. Totally unprepared and surprised by the massive attack on Yom Kippur, Israel almost lost. Only a total national effort and the saving airlift by President Nixon brought us back from certain defeat. We lost over 3,000 soldiers.

That Yom Kippur morning, I was worshipping at Or Hadash. During the service, one of the members rushed to the *bimah* to announce the surprise attack and that all men in the reserve should immediately ascertain if they had received a call-up. One of my tasks in the army was as a *Pe'il Giyus*, responsible for assuring that the members of my unit would be conscripted quickly and efficiently. I left the synagogue, ran home, picked up my ever-ready military backpack, and headed for my unit's base headquarters. I spent the rest of the day assuring that all of the members of our unit, except those who were abroad, arrived, were outfitted, and sent to the field. We were in the Israeli Air Force anti-aircraft artillery. We had been trained in the firing of thirty-seven-millimeter shells from Russian-made cannons captured in Sinai in the 1967 war. Five cannons made up a unit. Six such units were assigned to Haifa Bay, to encircle the Israel petroleum refineries and the electric company's power station against possible air attack from Syria. We arrived on the sands of the Haifa Bay late Yom Kippur afternoon. Our unit was disbanded and released on the fifteenth of February, four and a half months later.

This was a defining moment in my personal career, as I had been requested to stand as a candidate for the Knesset together with Shulamit Aloni, who had formed a civil libertarian party called *Ratz*. She wanted a Reform rabbi as a symbol, for I had worked with her, believing in her advocacy for consumers, women, Arabs, liberal Jews, gays and lesbians, and the poor. She asked me to be her number two candidate, and Marsha Friedman, a Haifa University professor who was an open lesbian, to be her number three. Because of my military responsibilities during those four months, fundraising responsibilities for Leo Baeck, and organizational planning for the first year following Dr. Elk's retirement, I had to say no to Aloni. *Ratz* did receive enough votes for three seats in that eighth Knesset. Who knows what our life would have been like, or my influence would have been, had I been a member of Knesset beginning in 1974.

Following the war, our unit had to be on our guns only at sunrise and sunset, when there was danger from a kamikaze plane coming in, hidden by the rising or setting sun. We had several hours of free time during the day. I brought a card table down to the base, which I would set up daily next to the *Shin-Gimel*, the gate leading into the base. Colleagues from Leo Baeck would come down to the base, sit at the card table, and strategize how to fulfill our goals and solve our problems.

Leo Baeck's finances have always been precarious. If contributions ever stopped coming in for any reason, the budget could fall altogether, and the school could default. That academic year, 1973–74, was no different. I searched for a way to fundraise despite being mobilized in the field during those crucial months. Our base had been set up near the Mercedes automobile salesroom and shop. The manager was happy to agree to our commanding officer's request that the men be allowed to come into the plant at night in order to shower. I was pleased to see a telephone booth in the auto shop. We arranged that I would be able to telephone anywhere in the world from that public phone, and the charges would be sent to Leo Baeck. When I told Leo Baeck's friends abroad that I was unable to come to see them this year, as I was in a base defending two of Israel's most sensitive strategic targets, there was an outpouring of support.

One major gift had an unpleasant twist, through no fault of the donor. Kivie Kaplan, the Boston industrialist who retired in his fifties to do social justice work, had become the only white president of the NAACP, the National Association for the Advancement of Colored People. Kivie had funded the establishment of the Religious Action Center in Washington, Reform Judaism's outreach arm for social justice in America. He was an authentic character, beloved by white and black social activists. He gave out "Keep Smiling" calling cards by the thousands and beautiful ties with the symbol of justice or peace in the fabric. On the backside of the tie was always the quote from Deuteronomy: "Justice, justice shall you pursue."

Kivie had become a personal friend and a devoted supporter of Leo Baeck. When I called him from that public phone, he said to me, "Bob, if you're defending Israel, I will give you $100,000."

He sent the check, but the leadership allocated $90,000 of it to other uses without informing me. Those were difficult times for Israel, for Leo Baeck, and personally, for Annette and my family. The Yom Kippur War and its aftermath was an enormous trial for the Israeli people. Unfortunately, this had happened before with donations, so we set up a non-profit 501(c)(3) Leo Baeck Education Center Foundation in Houston under the leadership of my brother, Vic. That foundation has been the backbone of our North American friends and partners now for forty years. It has ensured us support even in difficult fundraising years.

Succession

In 1972, Dr. Elk announced he would retire in the summer of 1974. There was to be a conflict for succession. Dr. Elk had promised Dr. Daniel, his colleague from the Breslau seminary in Germany and his faithful deputy for many years, that when he retired, Daniel would succeed him. The promise was made in 1964, when Dr. Elk was sixty-five and Dr. Daniel was fifty-five. At that time, they had not even dreamed of the kind of school Leo Baeck was to become. Now, in 1972, Dr. Elk was seventy-three, and Dr. Daniel was sixty-three. Dr. Elk pleaded with me to let Dr. Daniel have the position for a few years so that he could keep his promise. I said no, and the board agreed. Leo Baeck could not be developed by a man on the verge of retirement. Dr. Daniel was respected by his colleagues and his students for his knowledge and for his omnipresence. But Dr. Daniel was not only very Orthodox; he was, in fact, anti-Reform. Dr. Elk had a dilemma. I certainly would not have stayed in a school directed by an anti-Reform Orthodox rabbi. I told this to the board of directors, and they understood. They also understood that if I left, Leo Baeck would not survive as a non-municipal, independent school. So they decided to recommend to the Headmaster Selection Committee, consisting of the Education Ministry, the Haifa Municipality, and the two teachers' unions, that I be the preferred candidate of the Leo Baeck board. In 1974, I was chosen to become Leo Baeck's second headmaster and general director. Dr. Elk and Dr. Daniel retired together, with honor and with grace. Neither of them ever set foot in the building again.

The board and I continued to honor Dr. Elk until his death in 1984 and even beyond. On his eightieth birthday, we took eighty students to Jerusalem to plant eighty trees in the *Ya'ar HaShalom*, the Peace

Forest. Under my direction the students prepared a presentation on Rabbi Meir, the great third-century tannaitic leader and Dr. Elk's given name. Following Dr. Elk's death, the central inner courtyard of the high school was named for him, and sculptress Ursula Malbin was commissioned to sculpt a bust of the school's founder. The inner street leading into the campus was named Derech Meir. Dr. Elk's well-preserved legacy is best expressed by his affirmation: *"Our School must always strive to teach its young people tolerance, understanding, and respect for any honest opinion that enhances humanism in the spirit of Rabbi Leo Baeck."*

CHAPTER 4
REALIZING THE VISION

PART 1
Education for Values

An Israeli Educator

In 1974, I received my appointment from the Education Ministry as headmaster and general manager of the newly named Leo Baeck Education Center. At a combined meeting of the board of directors and the staff, I said:

> On September 1, we will inaugurate the thirty-seventh year of our precious institution. We have been led through the years by Dr. Elk, Dr. Daniel, Elisheva Egozi, and by many learned men and women of the spirit. We who are to lead, to teach, and to educate the next generation stand ready for these tasks because of all that the generation before us has done. Dor dor v'dorshav [Hebrew for "each generation and its leaders"]. The mantle of opportunity and responsibility is now being passed to us. I hereby declare that we will continue to develop the School and to inaugurate a Community Center based on those values which have characterized Leo Baeck through the years, a humanistic Judaism generated by social justice and equality for all. We will prepare all of our students, intellectually, socially, and morally, for a life of value in Israel. We will teach our traditions in a spirit of the search for truth; we will gladly receive all immigrant teens who come to us and give them their first spiritual home in Israel; we will teach the language and culture of the Arabic-speaking people among whom we live; there will be absolute equality between females and males; and, thereby, help build an Israeli society based on pluralism and egalitarianism; we will open our doors to young Jews from the Diaspora and send our students to their communities; and all of this in the spirit of Rabbi Dr. Leo Baeck.

I appointed my first senior staff. The key was to find a partner of the spirit who loved adolescents, believed in a democratic education, and was creative and resourceful. I found that in Tzeira Trifon, who had been a senior teacher in Ironi Daled High School, which had merged into Leo Baeck. She and I became a team with perfect understanding of the role of education in creating knowledgeable, moral, and motivated teenagers for tomorrow's leadership. I had worked with Tzeira for four years following the merger with Ironi Daled. Since those students were mostly studying education and pedagogy, it had been her task to integrate them, and she did so with perfection.

I saw her as a partner from the very beginning. Tzeira was a secular Jew who loved the language and the culture of our People; I was a Reform rabbi who loved the ethical traditions of our People. We were a perfect match for the kind of education we sought. We had been discussing the proper paths of education in order to create citizens for Israel who would be *menschen*, loving human beings; citizens who would become knowledgeable in their own traditions and culture and in the traditions and culture of others; who would get a fine grounding in the natural and social sciences, the humanities, and the arts. In order to do this, it was important to treat the students as citizens already, not just teach them civics. We would try to create a student body that made decisions for themselves, where the responsibility for their behavior rested on *their* shoulders and not on our discipline. Tzeira and I had come together from totally different traditions, but both led to the same democratic and Jewish values.

I had studied educational philosophy and management, curriculum development, and educational models at Haifa University prior to being chosen as the second headmaster and general manager of Leo Baeck. But there was no course at the university in how to integrate the principles of democracy with the traditions of Judaism, nor was there an educational institution based on that combination. Dr. Elk had begun. It was to be our task to develop the educational principles, curriculum, and atmosphere to internalize in our staff, students, and community this vision for Israel.

I needed partners in addition to Tzeira in order to reach those values. Two such people were Herbert and Miriam Bettelheim. Herbert had worked in administration in the Education Department of the Haifa Municipality. He was very active in Or Hadash, both as chairman of the board and as the first chair of the Movement for Progressive Judaism in Israel. He became the director of administration at Leo Baeck. I made him a member of the senior staff, together with the principal of the senior high school. In order to have a proper administration, we hired a director of finance, Emanuel Yagol. He was not a soulmate with regard to either education or Jewish tradition, but he was straight as an arrow, and for a decade, he and Herbert kept Leo Baeck honest and accountable, with an administration open and transparent for the board, the government authorities, the parents, and the public. Miriam was my secretary and responsible for the administration of our fundraising and development. She was a partner in ideology, and her exceptional secretarial skills and phenomenal memory served Leo Baeck for forty years.

Starting in the late 1980s, Herbert and Miriam, both native German speakers, took pride in representing Leo Baeck in Germany as we developed programs of exchange of views and people, healing the wounds of the past and building friendships with people of principle in our two worlds. They established a board of directors in Germany, consisting of leaders in business, churches, and national and state governments to fund these programs and our work in interfaith and pluralism. Upon his retirement Herbert became a member of our board of directors, where he served as chair of the finance committee for many years. The work and council of the Bettelheims were a major contribution to Leo Baeck's success.

On the other hand, Ruth Miller and Hannah Bar-Yosef, the two principals of the junior high school who succeeded Yair Magen in the early 1970s, demanded independence from the Leo Baeck Education Center, refused to participate in senior staff meetings, and received the backing for this from both the Education Ministry's School Supervisor and the Haifa Municipal Director of Education. Ruth Miller told me, "I'm the principal of a school. I will not sit with administrators and finance managers." Though I had been appointed headmaster of the six-year school, the authorities decided to give her independence from my leadership. Dr. Hanan Brin, my beloved long-time partner in developing Progressive Judaism in Haifa and in paving the path for the board of directors, fought together with me in order to ensure that Leo Baeck would not lose control of the junior high. The Ministry of Education stated that the junior high, which was a public school, should not be under the influence of Reform Judaism. We responded that our approach was not *Reform Judaism*, it was *Judaism*, as legitimate as the controversy 2,000 years before between Beit Hillel and Beit Shammai for the direction Judaism should take.

It was, in fact, not an ideological issue, but rather, a power play. So all of our conjectures regarding the role of a progressive interpretation of Judaism in a progressive country with a progressive curriculum were irrelevant to the true cause and, therefore, to no avail. They did separate the schools, and both Ruth Miller and her successor, Hannah Bar-Yosef, took control of the junior high for the period 1981–93. We cooperated on some projects and several teachers taught in both divisions, but there were no progressive educational principles in the junior high school. I taught Judaic Studies in the eighth grade for twenty-eight years and had a free hand to work with my students in selecting texts with ethical implications, celebrating Shabbat and the Jewish festivals, visiting synagogues of all Jewish denominations, and creating our own modes of creative meditation and worship.

The senior staff of both divisions worked together on the transition from ninth to tenth grades. In the early years, there was tension over the junior high staff's recommendations to the best students and their parents as to where they should continue their senior high education. Generally, the twenty-five best students graduating ninth grade chose to continue in the large technical school, Bosmat, and in the prestigious Reali School.

By 1985, however, the tables began to turn. No one any longer called Leo Baeck a "day camp." The word was out that Leo Baeck's senior high students were achieving at a high level and were very happy in their daily environment. Now the pressure came from the junior high for us to accept a larger percentage of their graduates. But the administrative decision by the local and national educational authorities had profoundly affected the level of academic studies and social cohesion in the junior high. The longer the separation lasted, the greater the gap between the two divisions.

The four mayors of Haifa during that long period (1978–93) allowed this to continue. Only when General Amram Mitzna was elected mayor in 1993 was the error corrected. Mayor Mitzna understood educational philosophy, saw the discrepancy, and agreed with me that we should have control over the junior high's formal educational policy and enrichment programs. Only then could we influence the pedagogic philosophy. In 1997, after several years of negotiations, we signed a contract whereby Leo Baeck could appoint the junior high principal. The principal would be an integral partner of Leo Baeck's senior staff, and our headmaster-general manager would determine or approve the educational philosophy, pedagogy, enrichment, and social programs. We agreed that over a period of three years, the senior high would take almost 100% of our ninth grade graduates. Dani Fessler, a graduate of Leo Baeck's Class of 1981 and designated the next headmaster and general manager of Leo Baeck, took on the task of integrating the two divisions of the now once-again six-year high school.

For the past two decades Leo Baeck has appointed the junior high principal from among the senior educators of the institution. That principal is a full member of the senior staff, sitting in weekly staff meetings and consulting regularly with the headmaster. As a result of the seamless uniting of the two divisions, the junior high has also become one of the finest schools in Israel.

The *Amana* Social Contract

When I took the reins in 1974, I faced the crucial issue of appointing a vice principal responsible for student affairs. I believe that young people have the ability to make decisions for themselves. If adults are honest with them, youth have a basic sense of the ethical and moral path. But they also have a need to decide for themselves, and therefore when adults (parents or teachers) decide for them, they will object not only to the coercion but also to the principle involved.

I was ready to launch a new direction in student affairs. My whole life had prepared me: my own home training in my "democratic" family, my independence in late adolescence at Brandeis University, and my personal experience in leading teenagers both in the American Reform Movement and then with the Israeli students under my wing at Leo Baeck and Or Hadash. All these came together to help me formulate a new path in student decision-making as I launched my career as head of a major Israeli educational institution.

In 1973, when I was appointed headmaster, and one year before being installed, I asked Dr. Elk to let me determine who would be responsible for augmenting this policy. Dr. Elk, however, felt obligated to a veteran history teacher, Aryeh Steinberg, and one year prior to his retirement, Dr. Elk appointed him Assistant Principal for Student Affairs. I pleaded with him not to do so, as I knew that Aryeh had been a sergeant major in the IDF, and he treated his position as head of the student body not as a senior colleague of the students, but as a sergeant keeping discipline and making demands. This was to be a failure.

Many educators, even on our staff, were inexperienced with student governance. They could not identify with Dr. Janusz Korczak's skillful handling of the very young children in Poland before World War II.[4] So, one year after becoming headmaster, I appointed Moshe Klein, a math and science teacher. Moshe, Tzeira, and I led the staff in finding paths to partnering with our students. It took some ten years for the community of staff, students, and parents to internalize this principle. The school began to gain in popularity, the students' achievement level rose, and people felt better in and out of the classroom. The staff came to accept that social openness and responsibility-sharing, not discipline, made us partners with our students.

In 1994 Leo Baeck experimented with creating an *Amana*, a social contract, for all constituents in the institution. The experiment succeeded. Each year a committee is chosen by the parents, teachers, and students. Each group chooses six representatives. The eighteen members of the *Amana* Committee are responsible for determining the rules for that academic year.

The principals are not a part of this decision-making. The committee sets the standards governing clothing, absences, tardiness, cleanliness, conflicts, student responsibility regarding exams, time limits for teachers' returning exams and homework, smoking, drinking and drugs. The committee also set rules for use of phones, school property, student property, cheating, volunteering, student participation in extra-curricular activities, representing the school internally and externally. They were responsible for staff and student leadership in advancing the values stated in the *Amana*.

Throughout the years, the students never disappointed by making a determination the administration could not live with. I didn't always agree with their decisions, but they were never of a sort that was against the spirit of the institution, such as inequality or discrimination of any kind. We always tried through this *Amana* to have a reaction, rather than a punishment, to any breach of the rules laid out.

---

4. Korczak was a famous secular Polish Jewish physician, influenced by Dewey and Montessori, who devoted his life to the democratic education of children. As head of both a Jewish and a Christian orphanage in Warsaw before WW II, he instituted self government, non-coercion, and social and gender equality among his wards. He was known for his work in promoting the principle that the poorest classes of society had the universal right to live in dignity. In 1942 Korczak marched to his death with his pupils at Treblinka.

The key to such a home and school is in the motto that Leo Baeck took from Psalm 85: "Truth will spring forth from the land." Parents and teachers must be absolutely truthful with their offspring or pupils. They cannot lie. If you lie to children, they will know it and will lose their faith in you. Let them be part of the process of amendment, rather than hiding and denying problems.

The *Amana* philosophy by which the school is governed is based on the post-Holocaust writing of Rabbi Leo Baeck:

> *Life brings historic revolutions. We can no longer continue in the old ways. New challenges appear; new methods must be devised. This is the situation which Judaism must meet today. It will be possible to solve these problems today (as far as it is possible to solve a problem) only by a strong covenant whereby the old generation and the new will unite. Through mutual help—the adult will help the young and the young will help the adult; the teacher will help the pupil, and the pupil will help the teacher—[we will] forge a new way for today and tomorrow.*

This message is extremely important to all three groups. The teachers internalize the school's philosophy; the parents learn how to share with their own teens at home; the students are given the same power of decision-making as the adults in their personal and social behavior.

The *Amana* also states the direction of the school in enforcing the rules. The principle is not to punish but to help correct the error. The members of the committee and other leaders of the institution are encouraged not to use the Hebrew word *onesh,* punishment, but rather *t'shuvah,* to return to the straight path. The person whose action has been against one or more of the rules of behavior is called for a peer or teacher conversation and consultation in an attempt to have the student self-correct. Punishment comes only if the privilege of self-correction is ignored or abused. Even then, the principle of helping the person take responsibility is desired and promoted.

This educational method is based on a powerful process within Judaism, the tradition of repentance, of turning from error to wholeness. Before Rosh HaShanah, the five steps of repentance are taught in an attempt to internalize them. All people err, openly and secretly. Elul, the month before the New Year, is a time of *s'lichot* (forgiveness), when we must first have (1) *vidui,* acknowledgment to ourselves that we have erred, and then (2) *charatah,* feeling sorry for what we have done. We are directed to look inside and feel regret for not having lived up to our ethical standards. Rosh HaShanah is the day of (3) *t'shuvah*, repentance, returning to the straight path by asking for forgiveness for our transgressions. We then have eight more days to make things right with others. "I took your pen. I must return or replace it." "I started that rumor. I must confess that it was I and say that I am sorry." On the tenth day, Yom Kippur, the Day of Atonement, having honestly gone through those first three difficult stages, I am now ready for (4) *kaparah*, atonement, to relieve guilt, to try to rid myself of those bad things, to try to make myself clean of the error. But there is one more stage, and it is the critical one: (5) *t'shuvah sh'lemah,* complete repentance. Most of us walk a crooked path throughout our lives. We return to the same errors over and over. Complete repentance means that when you have erred and gone through the four stages, and now you are faced with the same urge, conscious or not, to make the same error once again, this time you do not. That is true repentance. Once a person understands the process, it can be applied at any time throughout the year.

All of us in the Leo Baeck community are asked through the *Amana* to live in such a way that we follow the rules, not because of fear of punishment from those with more authority, but because those rules have been set by our peers and are a better way than any other for ourselves and for our society. The process takes much more energy than *quid pro quo* punishment for non-observance of rules, but it is decidedly better for all involved and by and large helps adolescents love and respect elders, parents, and teachers, and not fight against them and their authority. Leo Baeck's *Amana* is an attempt to wed our Jewish heritage to our democratic heritage in the individual Israeli's basic human relationships.

A New Beginning: Vision and Goals

These are the goals and tasks that we set before us in 1974 as we began a new period in the history of the Leo Baeck Education Center:

> *To strive for excellence in all aspects of our Center's life.*
> *To maintain the highest standards of employment and build a worker culture of sharing of tasks.*
> *To have absolute equality between males and females in student recruitment and academic pursuits; in hiring, salaries, benefits, and professional advancement.*

To prepare all students to read critically and write intelligently as tools for a satisfying and enriched life.

To educate students to research and to analyze with the goal of opening new vistas in their chosen disciplines.

To see each student as unique and to guide their development toward a healthy and positive attitude toward life.

To bind the generations together in a learning community of joy, hope, and optimism.

To teach the philosophy, traditions, and world view of all streams of twentieth-century Judaism with an emphasis on an objective search for truth.

To interpret Judaism in the light of humanistic, democratic, and universalistic principles.

To develop Israeli Jewish traditions based both on historic Judaism and on the modes and mores of modern Israeli life.

To teach Bible, Rabbinics, and Jewish Thought through the ages with the goal of helping each teacher and student to build their own Jewish identity.

To teach the value of civil equality for all Israeli citizens and residents in spite of differences.

To challenge teachers and students to constantly increase their knowledge of the exact and social sciences, the humanities and the arts.

To strive for love of Israel, including a critical evaluation of its social, political, cultural, and economic progress, and to develop future leaders for our country.

To strive for the integration and equality of all Jewish ethnic groups.

To build a synagogue in the Center which will help to develop a life of the spirit; a holy space based on voluntary membership and participation with no religious coercion.

To accept with love all immigrants who come to live and study with us and to make their first home in Israel welcoming and productive.

To teach Arabic language and culture and strive for acceptance of Arabs and especially those living in our community.

To welcome people of other lands and cultures to our Center, especially Progressive Jewish Youth, and to offer them educational programs.

To send our students and staff on programs of exchange in order to expose them to other peoples, their cultures, and ways of life.

To encourage students, teachers, and parents to take an active role in determining the rules of behavior in the Center in order to develop a multi-generational covenant of felicitous human relationships with a culture of Tikkun, repair, rather than punishment for non-acceptance of those rules.

To build a community of all residents in the vicinity of our Center, linking people of difference together: young and old, men and women, wealthy and poor, Ashkenazic and Sephardic, Jews and non-Jews, intellectually gifted and others challenged.

To strive for social justice within the community and to create the conditions for it in the neighborhoods around the Center.

To challenge all in the Leo Baeck family to volunteer their talents, interests, and material means for the constant betterment of the community.

To encourage in our student body and our community a healthy body through education, diet, exercise, and sport.

To develop in the Center a financial and management culture which is open, transparent, and honest in order to encourage trust in us in all segments of the public.

To work closely with the Board of Directors on pedagogic, administrative, and economic issues in order to ensure that the Center will always maintain the highest academic, financial, and community standards, and will build partnerships with local and national government, corporations, foundations, and individuals to sponsor and to support the programs and people in the Center.

What follows are some of the key strategies and programs we developed to realize these goals during the twenty-five years of my leading Leo Baeck, from 1974 through my retirement in 1999.

Symbols

What we repeatedly see and hear becomes a part of our identity. From the day we are born, if our parents tell us "say thank you" every time it is appropriate, we will internalize and identify with that as a value.

Students know quickly what teachers believe by how many times they repeat themselves. If you want to emphasize a value borne out in a painting or a sculpture, place it in the most appropriate place in your home for all to see and internalize.

In that vein, we determined a few symbols to be seen or heard repeatedly at Leo Baeck. Here are two of them:

EMET M'ERETZ TITZMACH, "TRUTH WILL SPRING FORTH FROM THE LAND." Dr. Elk had chosen this marvelous half verse from Psalm 85 as his school's symbol. It emphasizes the search for truth, which should be a supreme value in every educational endeavor, but often is not. The verse values our return to our Land and our need to be truthful in building our very diverse society. It also tells us to be sensitive to nature, to learn its secrets and not abuse it, and it encourages adolescents to see themselves truthfully as they grow and develop.

If this is a Leo Baeck symbol of our values, we should teach our community of learners subliminally by placing it in front of them in the most central spots on campus, and we did. It is the face of the clock in the central inner courtyard, and it spreads across nine meters of the wall above it in a beautiful artistic piece by kibbutz artist Yochanan Ben Yaakov. It is the central theme for the *aron hakodesh* in Ohel Avraham, the Leo Baeck synagogue, emphasizing values that come from the Hebrew word for truth, *Emet.* The Psalm is read at every public ceremony. It is on all of our stationery. It is ubiquitous at Leo Baeck.

"LEOBAECKIUT." The suffix "iut" at the end of a Hebrew word means "belief in," the same as "ism" in English. We began to use *leobaeckiut* for acceptance of the other as equal, for volunteering, for partnership between students and teachers, for outreach to people in need in our neighborhoods. We took concepts from the life and writings of Rabbi Leo Baeck: *leobaeckiut* is faith that all people are created in the image of God. *Leobaeckiut* means that we are striving for ethical perfection. *Leobaeckiut* says we have a threefold faith—in ourselves, in those who touch our lives, and in all of humanity. *Leobaeckiut* is the spirit based on the twenty-five set goals. We used as many tools as possible to help everyone in the institution "get into the spirit." Teachers' meetings, retreats, top-down training, classroom observance and critique, parents' conferences, student government, and eventually community residents were recruited to get into the *leobaeckiut* spirit.

Finding Role Models

Tzeira and I retained and hired teachers and workers of quality. They had to be very good not only at their profession, but as leaders of people. In Israel, a new teacher has a year to prove those qualities. If the teacher has not been notified of dismissal by May 31, that person has tenure and the path of dismissal is strewn with thorns. When seeking excellence, that first year of teaching, therefore, is crucial. Tzeira would warn each new recruit of this. Often, reluctantly, we determined to terminate a good, but not-good-enough, teacher at the end of the first year.

On the other hand, teachers or workers who are skilled in their tasks and whose lives and personalities are obviously representative of *leobaeckiut* are to be nourished, encouraged, and retained. Though it is impossible to pay more to some than to others for the same jobs, there are many opportunities to reward employees whose tasks bring them to the center of Leo Baeck's vision. Often, we have thought "outside the box" in order to retain leaders who are partners of the spirit.

The Gifted

Without compromising our social justice beliefs, we now sought out students with outstanding qualities: students who could be taught for academic excellence and students who displayed other qualities of excellence in such areas as sport, the arts, and leadership.

In 1976, I heard that a small department had been set up in the Ministry of Education for educating some of Israel's gifted children. A program was to begin in the fourth grade at the Henrietta Szold Elementary School in Tel Aviv. The children chosen for this pioneering class had scored in the upper one-half percentile on the national test given to all third-graders. This examination tests intelligence, reading comprehension, and mathematical skills. I hurried to Jerusalem to meet with the initiator of this national project. He was delighted to hear that I was interested in having such a class at Leo Baeck.

Tova Ben Dov was the Director of Education at the Haifa Municipality. When approached, she, too, liked the idea. All third grade children in greater Haifa were tested, and the students in the upper one-half percentile were offered a place in the fourth grade *mechonanim* (gifted students) class to be opened in the Mt. Carmel David Yellin Elementary School in September 1977. They entered our junior high in 1980. We knew their education had to be at a higher level, but we also knew their emotional level was equal to or even behind that of their peers. We believed that it was important for them to integrate with students their age wherever possible.

Our approach has always been to have the intellectually gifted study parallel with their age group, often learning the same curriculum, but with the caveat that they should go deeper into the material in those disciplines. They should have as much contact with their school peers as possible—in sport, the student council and government, school outings and school-sponsored travel, assemblies and cultural events, volunteering, and just meeting in the open public spaces. Of course, there are teachers and then there are teachers. It takes a love of the brilliant mind, a great talent, and deep knowledge to teach the gifted. They are a challenge. The principal must look for teachers that have the tools and love that challenge.

One example—I taught each tenth grade class a mini-course on "The Streams of Twentieth-Century Judaism." In introducing the historic background of the ability of Jews to choose their religious conceptions, I would ask the class if anyone had heard of Jean-Jacques Rousseau. Invariably, one or more of the gifted students would give us a summary of the man's life and thought right out of the encyclopedia. I would often finish my lesson plan in ten minutes in the class for the gifted and then spend the next half hour going deep into the subject for that hour.

One known characteristic of the highly intellectually gifted is that they are often slower to develop emotionally. It may take several of their first years for parents to recognize how intellectually gifted and in need of special stimulation they are, often disciplining them every time they act out their boredom. For this reason we felt it was crucial for a gifted child to be integrated into a normal school environment in order to enhance their social development. If the educational setting can both stimulate them intellectually and integrate them socially, these highly gifted young people have a chance for a creative and spiritually satisfying adulthood.

There are some educators who do not believe in intellectual enrichment within a school setting for the highly gifted. At the same time, there are others at the opposite end of the spectrum. They believe these young people should be advanced according to their intellect so they can finish twelve years of schooling in nine or ten and be well on the way to their first academic degree before they are conscripted into the army. After a professional lifetime of experience with a class of approximately twenty-five highly gifted students in each grade, I am convinced the middle way is preferable.

There is another advantage to this track, namely, leadership. One characteristic of the highly gifted is that they are able to accomplish many tasks simultaneously. It does not detract from their academic achievement if they are leaders in a youth movement, in the school play, musicians, and in school government all simultaneously. Quite the opposite. The stimulation of an artistic or sports achievement or a volunteer experience or a role in school and community leadership enhances their energy for academic achievement.

Another goal of the gifted students program has been to internalize in these students a sense of good citizenship, volunteering, leadership, and respectfulness for those less intellectually gifted without a sense of superiority. Finally, I believe that adding these 150 gifted young people to the six grades of the school has lifted both the academic level of all the students and increased leadership in the student body.

In 2010, Leo Baeck held a reunion of the first *mechonanim* (gifted) class that graduated in 1985. These gifted people, now in their mid-forties, were such a pleasure to behold. Successful in their careers, and even more importantly, most with loving families, they are living lives that give them great satisfaction. In addressing them, I challenged them to use their gifts for the enhancement of Israel, ecologically and spiritually. Their response to this challenge was heartwarming. Many of them have remained in the Haifa area, and one of the reasons is to be able to enroll their children, who may also be gifted, while another is certainly to live in Leo Baeck's liberal environment. There is no better criterion for the program's success. I personally am more satisfied that their affective personality was normative, that they were better able to enjoy their lives as well as succeed academically and professionally.

I have no doubt that our program has led to excellence in knowledge, character, and performance of the graduates over these thirty years. It has also lifted the standard of these three qualities in the other students who have worked, played, and lived with such outstanding minds through the years.

Reading Critically and Writing Intelligently

In 1985 I was approached by Yosef Greenblatt, a financially successful Israeli businessman who had used the principles of international trade he had learned in Romania. He was looking for a school in Israel that would teach those principles. My staff liked the idea, and we decided to offer such a major in our curriculum. Dani Fessler, a graduate of Leo Baeck, who would later become my successor, had studied and taught management and economics at Haifa University. He took on the task of creating the curriculum. Mr. Greenblatt established a fund for this purpose.

We went to the dean of Tel Aviv University's Business School to show him the proposed curriculum and to ask him what he would want his first-year students to know before they arrived. "You teach them to read critically and write intelligently in both Hebrew and English. We will teach them business." I was surprised but then recalled my own training at Brandeis. He was partially right. We consulted elsewhere and received some suggestions for the curriculum but were always told that reading and writing skills were most important for university studies leading toward economics and an M.B.A. We did start the high school business program, and it has been very successful. But the "heads up" about the foundations of reading and writing have become a major part of our overall curriculum.

Using the Sources for Teaching Values

One crucial factor in teaching tradition is to free it from its authoritarian source. If Exodus says that the Red Sea split, in a secular school one must explain this not only by trying to show what could have happened in nature but also a plausible ethical reason for the text saying so. For example, the midrash tells us that God scolded Moses and the people for cheering when the Egyptians drowned in the closing sea. "No," says God in the midrash, "my creatures are drowning, and you are singing praise before Me?" But it is not only the miracles that must be redefined as the rabbis often did but basic conceptions, such as to whom you are praying in Jewish prayer. Can God respond to prayer? Certainly it will not rain because you prayed for it three times a day, but how should we use the elements of nature to best preserve our planet and produce the nourishment we all need? If the rabbis of the first centuries of the Common Era could change laws from Leviticus in order to meet the needs of Jews who were not farmers, why can we not continue to do so in a post-industrial age of communication? We are not a religious school that demands adherence to the halachah. We are not a secular school teaching Bible only as great literature or as historic roots. We are a Jewish school that respects and conserves our tradition by modernizing it and carrying it forward to help show us the right way.

This takes a generation of instruction and convincing adult teachers in order to uproot, or at least minimize, conceptions ingrained from childhood and motivate them to find a universal ethical lesson in whatever Jewish text they teach. It is a never-ending process.

What I have never done, but should be done, is have sessions for parents in this positive use of Jewish texts. Hopefully, the parents of our students will be open to changing long-held prejudices against the literal interpretation of the text. As the students mature and become more sophisticated intellectually, they can be taught difficult texts accompanied by the historic circumstances prevailing at the time. The key is graduating eighteen-year-olds who have gone through a process to help them love their Jewishness.

Creative Curriculum

Following the 1967 Six-Day War, Israel held the entire Sinai Peninsula for eleven years until Egypt's president, Anwar Sadat, shocked us by coming to Jerusalem in 1978, speaking in the Knesset, and offering us a non-belligerence treaty. In order to secure that treaty, Israel had to return the entire peninsula to Egypt.

During those eleven years, however, Israel developed a broad infrastructure of roads, residences, and tourist facilities. The eastern coast of Sinai has some of the world's finest coral reefs, which were explored and mapped by Israel's top naturalists and entrepreneurs. A year after the Yom Kippur War, once I had my feet on the ground again, I went down to Eilat with my sons, Ami and David (then sixteen and fourteen) to learn to scuba dive. Having passed the course, we drove down the Red Sea coast to the beautiful Naama Bay at Sharm El Sheikh to dive. That underwater world is a natural treasure, full of exotic fish and exquisite corals. This world became a regular vacation for our family, as Tamar, our daughter, also learned scuba diving. We explored that coast from Eilat down to the southern tip of Sinai at Ras Mohammed, and even beyond.

It was natural, then, that I began to inquire into the Department of Sea Studies at Haifa University. Two coastal kibbutzim, Ma'agan Michael and Sdot Yam, had founded a small shipping company based on the principle of crew equality and had become a curious economic and social venture at ports throughout the world. A kibbutz member, Elisha Lindner, had begun to study the history of maritime civilizations along the eastern Mediterranean. Together with Avner Raban and Ruth Aronson, Lindner founded this fascinating Haifa University department. A consortium of eight universities from around the world, led by an academic team at Haifa University, had begun a multi-year exploration of the sunken Roman port at Caesarea, the only Roman port to remain intact during these almost 2,000 years.

I wanted our students to take advantage of this marvelous world being explored and researched at our doorstep. Leo Baeck's approach to Haifa University was welcomed. We developed a curriculum and inaugurated a major in Maritime Civilizations, with the following offerings: "The History of Maritime Civilizations in the Eastern Mediterranean;" "Ancient Ports; Coastal and Underwater Archeology;" "Underwater Exploration" (including diving with experts); and "Marine Biology." The curriculum was supervised by the University and, after a number of years, Dr. Aronson became the dynamic teacher of the curriculum. Each year I took our students to Sinai to dive, explore the fish and corals, and write about one aspect of that magnificent underwater world. Unfortunately, when it became a security risk to send our students to Sinai, and Dr. Aronson ceased to teach, we closed this major. That period in the history of Leo Baeck, 1987 through 1995, offered a treasure to our students because of our proximity to the seas at our doorstep and the University on the Carmel.

Although this major closed, others took its place, including Leadership Training and Management and International Trade. Every school should offer its students something exciting outside the box.

A Culture of Giving

The natural corollary to self-discipline is volunteering, not just keeping the rules, but improving the social fabric. My father's question, "Bobby, what happened today?" will reverberate in my psyche forever. Could the answer to that question become the norm in a large educational institution? I outlined my answer on a sheet of paper in 1973 while manning our anti-aircraft cannon following the Yom Kippur War. Leo Baeck would need four ingredients: the staff's internalization of the value, a study of the community's needs, a method, and a budget (institutional organizing of volunteering is costly).

In order to get to a basic consensus that helping others is a mitzvah, a supreme value, we would need to move from the macro to the micro. Could we convince teachers they should "volunteer" *their* time, over and above what we paid them, to help students improve their learning skills? This was to be the basis for an institutional culture of giving. We speculated that this mitzvah, internalized in the staff, could become the norm of behavior in the student body and in the community. We introduced the concept to the staff. Tzeira and I were the first among equals to give of ourselves tirelessly. Tzeira worked with the teachers, creating among other projects a small team to "adopt" a few very needy immigrant and Sephardic students and their families in a neighborhood adjacent to Leo Baeck. I worked with our non-teaching staff—secretaries, librarian, lab assistants, maintenance and cleaning staff—leading them to such a culture. Students began to see that their individual and communal needs were a concern of their educators. Moshe Klein and the homeroom teachers worked with student leaders—heads of the student council, homeroom representatives, and student volunteers—in giving their free time for internal school enrichment, such as newspapers and yearbooks, dances and events, room and furniture maintenance, audio-visual equipment, and student clubs. We were channeling the sizable extra energy of the teens toward mitzvah, giving of themselves for the benefit of others. We reiterated that this is what was meant by being a citizen in "a *Jewish* State," as well as in "a *democratic* State."

A Leo Baeck graduate, a teacher of Hebrew, Miri Wolf, became one of Israel's leaders in the profession of student volunteering. For thirty years she had a full salary as coordinator of student *hitnadvut k'hilatit*, community volunteering. Miri's high energy, love of teenagers, study of the principles and psychology of volunteering, and years of experience have been a major influence in this process. Her room became a hub of activity as hundreds of teenagers took on serious community projects. As our Community Center developed, we were able to integrate the needs of the community with the outreach of the student body, and as the number of students increased, we were able to offer our students more diversified opportunities to serve the community.

The Dworkin Camp: 1,000 Days Together

How to introduce *leobaeckiut* to incoming students? Let the senior students do it! A family tragedy triggered the solution.

Sue Dworkin was a grandmother in Rochester, New York, who started a camp for teenagers in her Reform congregation in memory of her twenty-year-old son, who died of a sudden seizure. Sue and I became friends. I helped her buy an apartment in Haifa, and she was our guest twice a year. Sue's daughter, Nina, had two wonderful children, and Sue was a happy and proud grandmother. One night Nina went to sleep and never woke up. It was a tragedy that is hard to describe. I flew to Rochester to be with Sue, to comfort her, and together with the rabbi of Brith Kodesh Congregation, help her arrange care for her grandchildren.

Sue asked me if I would consider starting a camp for our students in Nina's name. A flashbulb went off in my head. This was a perfect opportunity to introduce our incoming tenth graders to the philosophy and spirit of Leo Baeck, to *leobaeckiut*. So, in 1981 a combination of our teaching and community staff, together with fifty senior students, created the first Nina Camp at the Poriya Youth Hostel above Lake Kinneret. The seniors were self-chosen and chosen by their peers. They prepared the program during their summer vacation, and the camp took place on the weekend before the school year began on September 1. Sue Dworkin attended. The students fell in love with her and decided to call the retreat *DWORKIN*. The name stuck, and the pre-school-year Nina Camp became a tradition.

The tenth graders had not been introduced to our spirit in the junior high for the reasons previously outlined. But from the first moment on the buses the seniors put our spirit into action. The school song, written by Tzeira Trifon; the joyous singing of Israeli and liturgical songs; the personal conversations between the younger and older students; the hours with the tenth-grade homeroom teachers; my introduction to them of "our common 1,000-day journey"; the Erev Shabbat and *Shacharit* songs, blessings and prayers; the introduction to decision-sharing and volunteering; the opportunities in the Community Center; the Havdalah friendship circle all gave our incoming students a sense of belonging, a package of Jewish and democratic values, and a feeling of being respected and cherished.

In 2014, *DWORKIN* was duplicated in our junior high. We call it "The Beit She'an Gibushon" (Integrator). The incoming seventh graders are greeted by the staff and a select group of ninth graders for a three-day conclave in Beit She'an with the same results based on the same goals. It's a wonderful fun-filled weekend where homeroom teachers for each seventh-grade class are responsible for centering in on *leo-baeckiut*. The kids come back very enthusiastic, but also beginning to understand what their new school stands for.

CHAPTER 4
REALIZING THE VISION

PART 2
Fulfilling the Mission

Making a Home for the Dispossessed

Burstein and the Early Russian Immigration: 1974
One day he appeared at my door. I had never met the Supervisor for New Immigrants before. He walked through the door as if he were at home. "My name is Burstein, but you can call me Aharon. You and I have a destiny together. I know of your work with new immigrants. I need you and you need me."

"Aharon, please sit down," I replied. "I have a feeling you're about to change my life."

My secretary brought him a cup of tea, and an astounding partnership began at that moment. The year was 1974. We already had a scattering of new immigrant teens throughout the high school. Burstein immediately explained to me his dilemma. Unbeknownst to me, the Haifa Municipality had started an *ulpan* in our old building at Hillel 47. The director had no clue how to accept new immigrant kids. In the 1970s, the USSR opened its borders slightly, and Jews were crossing them. Many arrived in Haifa, but Israel determined in which communities the new immigrants would live. With this new Soviet migration, Haifa chose *European* Jews from Moscow, Kiev, and Leningrad.

Burstein was responsible for the new immigrants in the Ministry of Education and he had appointed Hannah Or as a director of the *ulpan*. When I became headmaster, he decided to approach me. I was more than delighted. Leo Baeck received Haifa's *ulpan* lock, stock, and barrel. It was a blessing. He would supply me with the immigrants and tuition, and I would supply the teachers, infrastructure, and loving environment to make them feel at home. On that September day a covenant was sealed that brought thousands of teenage immigrants to

Leo Baeck in the coming years. This covenant not only provided an education for those teenagers, but in fact was to ensure that families would remain in Israel and become absorbed into Israel's culture and language.

I knew I was actually continuing Dr. Elk's vision of providing a home away from home for teenagers separated from their birth culture and homeland. For Dr. Elk, it was the children of those middle European German-speaking Jews who had been so dispossessed. But with our expanded campus, we had the ability to take in all new immigrant children who arrived in Haifa and environs. We had built a beautiful physical structure and had the room to absorb these immigrants and make them feel at home with *sabras*. As soon as we got to know those youngsters, we were astounded by their talent: Olga, the champion ballet dancer from Moscow; Alex, the mathematician who was the USSR's junior champion chess player; and Vitali, Leningrad's champion skier.

Hannah Or and I had endless discussions on the character of the *ulpan*. We were generally on the same page and believed in treating each student individually. She knew how to run an *ulpan,* and she was to be the supervisor of our new immigrant program for the next thirty years. A history teacher, she became devoted to teaching immigrant students. Hannah had tenure for her hours as a history teacher. I asked her if she would be willing to administer the entire immigrant program. I couldn't offer her tenure for her hours, as I had no idea if the immigration would continue or not. She made a very gutsy decision to do so. And so it was that Hannah got a one-year contract from year to year for over thirty years. She provided the teachers and the atmosphere, which was not only good for the new immigrants but also for our *sabra* students.

The Interim Period: Late 1970s to Early 1990s

On ideological grounds, Aharon Burstein and I were ready to keep the program for the dispossessed open until such time as there would be another massive migration. From 1974 until 1990, we made it Leo Baeck's mission to take every young person arriving in Haifa into our immigrant structure. *Flexibility* is a key to a young person at the bottom of the barrel feeling a first ray of success; instead of feeling "I can't....," starting to believe, "I can!" They started in *ulpan* number one and were able to move up five levels according to their individual progress, irrespective of their group. In fact, they could move out of the *ulpan* structure itself and into a class for new immigrants at their grade level at any point. The immigrant classes were based on a different Hebrew level and a different level of knowledge of the humanistic and social sciences. However, they studied math and science together with the *sabra* students. In effect, a bright and diligent immigrant student could eventually end up with the same matriculation as a fourth-generation Israeli.

Regrettably, the immigration of Russian-speaking Jews stopped when the Soviets closed the gates again in the mid-1970s, but all was not lost. Burstein seemed to be able to find dispossessed Jews in Haifa and its environs from the four corners of the earth. This provided us sustainability, that is, enough income per student to maintain a staff. We did have to fundraise, but this was not a difficult task as American and British Reform Jews were ready to sponsor our program to give a first home in Israel to Jewish immigrant children. However, in addition to our regular staff, this new type of immigrant program demanded we find teachers with language skills hard to come by, since the Ministry of Education allowed each immigrant to major in his or her own native language. We needed to find teachers of such languages such as Farsi, Azerbaijani, and Hindi. One year we had a class of eighteen students from fourteen different countries.

I had the opportunity of teaching these young people from time to time. One of my students, Anna, a Russian-speaking girl who was angry with the world because her parents took her away from her friends, fell in love with one of our students, Meir Azari. Today, Meir is a Senior Reform rabbi in Tel Aviv and Anna has been Israel's ambassador to Ukraine, Moldova, Russia, and Poland.

Another interesting student in that period was Yisrael Bronstein. He came to Israel at age twenty-two from Colombia. He was totally alone and a brilliant young man. Burstein introduced him to me as a special case. The only possible framework for him seemed to be to spend the year finishing high school. He lived alone in one of the rooms of the Jewish Agency's homes for immigrants in downtown Haifa. Burstein invited him often to his home, serving as his mentor. I accepted him as a senior into the school, and we put him in wherever we felt he might have a shot at success, with massive tutoring support. He was placed in three-point math, the lowest level. After a week he came to me and said, "I will never be able to use this math. I want five-point." At that time he barely knew Hebrew.

Yisrael was phenomenal. He actually succeeded in all of his studies. He stayed at Leo Baeck for another year because he needed a social framework. During that year he was accepted into the Technion. We helped him overcome issues with the army, and he began his Technion studies, for which Leo Baeck paid. Yisrael says it was only at the end of his four years at the Technion that he began to feel at home in Israel. As I write this, Yisrael is in his mid-fifties, married to a wonderful woman, and has two grown children. He works as an engineer for the Tel Aviv Municipality in the new light rail system and is the light of the office socially, helping younger colleagues every day. Leo Baeck saved this young man, and he is today a fine Israeli citizen.

As an immigrant myself, I came to understand the trauma of leaving your birthplace, your home, your culture, your language, your friends, and sometimes even your family. Perhaps the hardest times in life to do this are the years between fifteen and twenty-five, for you must also leave your social milieu. I always saw it as a challenge to create the conditions for young people to feel at home in spite of the enormous challenges they had to overcome within the family and outside of it.

Two Major Explosions: The First Ethiopian and the Second Russian

Leo Baeck truly changed forever with the massive immigrations, starting in 1985 with the Ethiopian Airlift, Operation Moses, and then the colossal exodus of Jews and others from the former Soviet Union in 1991. Also in 1991, Operation Solomon brought us 14,000 Ethiopian migrants in a 24-hour period. Each of these is a huge story.

The first of these was Operation Moses. I sent a letter to the Minister of Education when I heard surreptitiously that Israel was about to bring in the Jews that had made the trek to Sudan from Gondar, where most of the Ethiopian Jews lived. I could have given a new life to somewhere between four hundred and six hundred new kids. I was ready to take in as many as the Ministry would give me. I did not get an answer to my letter to Yitzhak Navon, at that time Minister of Education and Culture. I wanted to make sure he would be home, so I called him at his private residence. He said, "I got your letter, Rabbi Samuels, but my hands are tied. There is a secret agreement between the Jewish Agency and the National Religious Party that all Ethiopian children and youth will study in Orthodox schools." I was at the end of the line at grappling with power.

We got no Ethiopians at Leo Baeck's finely honed *ulpan* program. There was nothing for me to do. I had the techniques, I had teachers who would put their hand on each of the backs of those under-nourished, under-educated youngsters. We would have provided whatever pedagogical structures necessary, but were not to get a single teenager. I knew they would be segregated in the religious youth villages, as they were, giving them a sense of unworthiness, of disrespect, and worst of all, of being sent away from their parents. I was not ready to give up. Eventually the day came when it was possible to teach Ethiopians without having to grovel before power.

In February of 1985, we heard that eighty-five young Ethiopians had been brought to the youth hostel in Kfar Zamir, at the foot of the Carmel on the southern approach to Haifa. These were young people, most of whom were the sole survivors in their families of the trek from the Gondar section of Ethiopia to Sudan, a 700-mile journey by foot, where they were attacked by bandits and fleeced of their belongings. Many were killed. Most of the older parents and grandparents who tried to make the journey did not succeed. So I hurried to Kfar Zamir with several senior staff and workers from the community center to meet these young people in order to ascertain how we might help them be successfully absorbed into Israel. I felt this was not just any opportunity, but rather a once-in-history opportunity for a Western and white nation to bring blacks out of Africa not to serve us, but to make them free.

Fifty of these eighty-five young people had never seen a classroom, twenty of them had all or some elementary school education, and only fifteen had some high school education. None of them had achieved high school matriculation. We, including some Leo Baeck staff, and students, made two decisions as a result of that visit. We would prepare a *Kabbalat Shabbat* and *Oneg Shabbat* for them on the next Friday afternoon at the hostel. We would also prepare a plan for bringing them to the Community Center and having each adopted by a *sabra* family. On that first Friday afternoon we brought candles, wine, and challah. Each person received a small cup of wine, and as I lifted my cup to sing the *Kiddush* in my Western mode, it occurred to me that perhaps they had their own tradition for *Kabbalat Shabbat*. Through the translator, I asked if one of them would like to make *Kiddush*. All of a sudden this group, which had looked depressed, lit up with smiles. One of them stepped forward, lifted the *Kiddush* cup, and began to sing in an African mode. After approximately thirty seconds, the entire group answered him. This went on for at least five minutes. The ice was broken, and a more relaxed atmosphere followed.

When we arrived the next Friday night for a similar occasion, we found them sitting with a white, Ashkenazic Orthodox rabbi, who was telling them, chapter and verse, the laws of Shabbat. They were, of course, the laws of Jews of Poland and Eastern Europe, with no connection or even hint of how Ethiopian Jewry may have developed outside medieval European Jewry. When I interrupted the rabbi and asked if he would like to ask about the traditions of Ethiopian Jewry, he looked at me incredulously, as if to say, how could these "black people" have any responsible Jewish tradition. I offered to demonstrate. We filled the cups and passed them out for these young people to make their own *Kiddush*. This horrified the rabbi, as the language of the *Kiddush* was Amharic, not Hebrew. It was an unbridgeable religious and cultural gap, which I saw as a dangerous precedent that would profoundly affect these new immigrants. The chief rabbis had already declared that the Ethiopians were not to be considered Jews because it was impossible to find the *ketubot* of the married couples, therefore, *ipso facto*, all immigrants from Ethiopia would have to go through a process of conversion. How cynical that the Chief Rabbinate rejected their Jewishness, whereas the National Religious Party declared that the children would all have to go to religious schools because they came from a "traditional background."

The absorption program worked wonders for both these young Ethiopian Jews and the members of our Leo Baeck community. For six months these young people studied in an *ulpan*. We followed their progress and it became clear toward the end, that eight of the eighty-five had the necessary background, intelligence, and motivation to prepare for university entrance. We met with the leaders of the academic *ulpan* at the University of Haifa. Together we determined they needed a two-year preparation in order to be accepted for the first year of university studies. Leo Baeck was to prepare them in one academic year to be accepted into the pre-academic year at the university. We called this the ELTP, the Ethiopian Leadership Training Program.

In September 1986, these eight students began the first year of a program that was still running in 2011. Several agencies became partners with us in this effort. The Jewish Agency provided dormitory rooms in their absorption center in downtown Haifa. The students climbed the mountain every morning in order to get to classes. The Ministry of Education provided the funds for their teachers. The City of Haifa gave them special holiday packets on all Jewish and national holidays. All eight succeeded in the program and continued in the pre-academic program and then in universities. Half were accepted at Haifa University, and half went to Bar-Ilan University. The four at Bar-Ilan studied social work. One became the head of Ethiopian absorption at the Jewish Agency, and as a member of the Kadima party, is now a Member of Knesset. I believe the training he received at Leo Baeck has affected his pluralistic and egalitarian approach to Israel's social welfare, which is reflected in his voting record and work in the committees of the Knesset. Leo Baeck as an institution, and I personally, have followed these hundreds of young people from the ELTP program and continue to provide them with advice, aid, and encouragement as they prepared themselves for life in Israel.

An interesting item regarding the personal identity of Jews who come to Israel from other countries is that when you ask a Russian-speaker, "Who are you?" the answer will invariably be, "I am a violinist. I am a doctor. I am an engineer." They identify through their occupation and work. If you ask an Ethiopian, "Who are you?" the immediate response will be "the father of," or "the son of." They identify as family. I have always felt that especially for this reason, it was a crime to take the Ethiopian children away from their parents and put them in boarding schools upon their arrival in Israel. It broke the close family tie, on the one hand, and did not allow for successful absorption into the Hebrew language and Israeli culture for the parents, on the other hand. As the Ethiopian teenagers drifted away from their traditional family identity, a crisis between the generations often began.

The policy of the Israeli government and the Jewish Agency was to move the families out of the absorption centers as quickly as possible and provide them with an apartment, for which they received a mortgage of up to eighty-five percent of the cost. A wonderful aspect of that was that if the family was successfully absorbed into the community within one year, the assigned social worker could recommend that the government loan become virtually a grant, and the monthly cost of the mortgage would be no more than NIS 600 ($125). My personal experience with this is that one or both of the parents of Ethiopian teenagers do not work and remain at home from day to day. We had to become family for these twenty-somethings and restore whatever family links they had, if any.

During Operation Solomon, the Israeli Air Force went into action using El Al planes. It was an up-and-down, around-the-clock airlift in which, imagine, 14,000 were brought from Addis Ababa. They were sent to centers in order to be absorbed quickly and sent out to live in the country. We Israelis made many mistakes in how we absorbed them, but one thing white nations absorbing blacks have never done was offer them housing. They were able to buy an apartment because 85% of the mortgage was taken over by the state. They were only required to pay the other 15% over a long period.

Many of those apartments were on the western slopes of Mt. Carmel descending toward the Mediterranean Sea. It happens that these had become slum areas during the previous *aliyah* of Sephardic Jews from North Africa. We took it on as our task to make our new African brothers and sisters feel at home there nonetheless. We set up a center for errant and distressed youth. It is still functioning some twenty years later. We set up handwork workshops for elderly women and men. The men repaired equipment for companies we contacted: radios, transistors, telephones, and fans. The women made clothes, *mezuzot, chamsot* (artifacts in the shape of a hand), embroidered challah covers, and crafts, all of which we marketed. One of our finest successes was producing 800 *mezuzot* for the handsome new offices of the Israel Electric Corporation.

Operation Solomon was but the battering ram for opening the gate to Israel for all the Beta Yisrael, as the Ethiopian Jews are known. After the airlift, another 20,000 arrived in its wake. A huge outgrowth of this work with the Ethiopians in our neighborhood was the establishment in southern Haifa of a caravan city built for 2,000 Ethiopian immigrants as a first stage in their absorption in Israel. Prime Minister Ariel Sharon arranged that thousands of family caravans would be set in open fields in Israel for the absorption of hundreds, if not thousands, of the immigrants in the 1990s. It was run by Peter, a member of Kibbutz Nachsholim, on behalf of the government of the Carmel Coast. We joined them as partners and hired staff as we took on projects.

In 1990 the Jewish Agency and the UJA of North America invited me to go to Moldava in order to search out the situation of Jews in Kishinev. There were 35,000 in Kishinev, half of whom had a direct need for an *ulpan* to prepare for their eventual *aliyah*. There were two Jewish teachers there altogether. The idea was that I would find a school that taught half in Russian and half in English. We would send a group of our students who would study in the morning and teach in a massive *ulpan* in the afternoon and evenings. It was a daring and excellent idea.

I found such a school which had undergone an astounding overnight change. I sat in an eighth grade classroom at a double desk next to a handsome young man who shared his English textbook with me. I couldn't believe the spirit in the book. It was beautifully colored, it had flags of all nations, it was foreigner-friendly, and in fact it was all about international friendship.

When the lesson was over, I approached the teacher who said, "You don't realize what a revolution this is. Please come with me."

She opened the doors to the classroom's cupboards and extracted last year's textbook. It was grey, had Lenin all over it, was about the clash of the proletariat with the bourgeoisie and the downfall of the US. It was easy to realize that Communism did not just fall for economic reasons; it was brought down in a cultural clash. The headmistress was delighted with our project, at which time I went into action to see if it would work.

Two factors I could not overcome stood in our way. Everyone knew that Moldava was about to have a major cultural clash. The population was divided, even within households, on whether it should become an independent state and attach itself to Russia, or become part of Romania. Talking to the senior students there, I realized this debate would tear the country apart, and we should not be there when it happened. There was also no infrastructure for communication. It would take two days to make a phone call to Israel. I could not put my charges in that danger. So the program was dropped. For me, however, it was the wakeup call that a major *aliyah* was on the way. If tiny Moldava was in this quandary, certainly giant Ukraine and all the rest of the Soviet states would also be. The Jews wanted to leave.

A sociologist in Haifa told me that Haifa was going to have a huge part in the absorption of these expected Russian speakers. I went to HUC-JIR. I needed more rabbis and teachers to help support this enormous influx of immigrants. Leo Baeck was filled to capacity with excellent *sabra* students.

There would be no classrooms available for such a massive *aliyah*. I went to Sallai Meridor, who had a major position in the Jewish Agency, told him my story, and asked for his support. I would need four caravans. He agreed to send them if we had a place to put them. I then went to the municipality and got them to agree that the turnaround parking lot in front of Leo Baeck would now be used for the installation of eight *ulpan* classrooms.

Hannah Or now had a huge new responsibility, finding the teachers. Fortunately, many of them were already there because of our interim period. We spent long hours talking about both pedagogy and social integration. We decided that pedagogically, each student should be considered a world into him/herself. There would be no minimum or maximum time to remain in the *ulpan*. We now needed to greatly expand our two major principles of flexibility and sustainability. As we added new staff to this program, we needed to train more teachers in the Leo Baeck concept. Many of these teachers were so good they were later integrated into the regular Leo Baeck staff, often taking leadership roles in pedagogical projects.

It was our great fortune that in the waning years of the 1980s we had built our $3 million sports center. And for these students, the campus was complete. They could now play basketball with the *sabras*, swim with the *sabras*, and work out in the weight room with the *sabras*. They could be in a theater group with the *sabras*, in a dance performance with the *sabras,* and in a band with the *sabras*. They could volunteer with the *sabras*, they could sit on the student council with the *sabras,* and they could run the internal radio program with the *sabras*. It was our opportunity to offer them the whole gamut of integrated student activities.

In the early 1990s, as the new immigrants poured in, we found a space underneath the chemistry lab, which we excavated in order to make a floor upon which we could put shelves, tables, and refrigerators. In this area we opened a grocery store called "Oleh L'Oleh" run by the *olim* (immigrants) themselves, providing food at sharply reduced prices for people who had as yet no income. The Clore Foundation of England gave us an initial grant, followed by a grant from the Cummings Foundation. We negotiated with the Histadrut supermarket (Tzarchaniya) for all the supplies we ordered. This allowed us to sell the food between 30%-50% cheaper than anywhere else. In order to buy at Oleh L'Oleh, you had to show that you had made *aliyah* within the last thirty-six months.

The store lasted six years, from that critical moment of the lifting of the Iron Curtain. During that entire period, the professional staff members were immigrants themselves: Fausto from Brazil, Tatiana from Ukraine, and Dina from Russia. They were supported by hundreds of student volunteers. There was a daily march from Sprinzak near the sea all the way into Oleh L'Oleh so that all these immigrants could also save the bus fare. The need was so great for these people. Oleh L'Oleh is a perfect example of the intensity of the commitment and labor to give each person in this huge *aliyah* a feeling that in Haifa and at Leo Baeck they had found their second home.

Softball in Israel

One day my phone rang, and Gadi was on the line. "Bob Samuels?" "Speaking." "Would you like to play softball?" "I'd love loooooooove to play softball!" "Well I'm organizing a team in the North of the country and I'd like you to be my first baseman." "Well, you're on." It was a ray of sunshine for me. Another American émigré lived at Kibbutz Shomrat. He borrowed the kibbutz tractor, put up side fences, and lo and behold we had a field, and the Shomrat Cubs came into existence. We had a ball playing against other Anglo-Saxon teams. We had picnics and BBQs, and we loved playing together in spite of the fact that a clod of dirt could bounce the ball up and hit you in the head.

When Kibbutz Shomrat said it could not afford to keep leveling the field, I asked my brother Tom if he would sponsor the team. And we became the Triple Ts: Tom's Terrible Tornadoes. Every year, Tom ordered new shirts and hats, and our team struggled on. A real field was built, believe it or not, by Israel's Baptist Village. In addition to loving baseball, there was a member of the Baptist Village who had business acumen. He developed the fields for the long haul, anticipating these sports would be popular in Israel and would make him money.

I was recruited by the best baseball team in Israel and, for a period, played on the national squad. In 1993, when I was sixty years old, I was recruited as the manager of Israel's national softball team, which was to play in the sixteenth National Maccabiah games. We raised the money through Israel's national door lock company. I took them to Holland and Denmark for training in fast pitch. Knowing that in the Maccabiah, the American and Canadian teams were much superior, it was our goal to beat Argentina and all the other teams in order to come in third. It was a supreme effort but much admired. The Israel national softball team won the bronze medal in the 2009 Maccabiah games by beating Mexico 5-4 in a dramatic ending.

Meanwhile, back in Israel, we were developing a new generation who have subsequently taken over. Both baseball and softball have become accepted sports, and not only for Anglo-Saxon immigrants. More softball fields dot the landscape, and the younger generation is just as keen on the sport as we were. Sadly, Dave, one of our Triple T players, was killed by a rocket on his northern kibbutz. We decided to hold a tournament in his memory every August. It is now a two-day affair with almost all new teams and has become a wonderful tradition for all of us who love the sport.

In 1999, after I retired, I had more opportunities to satisfy my love for baseball. My grandson Gilad in Caesarea wanted to learn the game. I coached him personally and then a few of his friends, too. When he was in the fifth grade, together with Gilad we organized a team, the Caesarea Crocodiles. At the end of their seventh grade, we lost the Israel Championship game by only one run. It was a great experience for all involved.

With Our Arab Neighbors

When I arrived at Leo Baeck, the junior and senior classes had six to ten students studying in the *Megama Mizrachit*. This is a Middle Eastern major that focuses on classical Arabic and Middle Eastern culture and politics, preparing students for work in the IDF as a part of Israel's security. The students did not necessarily have contact with Arabs. I felt, early on, that this approach might be necessary for Israel's short-term security, but long-term security, for Leo Baeck and for Israel in particular, needed programs that brought Jews and Arabs together as friends, common citizens, and neighbors. As we made some improvements in our home, an Arab carpenter worked for me, making a dollhouse for Tamar and also the *aron hakodesh* for my new congregation. I had occasion to speak with him about this. He was a many-generation Haifa resident who said that when he was a child, many Jews conversed with him in Arabic, but this was no longer true. I was determined to see if we could break through that at Leo Baeck, but, for the most part, I did not succeed.

One case proved to be the opposite. Following the Six-Day War, one of our Leo Baeck graduates, Aharon Zveda, who taught Arabic at

Leo Baeck, had been born in Iraq and spoke perfect Arabic. He was also a high-ranking officer in the IDF and was called to set up a series of schools in Western Sinai. Once a month, the army flew him down to Abu Rudeis, where a jeep met him and off he went into the desert to set up schools for the children of the Bedouin tribes there. I asked him to take me along. I found myself in five little shacks in different parts of the desert where twenty-year old Bedouin men were teaching five to ten children of their tribe. I did not understand the Arabic, but it seemed to me their pedagogic skills were close to zero. I asked Aharon if we could bring the teachers to Leo Baeck for a few days of pedagogic training. He not only agreed but arranged with the army to fly them up to Haifa. These Bedouins knew no Hebrew, so the language of communication and instruction had to be Arabic. This project continued for three years, until Aharon felt the teachers were adequate.

During one of the Dworkin Camps, I sat in on a session where the homeroom teachers gave orientation to their charges. As we walked out of the classroom, one of the fifteen-year-old boys approached me with the following conversation:

"Rabbi Samuels, I have a problem with your school."

"What is that?"

"I'm in the gifted student class, right? That means I'm smart, and I can learn anything. Well this summer, I worked in my grandfather's plant, and I was the only Jewish boy there. I studied Arabic for three years in your school already, and shame of all shame, I could not speak with those boys."

I said, "Cliff, you're absolutely right. That embarrasses me because we are not allowed to teach spoken Arabic."

"The embarrassment gets even worse," he said, "because I picked up a book in spoken Arabic and learned it on my own in three weeks! Now those boys from the village of Tamra are my buddies. I'd even like to try an experiment. If I can get the students in my class to agree, would you help me set up a joint after-school program with those boys in Tamra?"

"Absolutely."

And so it was for the three years of their senior high school experience. At this point I pleaded with the Ministry of Education to help me start a program of spoken Arabic in the four elementary schools that fed into our junior high. My plan was for those young children to learn only Hebrew in the first grade, Hebrew and Arabic in the second grade, and then add English in the third grade. I could not make it happen. My thought was that from the second through the fifth grade, the children would learn only spoken Arabic without the use of a book. Starting in the sixth grade, they would learn classical Arabic. By that time they would know how to have a conversation with an Arab-Israeli in the market, on the basketball court, or while waiting in line.

The Arab Orthodox School in Haifa has a fine reputation. They take students from all over the country, and they have a high rate of matriculation success. We decided to approach them to ascertain if we could have common programs. It was a huge success with the students. We developed a tennis club and a drama club. It was not without problems, as the Arabic students felt that the facilities at Leo Baeck were so much better than what they had and, in spite of our efforts, they preferred to meet at Leo Baeck.

Both schools received the Israel Education Prize for our work in coexistence, but then it broke down. The highly acclaimed principal, Hannah Abu Hannah, a recognized Arab poet, and I decided to have common staff meetings, which turned out to be a disaster. It was the time of the first Intifada. There was great tension on both sides. Abu Hannah and I decided we would hold two sessions on the subject of Arabic and Jewish proverbs, one in each session. The first session took place at the Arab Orthodox School. I walked into a large auditorium with my staff and there on the table was a beautiful spread of meat and milk together. I thought, in my innocence, it was a mistake. Many of my staff were offended. We sat around in a huge circle, and Abu Hannah commenced with Arabic proverbs on the theme of "the ruler and the ruled." He gave examples from the period of the Ottoman Empire and then from the thirty-one years of the British Mandate. Everyone on my staff sat with clenched fists awaiting the proverbs representing the period of the Jewish State. But he wisely closed his lecture.

Many of my teachers were so insulted they did not want to invite them for the reciprocal meeting. I persevered. The evening began with a visit to our very artistic synagogue. The Arabic teachers were highly insulted that I had brought them into a place of worship, as if I wanted to convert them. It was a disaster, and it never happened again. We adults were too far apart and too loaded with our own experiences and prejudices to understand the sensibilities of the other side.

Following our Volunteer Day in 1988, we set up a committee of Jews and Arabs in the neighborhood to work on projects together.

Among other things, we decided to have a monthly lecture by a Jew or an Arab on some topic of his or her choice. In spite of our previous experience, I invited Hannah Abu Hannah, and we agreed that his subject would be the Israeli identity of Arab students at Haifa University. These lectures drew about fifteen or twenty Jews and a similar number of Arabs. As I walked into Leo Baeck that night, however, there was an enormous crowd of Arabs. It startled me. How could it be that so many were interested in university identity?

I asked Abu Hannah what he thought, and he responded, "Wait until my lecture, and you will see."

He had decided to change the theme to the Palestinian identity of Israeli Arabs. He was straight to the point. Because of the Occupation and the infringement on human rights in the territories, Arabs with Israeli citizenship were beginning to identify more with their Palestinian neighbors. I argued with Abu Hannah during his lecture. But he was right, and I was wrong. It was in fact a wake-up call for all of us Jews in the room that night.

Nonetheless, we are plowing on and there have been some great successes. Thirty years ago, Yoav Yagol, the creative director of our *Matnas* (Community Center), began a joint Arab-Jewish summer camp with fifty children from each population. It has been a huge success and many lifetime friendships have developed. We have a no-religious identity policy for membership in our *Matnas* and hundreds of Arabs feel at home there, with absolute equality.

In addition to the main campus, Leo Baeck's *Matnas* has developed nine satellite centers within Haifa for mothers and their young children, Arab parents whose children have difficulties, at-risk youth, retired seniors, and a coalition of organizations for women's issues.

One of these centers is located on the coast in Ein HaYam, a mixed Jewish-Arab neighborhood. Believe it or not, it was started by two senior students at Leo Baeck. It has become a major center with a building donated by the Haifa Municipality and made into a neighborhood center through a large donation from the Clore Family Foundation. A powerful coalition of Arabic and Jewish residents, together with a very creative staff of Jews and Arabs, has turned that center into a thriving institution for community change. All programs for sport, culture, and crafts are absolutely integrated with the two populations. A group of lay people in Ein HaYam decided to build a path, the Ein HaYam Trail, through the neighborhood. Based on this project, Leo

Baeck's *Matnas* was invited to the president of Israel's residence to receive an award for creative Jewish-Arab coexistence.

How delighted I have been to know that a large group of Arab and Jewish parents have decided to enroll their children in a joint kindergarten and school environment in Haifa, where the language of instruction is dual so they learn Arabic and Hebrew side by side. They are having a hard time getting the Ministry of Education and the Haifa Municipality behind them. They must grapple with power, as I did in my early years. Nonetheless, they persist in developing this wonderful source of ultimate integration. I've been blessed to help them for several years.

Israel has overcome the fear of Arab armies pushing us into the sea. Can we overcome our fear of terror by developing a more humane attitude toward our Arab neighbors? I know that most Arab families want basically what *we* want: a good job, a home, a car, a little money left over at the end of the month, and a future for their children.

Europeans Looking for Reconciliation

The flip side of Arab anger and hurt is European guilt. I decided early in my career to search for good people everywhere. Germans of good faith, mostly from the churches, turned to us. We established joint programs for youth, for adults, and for clergy. We made friends. They were thrilled with our work in coexistence with our Arab neighbors.

One organization in the name of two German scholars of depth, Buber and Rosenzweig, decided to honor Leo Baeck with its annual award to be presented in Mannheim, Germany. It turned out to be an important event. They invited me, as the head of Leo Baeck, Dr. Brin, who was of German descent, and Herbert and Miriam Bettelheim, my faithful staff partners in Germany. The ceremony was on a Sunday morning. There were 3,000 people in the auditorium and 50,000 people watching on TV. As I gave my speech, a straightforward message, I said people need to be kind to each other. Never stir up a storm. On a national scale, values should follow today's Torah portion from Leviticus 19. It avoids war, and it is dedicated to peace. Ofek Meir trained a twenty-five student choir to sing this song in Hebrew at this event. Here are the words in English:

Thou shalt love thy neighbor as thyself.
Thou shalt not oppress thy neighbor.

Thou shalt not hate thy brother in thy heart.
Thou shalt not take vengeance, nor bear any grudge.
In righteousness shalt thou judge thy neighbor.
Ye shall do no unrighteousness in judgment.
Thou shalt not favor the person of the mighty.
Thou shalt not stand idly by the blood of thy neighbor.

Can a Person Be Authentically Jewish and Democratic?

I have said that the key components in the ideology of Leo Baeck are the values of the Emancipation: democracy, the rights of the individual, egalitarianism, and pluralism. We set these as our goals. Leo Baeck, the great rabbi, would not have been satisfied with that. The Jewish factor had to be introduced and absorbed. Could we do it in the secular context of our institution? We believed we could. There are enormous democratic values to be learned from Judaism. Let me give you some examples: Honor your father and mother. Remember the poor, and save them the corners of your fields. Clothe the naked. Love mercy and be humble. Let justice well up as water and righteousness like a mighty stream. Justice, justice shall you pursue. Love the other as yourself. All you have to do to be Jewish in a civil democratic context is to integrate those values into whatever democratic program you promote.

At first we began on a small scale. I introduced a mini-course in all tenth grade classes teaching the modern streams of Judaism. It was a course I called, "I am a Jew. What do I believe?" Most students began the course extremely cynical about their Jewish identity, but quickly joined the debates on God, Israel, and prayer.

Secondly, we increased the amount of Jewish content in our Bible courses, but the key was teaching Judaism from rabbinic sources. The only person who could accomplish this was Rabbi Gil Nativ. Gil was brought in to attempt to establish a major in Judaic Studies and modern Jewish thought. He started in 1979 with eight female students in the ninth grade. He taught them the subject *Eretz Yisrael* (The Land of Israel), divided equally between Bible and Oral Law. I provided the finances for this, and at the end of the year, all eight of them agreed to continue, with two young men joining them. In the eleventh grade, they studied the family, ethical dilemmas, the public sphere, and conversion. The texts were taught traditionally, but the ideology was open for debate.

The subjects of the settlers and the greater Israel land grab were in their infancy and were not brought up as topics before the first Intifada. However, the subjects became vital in the early 1990s both among the students and in the teachers' room. I invited a high-ranking Palestinian from the PLO to speak at Leo Baeck in order to open the debate. I was almost fired for doing so.

The issue of Jewish Israel facing the national dilemma and Gil's work paid off. Gil became a member of the board of the national committee of the Movement as Jewish advisor to the Reform Conversion Court. He was struck by the difference between an "overnight" conversion Chief Tel Aviv Rabbi Shlomo Goren performed for Christian-born kibbutznik Helen Zeidman for purely political reasons (see Chapter Five for the story) and the conversions by Reform's rabbinical judges. The controversy became a major Israeli debate, so much so that Golda Meir asked three Israeli Reform rabbis to stop converting in order to save her coalition. We refused. It was a debate we had been looking forward to. We now had both serious internal Jewish teaching for conversion AND a connection to the political nature of national religious issues.

In 1979, Gil became a major player as he took on the task of being the first rabbi of Ohel Avraham, the Leo Baeck synagogue, which opened that September. He created many congregational frameworks for Judaism: life-cycle events, especially b'nei and b'not mitzvah and the first youth group of the Israel Reform Movement. Gil had some very creative ideas for the thirty-five members of the youth group. They attended (1) *Kabbalat Shabbat* services at Ohel Avraham every Friday afternoon at 5:30 P.M., (2) a very popular *motza'ei Shabbat havdalah* service with creative music by the members, and (3) a Friday night program held in a small office of Or Hadash, in which we brought Israeli personalities to speak on their lives. They also joined a select group of youth who were ready to take upon themselves the mitzvah in *Pirkei Avot* (Sayings of the Fathers) that the world rests on three things: *Torah* (learning); *Avodah* (divine worship); and *G'milut Chasadim* (good deeds). Each member had to do a mitzvah in those three categories each week without instructions, sustaining a two-out-of-three average over three months in order to stay in the youth group. It was a great exercise in leadership training.

When we inaugurated the Community Center in 1978, it was clear that our first project should be the establishment of *chavurot* (social groups): young singles, older singles, young families, empty-nesters, and seniors. There was great excitement and acceptance of this, and each of those groups had at least twenty people. We determined leadership within each group, so that very quickly we had an excellent combination of both professional and lay leadership. As we moved into the 1980s, we were sponsoring projects in the neighborhoods around us, including a monthly newspaper, *Mi-Lev el Lev (From Heart to Heart)*.

Leo Baeck, because of Dr. Elk and myself, had always had a Jewish dimension. We taught Bible more than other secular schools. We taught Rabbinics more than other secular schools. We introduced Jewish traditions into every aspect of our school. It was now crucial to make sure that all members of the community knew that Leo Baeck stood for liberal, humanistic Judaism as summed up once again in Dr. Elk's statement, *"Our school must always strive to teach its young people tolerance, understanding, and respect for any honest opinion that enhances humanism in the spirit of Rabbi Leo Baeck."* I added that this would be the Leo Baeck approach in all aspects of the Community Center as well. We now had a link between formal and informal education at Leo Baeck, but with a third dimension, liberal Judaism. There was much opposition, but today it is the foundation stone on which our entire structure is based.

CHAPTER 4
REALIZING THE VISION

PART 3:
K'hilah

Initiating and Defining

Before the Emancipation, Jews lived in Europe in *k'hilot k'doshot*, holy communities. They were called synagogues, and they served three purposes: a house of study, a house of prayer and a house of meeting. The concept of *k'hilah* was expanded following the Emancipation to include all portions of the Jewish population in any given place and to include political, social, and economic needs. Often these *k'hilot* were without a religious element, and the leadership was both rabbinic and lay. As Jews began to move to North America in the beginning of the nineteenth century, *k'hilot* were formed in every city. They were intended not only for the internal needs of the Jews but also to provide an address for the civil society. When my family moved to the US from Holland in 1814, they knew the address of the Jewish *k'hilah* in Richmond, Virginia, with its 150 families. It would be their initial contact.

Dr. Elk had his internal *k'hilah* in those German-speaking Jews from Shtetin and other cities throughout Germany who fled with him to Haifa in the mid-1930s. They formed his congregation, his center for seniors, his food bank, his social circle, his kindergarten, and his school.

We needed a new focus for our new campus. We were in a section of the Carmel with several neighborhoods with some 20,000 Jewish and a few Arab families. How to make them feel like an integrated *k'hilah* became one of my central concerns. Meeting their felt and unfelt needs became a challenge.

We based our approach on the Leo Baeck philosophy, the interconnections between education, community, and liberal religious values.

This concept is integral to serving the broader community through the interlinking of the school with the Community and Sports Centers. Liberal religious and spiritual values are the heart and driving force of our *k'hilah,* as embodied in the Center's jewel of a synagogue, Ohel Avraham.

This concept of a school interwoven with the community may be unusual in Israel, but not in other countries. We are one of a number of community schools throughout the world based on a connection between the institution itself and community agencies that help the school develop beyond pedagogic achievement into emotive and affective achievement. At Leo Baeck, we believe that a mix of formal and informal education will lead to healthier, more satisfied students. We want our students not just to study civics but become active citizens in our community. We also believe that the residents in our community should feel that the facilities here can serve their needs.

Building Community Connection

First we needed proper facilities to bring the community in and to meet their physical, social, community, and religious needs.

By 1977–78, we were completing the construction of another section of the original plan for the campus. The school facilities that would finally make it possible to bring in non-students (parents, children, other adults, the elderly, and people with special needs) were now in place: a 700-seat auditorium, a beautiful 180-seat spiritual house of prayer, a large room for social events, and a kitchen for receptions. We still had not been able to build the gymnasium, the swimming pool, and other sports facilities. But the school building itself was inviting, and we had extra rooms that could be used for early childhood and for the retired in our community. Our large shelter could also serve for enrichment activities, such as ceramics, sculpting, and judo. In fact, we believed that *all* of the space we had built, some 4,000 square meters (38,000 square feet), should be available for the entire community when not in use by the school.

Another key task was staffing. I also saw my task as finding graduates of our school who would become the future leaders of the institution. I believed that Leo Baeck graduates who had excelled in our method as students could become the leaders of this new conception of community organizing. *Itzik Cohen,* '71, was perfect for this task.

He had taken early leadership of the Reform youth group at Leo Baeck and Or Hadash. He was dynamic and had the kind of charisma that would bring in people of difference for their enrichment. In 1978 Itzik began as the first director of Leo Baeck's Community Center. Itzik was followed by *Uri Marcus,* who later became a supervisor of several *Matnasim* (Israel Community Centers) in the center of Israel. Uri was followed by *Rabbi Arnie Gluck,* who came from the United States. Arnie was a fine Hebraist who served as rabbi of our synagogue and led in community social action. *Javier (Chavi) Simonovich,* who came to us from South America, now teaches social work in the Galilee. *Anat Fruend* took a leadership role in our Community Center and has had a distinguished career teaching social work at Haifa University. Three of these early directors were trained at the HUC-JIR School of Jewish Communal Service in Los Angeles under the mentorship of Professor Jerry Bubis.

Rabbi Gil Nativ '65 was the perfect choice as the first rabbi of our synagogue center. *Benjy Golan,* '85, was to become our Director of Administration and *Meron Tal,* '84, Director of Finance, and subsequently the first director of the Sports Center. These teams chose others, many of whom were graduates, to lead an emerging Community Center with full use of our facilities.

The Community Center

In 1977 our senior staff met to strategize regarding the Community Center and its relationship to the school. We determined the following goals: (1) every student of Leo Baeck will automatically be a member of the Community Center. If their parents or other family members wanted to participate in activities, they could join at a reduced rate. (2) The Community Center would offer enrichment courses based on both the perceived needs of the community as polled and needs as determined by Leo Baeck based on recommendations by experts in the field. (3) The outreach to meet needs in the community would be equal to the inreach of those who purchased services. The outreach would be in immigrant absorption, services for the physically challenged, coexistence between Jews and Arabs, and preventive health and wellness services. We prepared a document entitled *Programma for Informal Education at the Leo Baeck Education Center,* the basis for the structure of our new Center. It was time to fulfill the *Programma's* concept.

I began negotiations with the Haifa municipality to make Leo Baeck a community high school in 1977. Yonatan Gali was the Director of Education in the Haifa municipality. He encouraged Leo Baeck to pursue this concept and accompanied me to the much anticipated meeting with the board of the *Chevrah L'Matnasim*, which met in Tel Aviv. *"Matnas"* is a Hebrew acronym for the culture, youth, and sport centers of Israel (*Mercazei tarbut, no'ar v'sport*). It is like the American Jewish Community Centers (JCC), but in Israel, it is not only Jewish. Every community is Israel has the right and the responsibility to establish such a center for its citizens. Today there are 160 *Matnasim* in the country.

A quasi-governmental agency, the *Chevrah L'Matnasim*, the Israel Association of Community Centers, has become one of the truly progressive, democratic, and egalitarian institutions of the country. Gali and I traveled to Tel Aviv to convince the board to include Leo Baeck among the first *Matnasim* of Israel. Haim Tsipori, the great pioneer of community development in Israel, and Yael Posner, the powerful political leader, listened carefully to our proposal but turned us down. "The only way we can agree to putting a *Matnas* in your building is to have a totally separate management. There can be no connection between the school operating in the morning and the *Matnas* in the afternoon and evening. Each director must be totally independent," they said. "If you would like, you can go to Upper Nazareth to see the school building built by the Israel Education Fund, which is now also being used as a *Matnas*." I argued that the integration of the students in the community and the community in the school would add to both, and that I would never agree to have no responsibility or authority for the *Matnas*. It had to be integrated. They turned me down cold. We were now faced with either dropping the idea or going out totally on our own. We chose the latter, and I had the responsibility to raise the necessary funds. Four needs for Community Center activities had to be determined before we began. We needed a great director and an adequate budget. We also had to find out the needs of the community and what facilities to use.

The "great director" decision was not difficult. Itzik Cohen became the first head of Leo Baeck's Community Center. He came to Leo Baeck as a ninth grade student in 1967 from the development town of Tirat HaCarmel on the southern outskirts of Haifa. Of Egyptian Jewish background, Itzik was brought to Leo Baeck as part of Dr.

Elk's program of offering a quality education to the children of North African immigrants. In fact, Itzik came with a rich family background of culture and learning. He had a dynamic and passionate personality, quickly becoming one of the leaders of the developing Reform youth group. He met his future wife there and, following his military service, became the leader of the youth group. Meeting in the old converted apartment house facilities of Leo Baeck, he brought it to its apex of over 250 members. Itzik studied social work at Haifa University and was, therefore, the obvious and best choice to inaugurate the Community Center.

As for the financing, when some of our pledges did not materialize as planned, we decided to increase the budget of the school by $30,000 a year to pay for our Community Center. We would find the independent sources to make up for the increase somehow, and we did. I was able to put together a coalition of donors who would spark the inauguration of the Community Center campaign. It was made more challenging by the fact that it was also a time of massive building of HUC-JIR and World Union facilities in Jerusalem.

Next, we needed to learn what would be most useful to meet our community's needs. Professor Hanoch Yaakovson helped us prepare a questionnaire to be distributed throughout the community in a one-kilometer radius around Leo Baeck, a population of 25,000 households. From the 2,000 people surveyed we determined forty-six needs in six general categories: security, integration of foreigners, tolerance and peaceful coexistence, activities for quality of life, the environment, and aiding families and individuals in distress. Noticeably, religion was not one of them. We were developing programs within the Center for the enrichment of our community members, but what had just opened up were the needs of the community itself for a strong social justice outreach program on a larger scale.

Finally, we wanted to make better use of our school building. A special committee was set up to determine what facilities used by the school could now be converted to double use. For example, classrooms on the senior class level, which surrounded the central internal courtyard, could be used for skating, dancing, aerobics, and community events. The extensive basement air-raid shelter could be compartmentalized and made into workshops in ceramics, woodwork, and metalwork. One of the classrooms on the top floor could be dedicated to a club for senior retired people. An afternoon daycare center for children could be situated in the room just below the senior center. Ohel Sara, the room directly across from the Ohel Avraham, used for *Kiddush* and after-worship events, could now be used by the Community Center.

Itzik and Amos (his assistant) decided to bring in twenty- and thirty-somethings by initiating *chavurot* (tight-knit social groups). After six months, when seven such *chavurot* had been formed and were successful, we held a two-day seminar at the Carmel spa. What we were searching for was a group of natural leaders who could then be harnessed for leadership roles in the Center altogether, and not just within their *chavurah*. Out of that seminar came nine young people who were either already active in their neighborhood municipal committee or who became active with our assistance. By helping to organize the neighborhood committee, we were able to influence several areas of communal life, such as recycling and mapping the neighborhoods for people who needed physician examinations for heart, lungs, and breast cancer.

From the beginning of the Community Center's life, we sought people who would volunteer their services for one or more aspects of help in the community. By 1985, we felt that we were ready for a major effort in full community volunteerism. We planned a four-day event to bring the concept of volunteerism to the entire community. Two weeks before the event we distributed a booklet to 25,000 homes. The booklet had practical information for the family: emergency numbers, how to remove stains, cooking recipes, basic first aid. On the bottom of each page were opportunities for volunteerism in six categories. The last page was a pullout sheet on which people wrote their names and the number of the activity for which they wanted to volunteer.

The volunteerism event started on Friday night, with a *Kabbalat Shabbat* service in Ohel Avraham, the subject of which was the difference between *mitzvah*, commandment, and *hitnadvut*, volunteering. Saturday night brought a large gathering to hear three of Israel's greatest volunteers speak about why they did it: Shulamit Aloni, the great lawyer-politician, champion of the underdog; Abie Nathan, Israel's most active and astounding pacifist peacenik; and Zair Armali, the Arab soccer player, who used his popularity among Arab youth to move them from gangs toward positive community activities.

On Sunday, the entire Leo Baeck campus turned into a volunteer fair. Sixteen agencies that were ready to accept volunteers demonstrated what they do, each in a different classroom. The central areas of the main building were turned into booths for throwing balls or rings, clowns, a magician, popcorn, cotton candy, and cold drinks. Over 2,000 people came through Leo Baeck on that day.

The last day, Monday, featured the campaign for gathering volunteers. Six hundred Leo Baeck students had been trained in how to knock on doors and say, "We have come to pick up your slip for volunteering." Over 1,000 slips were collected by the end of the day, and the Community Center was now faced with the happy task of organizing those volunteers. We quickly learned that volunteering is a very responsible and expensive activity. For many of those 1,000 people, volunteering was a one-time act, but for a few hundred, it became long-term and even, for some, a lifetime of giving of themselves. The event and the subsequent volunteering were so successful that we decided to do it again in 1988.

Another way Leo Baeck is influencing Israel's humanistic direction is through our Community Center leadership. Leo Baeck sponsored Itzik Cohen's studies at HUC-JIR for an M.A. in Jewish Communal Service. He became an expert in value-oriented public management, applying it to the entire staff at Leo Baeck and greatly improving our ethical management. Because of this expertise, he was head-hunted by a large and financially successful Haifa Bay chemical company to become Director of Human Resources. He has subsequently founded his own company, which he calls "Super Vision." He and his wife are experts in Israel and Europe, helping firms manage their human and other resources in a more efficient, humane way.

Itzik was succeeded by Uri Marcus, whom we also sent to the School of Jewish Communal Service. Uri has gone on to have a fine career in the world of the *Chevrah L'Matnasim*.

Chavi Simanovich, a dedicated progressive Jew, also a graduate of the School of Jewish Communal Service and director of our Community Center, was to have a profound influence on the community. Under his direction, we began to create satellites throughout Haifa. We helped Catholic nuns who direct the Arab Italian School in downtown Haifa to establish a program of activities for their community. We gave the use of our old building on the Hadar to several women's organizations, including a rape hotline. We established a youth club in Kiryat Sprinzak, one of Haifa's most neglected communities. We baked challah on Thursday nights and students delivered it to people who were homebound on Friday morning. We arranged transportation for these community members, both for shopping and cultural events and to community affairs where they were our honored guests.

Leo Baeck Comes Into Its Own

The fulcrum point for Leo Baeck was in 1985, which saw the beginning of a significant increase in students in the schools and members of the Community Center. Slowly but surely, families in Haifa were becoming aware of the significant differences in the approach toward both formal and informal education at Leo Baeck. One of the sure barometers of an Israeli educational institution's success or failure is what middle-aged couples talk about when they get together with their intimate friends. One such occasion is on Friday night, Shabbat. For secular Israelis there are two such types of Shabbat. One type begins with rest on Friday afternoon, in preparation for meeting four or five other couples at one of their homes, starting at 11:00 P.M. They have fancy snacks, cold drinks, sometimes with alcohol, and always with animated conversation. When a group of four or five mothers begin talking about their teenage children at one in the morning, you have a clear indication of the health of the institutions they talk about.

I have frequently been asked to join families for those Erev Shabbat late-night get-togethers to talk about Reform Judaism in Israel, liberal education, or one of my social justice passions. Many of the couples at these evenings I've attended have subsequently told me that in the mid-eighties, they began to realize that their teenage children at Leo Baeck were happy there *and* achieving at a high level. Often the conversations revolved around that, a clear indication for me that our quiet revolution in egalitarian-pluralistic-democratic-environmental education was succeeding. There had been many long years of non-recognition, when people in the community, and even educators, mocked our leftist liberal education and called it "The Leo Baeck Day Camp." Even some of the staff in our school was sure that this philosophy would fail, and Leo Baeck by necessity would revert to a more Prussian, *Gymnasia*-style regimented structure.

When the mothers began to praise our philosophy, Tzeira and I knew we were not only different, but better. More and better prepared students were turning to us for acceptance. We went from three parallel classes to four, and then to five in the 1980s. The Pedagogic

Council decided that five classes was not only optimal, but should be the maximum; between 180 and 200 students in a grade, in addition to a class of twenty-five highly gifted students and a class of new immigrants provided the optimum number of students and economic resources to provide a rich, varied curriculum, and at the same time maintain strong and close human relations with each student.

My vision was to create an institution where young people would be challenged for excellence in formal learning, and, through community outreach, would have the environment and community where they could volunteer and improve Israeli society. I wanted the environment to inculcate a feeling of responsibility for a lifelong giving of self to the community. At the same time, the Community Center could provide the enrichment every person desired or needed to improve their academic achievement and their skills.

Esti Shlyer, a graduate of Leo Baeck from the 1960s and a teacher who became the head of pedagogy for all of Leo Baeck, typifies the teaching staff's shift from initial resistance to enthusiastic acceptance of the radical concept of a school integrated with a community center. She observed, "You totally turned the *Matnas* from a small community center at odds with the powers in the school into an important large and recognized institution. Your concept regarding the intimate connection that needed to be established between the school and the community was so foreign at the beginning, and now it is the foundation stone in the thought of the Leo Baeck Education Center."

The Sports Center

It took us twenty years from the day we entered our new campus on the French Carmel to achieve excellence in physical education. Although I had been the laughing stock of staff and students regarding my dream of a swimming pool at Leo Baeck for all those years, I never gave up hope that we would be able to build the physical facilities and recruit the sports talent to arrive at excellence.

A gymnasium was in the original program for the new Leo Baeck Center on the French Carmel. We had been searching for a donor for the gymnasium since 1966. However, as the institution grew, and the community of users became larger, it was clear that a single basketball-sized gymnasium would be inadequate. Therefore, we decided that the remainder of the four acres that had been leased to us would be used for sports facilities.

Leo Baeck's pursuit of excellence in sports began with Rabbi Dow Marmur. He had been an outstanding rabbi in London before being called to the pulpit of the prestigious Holy Blossom Temple in Toronto, the largest, oldest, and wealthiest Reform congregation in Canada. He agreed to help me meet the leaders of the United Israel Appeal of Canada (UIA).

I came armed with drawings of a great Sports Center, designed by our architect, Moshe Gil, and planned to ask for the $800,000 needed for the gymnasium. Six people sat at a round table: Martin, the president; Bill, the vice-president; Jake, the treasurer; the executive director of the UIA; Rabbi Marmur, and I. Rabbi Marmur introduced me, and Martin asked me to tell them about Leo Baeck. After ten minutes, he asked how they could help us. I said that we had always wanted excellence in our Center and had many achievements, but not in sports.

"We hope to build a significant Sports Center for the entire community."

"What do you want from us?"

"The gymnasium."

"How much will that cost?"

"$800,000."

(Five seconds of silence.)

"How much will the whole Sports Center cost?" (I had no idea.)

"$2 million." (I threw out a number.)

"Jake, can we afford that?"

"Yes, Martin, we can do that."

"Rabbi Samuels, the Canadian UIA will sponsor your Sports Center."

It was a decisive moment in a fundraiser's life.

By the time the construction was finished, the Canadian UIA had contributed a total of $2.85 million. The Israel National Lottery paid $800,000 for the construction of our 400-seat gymnasium, and an anonymous Swiss donor sent us $500,000. We named the Sports Center for Allan Offman, one of the leaders of the Canadian UIA.

We finished the total construction in 1989. It includes the gymnasium, three swimming pools, jacuzzi, sauna, large workout and weight room, dance studio, rooms for spinning, pilates, yoga, karate, a spa, large grassy area, multi-sport outdoor courts, dressing rooms, administrative offices, and a small food area.

The dedication of the Offman Sports Center in 1991 was very emotional for me, as it brought together so many of the parts of my personality and leadership—sports, education, Zionism, management, development, community building, entrepreneurship. As both a former athlete and the principal visionary for a community-wide center for culture and wellness, I welled up with tears at the dedication ceremony. I thought it would be the last brick in the physical structure, creating the spiritual center we envisioned.

This addition to the school has become a central community integrator, providing a home base for *chavurot* (groups), and *chugim* (out-of-school-activities), from babies to the elderly, from the healthy to the physically challenged. It has provided non-athletes with wellness programs and superior athletes with basketball, swimming, volleyball, weightlifting, and gymnastics for highly competitive teams. It is an important center for physical education classes in the school and day camps for the neediest children in the community.

That year also brought us hundreds of students in the huge new immigration from the collapsing Soviet Union, some of whom were champion athletes in swimming, karate, basketball, volleyball, and artistic gymnastics. The Sports Center gave us the facilities to invite the community to our campus for every kind of activity. Meron Tal became the first director. It was his task to make it both popular and financially sound. The Center is now celebrating twenty-five years of activity and has brought great benefit to our residents and to Leo Baeck. A fine symbiotic relationship has developed between them and our students. We have total integration of Jews and Arabs, Christians, Muslims, and Baha'is; of rich and poor, and of men, women, and children. There are many programs for people with physical challenges.

Leo Baeck was given only four acres (sixteen dunam) from the beginning in 1965. The construction of the Sports Center almost completed the campus. Adding the Sports Center expanded the influence of the Community Center greatly in that we were now able to use other facilities in the community for the Sports Center—the gymnasium and outdoor court in the junior high, the gymnasium in the Tchernichovsky Elementary School, the playing field in the Kiryat Sprinzak Elementary School. Several of the rooms within the existing campus now became part of the Sports Center. A room was built in an open space for spinning, another room was built underneath the chemistry lab for judo and karate, and another space was found for the construction of a third swimming pool.

One of the programs of excellence has been the school basketball team. In 1997 I was approached by Meir Kaminsky, a nationally known basketball personality. He was moving to Haifa from Tel Aviv because his wife, a physician, had been appointed department head in a Haifa hospital. Feeling that he was leaving the heart of Israel, he asked who he should meet in Haifa and was given my name. I was excited at the prospect of a nationally recognized team sport at our school. Meir built a team of very tall and athletic teenagers, all of whom matriculated at Leo Baeck because of this coach. They came from everywhere in the country and quickly integrated into Leo Baeck's academic and social fabric. Within two years we moved up to the top Israeli high school league, and in the third year, we won the national title. It was a powerful experience in building school spirit, and it has continued to do so, another peg in the development of excellence in the institution.

The Sports Center has greatly increased the number of people that used our Community Center. It became a community-wide institution, which brought in people of every age and every walk of life.

I hoped that by doing this, eventually the *Chevrah L'Matnasim* would see the power in our model and would agree that we could become a formal institution, one of the 250 *Matnasim* in the country. It finally happened. In the early 1990s, I was approached by Dov Goldberger, CEO of the *Chevrah L'Matnasim*, with the possibility that Leo Baeck could finally become a *Matnas*. We had to meet the following criteria: The *Chevrah* demanded control over the board set up to run the *Matnas*. The *Chevrah* would then pay the salary of the director and train the staff and volunteers. Once again we were on a collision course. The *Chevrah* wanted the Community Center to be independent of the school, and I demanded that the director be a part of the senior staff of Leo Baeck and be responsible to the General Manager.

Ultimately the *Chevrah* did see the value of the Leo Baeck approach, and we officially became a *Matnas* in 1994.

The Lorry Lokey Center

In contemplating the future of Leo Baeck within the new facilities we were to build in the late sixties, one of the four specific goals was "to become an international center for Jewish youth throughout the world, and to create bonds between them and the youth of Israel."

One space was left on the campus for a multi-story building. I dreamed of erecting a building that would fulfill this fourth and final goal as an institution of Reform Judaism and the initiator of the EIE program. I envisioned bringing hundreds of teenagers from the Reform Movement all over the world to study at Leo Baeck for varying lengths of time, depending on the availability of the facilities and the requirements of their home schools. I also felt that Israelis, including children, adolescents, young singles, couples, families, and the elderly, could have a facility that would welcome them for various periods of time, from a half-day seminar to a weekend retreat or a month of study.

In order to do this, we would need a seminar center which, in addition to the multi-purpose rooms, would house both dormitory rooms for students and a high-grade hostel for seminar participants. One August I sat in my room at Kibbutz Sasa during the Dworkin Camp and drew up a program to establish an international learning center. The building was to be ten floors high, with three floors of underground parking built on the side of the mountain, and above that, seven floors consisting of three floors for reception, seminar rooms, and eating facilities; two floors of dormitory rooms; and two floors of a high-quality hostel. I gave the program to a Haifa architect, Yehuda Avidor, who drew a model of the building. We created a beautiful brochure, outlining the need, the method, and the facilities for an international academy of Jewish studies.

One fundraising story was a prolonged one. A man whose daughter visited us in the 1980s and who gave us increasingly larger gifts over the years announced to me that Leo Baeck's time had come. What could we do with $1 million? I told him that one part of our original conception of the task we could take on had never been implemented. We needed a building and a program for hundreds of dormitory students from around the world who would live with us and learn with us. Another section of the building would be for Israeli families who would come for a weekend Jewish retreat experience designed to enhance their Jewish identity within the context of their non-traditional lives. In response to his question, I said I would invest it in one floor of an eight-story building, but if he gave $2.5 million, it would become the Lorry I. Lokey Academy for Jewish Studies. He turned to me and asked the cost of the whole building. "$17.5 million," I responded. He said, "Well, I could do that, but I want partners." In the end, he gave us $14.5 million. Lorry Lokey has been a generous and great friend personally and to Leo Baeck.

Dani Fessler, who by that time had become headmaster, had other plans for the building. He appointed Ofek Meir as the head of the Lokey Center, which now houses the *beit midrash*, a great library, memorial corner, and state-of-the-art science center, a primary school all-purpose classroom, and a well-used small auditorium. It is my hope that someday it will also house a center for Jewish programming.

Ohel Avraham

From 1958 through 1962 I was one of the disciples of NFTY's national director, Rabbi Sam Cook. The Baeck School was Cook's passion in Israel. The "Cronbach Chapel" was one of Sam's brilliant ideas as a way to motivate all American Reform teens to donate to the Baeck School in the 1950s. Rabbi Dr. Abraham Cronbach was the professor of social studies at HUC-JIR in Cincinnati and the most committed pacifist in the Reform rabbinate. Rabbi Cook invited him as a faculty member to many of the National Institutes of the youth summer camps. He always interpreted Bible stories in his own way, making militant protagonists into pacifists. He would also ask each camper to give him a one-line prayer by Friday and then on a Shabbat afternoon would weave each camper's contribution into a remarkable prayer for peace and conciliation.

I found myself in a position to fulfill Rabbi Cook's vision of a chapel in Leo Baeck's new campus. Of course, we couldn't call it "Cronbach," so we took his first name and named the entire wing, including the *Kiddush* room and the library, Ohel Avraham. On another level, it is truly an *ohel*, tent, of Avraham Avinu, Abraham our Father. In the plaque dedicating the wing, we quoted the midrash about Abraham welcoming others into his tent.

In the master plan presented to the architects in 1965, we had envisioned a *beit knesset,* a synagogue. It was to be a room with 200 seats that would serve as a house of assembly, a house of prayer, and a house of study with a special spiritual dimension. We envisioned a space for *hidur mitzvah*, the beautification of the mitzvah. Any room can become a synagogue if it has a Torah and ten Jews, but a room filled with meaningful symbols can inspire a feeling of spiritual uplift.

Moshe Gil, the architect for our other buildings, created a beautiful space. The seats descend toward the *aron hakodesh*, and the ceiling ascends toward heaven. This makes for a large *mizrach* (Eastern) wall. We put the *aron hakodesh* under a ten-meter (thirty-two-ft.) tower, sunlight streaming from the top of the tower. We believe that *omanut mesaperet emunah*, "art speaks of faith," two words from the same root.

The substructure for this space had been built with funds left over from the previous stage of construction, when we built the Klorfein Auditorium. Now we needed $100,000 to finish the interior. A member of the UAHC board, Donald Millstone, agreed to donate $10,000 in honor of his wife, Naomi. Where would we obtain the remaining funds? As Queen Esther said in the Bible, "Help will come from another place."

Among the exchange students that studied at Leo Baeck in the early years was a sixteen-year-old girl from Decatur, Illinois, one of the small Midwestern towns settled by itinerant Eastern European Jews in the nineteenth century. Sixteen-year-old Ann Appelbaum was sent by her parents to study at Leo Baeck, as the sources for their Jewishness in Decatur were severely limited. Ann was significantly affected by her Leo Baeck experience. The parents, Irving and Cecelia Appelbaum, were so delighted with the education their daughter received in that one semester at Leo Baeck that they agreed to give us the $100,000, and we agreed to name the sanctuary "The Irving and Cecelia Appelbaum Beit T'filah." Ann, who married a Reform rabbi, Neil Borovitz, would become the chief attorney for the Jewish Theological Seminary of America. The Appelbaums have remained faithful friends of Leo Baeck through the years. These gifts and others allowed us to create a space that is truly inspiring.

I attempted to recruit the great artist Marc Chagall to design four stained-glass windows in the *mizrach* wall. When I had written that he could set his own price for the windows if he would sign one hundred lithographs of each window with the Leo Baeck seal imprinted within, he agreed to meet with me. I believe that had such a contract been signed, Leo Baeck's financial future would have been assured.

Chagall agreed to receive me at his home in Saint-Paul-de-Vence in the French Maritime Alps. However, when Annette and I arrived there at the appointed time, we were not allowed to see him. He was ninety years old then, and, for reasons we never learned, we were told he was not taking new commissions. This was a financial setback, but not an artistic one, as the windows that were created are perhaps even more artistic in concept than what Chagall would have done.

Rabbi Hugo Gryn, rabbi of the prestigious West London Reform Synagogue, told me of his close friend, Roman Halter, who had been with him in Auschwitz and who had become a well-known London architect of buildings for the physically challenged. Roman was thrilled with the opportunity to make these windows. He decided to come to Israel for six months to do two projects—the wrought iron gates leading into Yad Vashem and our windows.

Roman created a completely new technique for artistic stained glass. He made a sandbox, drew the pattern of the composition in the sand, poured molten bronze into the pattern, then epoxied the stained glass behind the pattern, thus creating a double artistic piece. During the day, it is the multi-colored glass that one sees with light streaming in from outside. At night, all of the glass, except for a Tree of Life going through from floor to ceiling, is black. The tree is opaque glass, reflecting the synagogue's lighting. Thus, at night it is the bronze that shines and shows the symbols.

One single window represents the first *mishnah* of *Pirkei Avot* (Sayings of the Fathers). "Moses received the Torah at Sinai. He passed it on to Joshua; Joshua to the Elders; the Elders to the Prophets; the Prophets to the Men of the Great Assembly" (1,000 years of Jewish history, from 1200 BCE to 200 BCE).

The window is a splash of color with symbols for the passing of both Jewish tradition and the Hebrew language from one generation to the next, two crucial tasks of our Education Center. There are two red hands at the top, facing down, and two green hands at the bottom, facing up. Symbols of Jewish tradition pass between them, while the two green hands have caught a piece of red. The hand on the right has caught from the older generation a red-hot *Yod, Hei, Vav, Hei* (the ineffable name of God), and the hand on the left an *Alef, Bet, Gimel* (the first three letters of the Hebrew alphabet), representing both our Jewish and our literary heritage that Leo Baeck seeks to impart. Also spilling out of the red hands are *tashmishei k'dushah* (Jewish holy symbols), such as a Torah crown, shofar, candelabra, Shabbat candlesticks, the four kinds or species for Sukkot, and a *Kiddush* cup. Our goal is for each new generation to gather these Jewish symbols into their identity and accept them as their heritage.

The three windows, which go from floor to ceiling, represent the second *Mishnah* of *Avot*. "The world rests on three things: *Torah* (learning), *Avodah* (divine service), and *G'milut Chasadim* (deeds of kindness)." The top window has students studying, and the middle window has students praying. The bottom window has one person holding up another. A Tree of Life runs through the entire piece, from floor to ceiling.

The challenge we gave to the young people in our youth group to ensure their membership has been to fulfill at least one mitzvah in each of those categories each week: to learn something for its own sake, to have a spiritually uplifting experience of prayer or meditation, and to help someone else at least once a week.

These windows were a gift of the artist and of Rabbi Gryn and his congregation, who saw to their transport and installation.

The *aron hakodesh* has a single concrete leg in the shape of a diamond, in which we placed the Foundation Scroll created for the groundbreaking ceremony in 1968. The Ark was designed to explain artistically the inner meaning of Leo Baeck's motto from Psalm 85, *Emet M'Eretz Titzmach*, "Truth Will Spring Forth from the Land." The *aron* itself has three Torah scrolls set on transparent acrylic, which makes them seem to hover in space. The background and the *parochet* (curtain screen) are the work of the American embroidery artist, Ann Harris. The floor, back, and sides inside the *aron* are picturesque representations of heaven and earth, based on the complete verse, "Truth will come forth from the earth, and justice will shine forth from heaven." The Torah scrolls are floating, anchored in the earth but striving toward heaven. The artist created mantles for the three scrolls with large letters, *Alef, Mem, Tav*, the first, middle, and last letters in the Hebrew alphabet, spelling *Emet*, Truth. Each mantle has words starting with its letter.

The first Torah, *Alef*, has the name of God, which Moses saw in the Burning Bush, *Eh'hehyeh Asher Eh'hehyeh* ("I will be what I will be"). Across the bottom of the mantle, stretches the word *adamah,* earth, and then *adam*, human, above it. And in the center are *ish* and *ishah*, man and woman, representing the human condition, as we hover somewhere between our physical presence coming from matter and our striving for spirit, in order to realize what we can become. Only through our covenant with God can we reach our potential.

The *Mem* Torah mantle has at both the top and bottom the word *mitzvah*. In the center is the word *masoret*, tradition, and above and below it is the word *musar*, ethics, both from the same Hebrew root, but representing two decidedly different kinds of commandments. *Masoret*, which we are commanded to do only as Jews, are obligations between a person and God, between a person and him/herself. These traditions are constantly changing and must be reconciled with the conditions of time and place in which Jews find themselves. These are the commandments each person and each community must decide for itself. *Musar*, ethics, are the universal commandments of morals and principled life that must be done not because we are Jews, but because we are humans, and they are obligatory of all peoples.

The *Tav* Torah mantle has as the base the word Torah, and at the top the two ways we interpret Torah, *t'kadesh* and *t'chadesh*. Just change the second letter and we learn that we must "renew the old" and "sanctify the new," the brilliant analysis of Rabbi Kook, the first Chief Rabbi of modern *Eretz Yisrael*. Under that is the word *t'kumah*, the renewal of the Jewish People after one third was annihilated, and then the word *yeshuah*, redemption, which the State of Israel is to give to us as a promise. The letters of *yeshuah* are increasingly enlarged so that the last letter, *Hei*, brings us back to God, where we started with the *Eh'heh'yeh*.

The *parochet* (embroidered screen) completes these amazing verses of Psalm 85: *Chesed v'emet nifgashu*, "Mercy and Truth have met together." *Tzedek v'shalom nashaku*, "Truth and Peace have kissed each other." The two sides of the *parochet* meet together and "kiss" each other, standing for the highest values of our faith. Mercy and Justice find themselves touching and kissing, a symbol of the two qualities of God, qualities that must be used with wisdom by parents and by teachers as they train children to live in a world of both order and love, both borders and forgiveness, both containment and compassion.

Above the *aron hakodesh*, hanging down eight meters from inside a tower, is the *ner tamid* (Everlasting Light), created by Helen Burke, the former artist in residence at the UAHC Swig Family Camp in northern California. On a visit to Congregation Sherith Israel in San Francisco, I saw a bronze art piece of hers. I was so taken by it that I asked whose work it was. A meeting was arranged, and it was love at first sight. Helen Burke was a spirit. She was a natural teacher, working with campers and with leaders of the youth movement in California to create great religious art.

In 1977 I invited her to come to Haifa to live with us for six months and to create pieces of art for our synagogue. She arrived as the sanctuary was being completed. We set up a classroom as a welding studio. She asked that we find forty old water boilers for her, so that she could smelt down the copper lining. This would be her basic artistic material. We talked a great deal about the symbols in the synagogue. I told her that the *ner tamid* was a light hovering over the *aron hakodesh* as a symbol of enlightenment and permanence of God's presence. Together we found a verse in Isaiah (31:5): "As birds fly, so God protects Zion." Helen created five birds, flying in a circle and held above the *aron* by three chains, each containing eighty links. In the center of the flying birds, and slightly under it, is a hanging nest with an everlasting light. Helen brought in every class in the high school, and each of the over 300 links was the creation of a different student. The wings of the birds represent the *Shechinah*, the ever-present winged symbol of the God of love and mercy, protecting the nest below, the symbol of Zion. The nest lowers from a pulley at the top of the tower and out of sight from the congregation. The original idea was to have *shemen zayit zach*, pure olive oil, daily rekindled and rededicated by a different group of students.

We created a short daily service of rededication of our sacred space and of ourselves, but none of the seven rabbis of Ohel Avraham have wanted to do that. For years, we lit a weekly candle and put it in the nest. Today, there is a fan in the nest that blows a piece of cloth above an electric light. It looks very much like a flame.

Helen also created a bronze balustrade for our choir balcony. It consists of four trees, representing both the history of the Jewish people and the Jewish family. One tree has deep roots in the ground, representing the biblical period. On the other side is a tree with a full trunk, but with few roots, representing the Diaspora from Babylon to America. The tree on the inside of the biblical period has a thinner trunk that is moving away from the biblical period but coming back to it, representing the emancipation of the last two hundred years. The remaining fourth tree has a very thin trunk, representing the latest stage in Jewish history, the birth of the State of Israel. Each of these trees has some two hundred leaves, each leaf made by a different student. The leaves spread from three branches, representing the letter *Shin*, for *Shaddai* (God). The four stages of our history, the Biblical Period, the Diaspora, the Modern Period, and the State of Israel, give us deep roots and dynamic growth, and if we constantly reach toward *Shaddai*, we will always see the blooming of many leaves.

The other deep meaning in these trees is that of the Family. The Father, with deep roots; the Mother, with roots in her trunk from which comes life; the Adolescent moving away from Parents but coming back toward them, the ambivalence of adolescence; and the Child, standing strong between both parents, and learning from them to stand erect and independent, with all the human values represented in the Jewish family.

As Helen departed from Haifa, she presented us with an exquisite set of candlesticks, a *Kiddush* cup and a *Havdalah* set. Her artistry and her spirit have inspired us now for almost forty years.

The last artistic piece in the sanctuary is our powerful symbol of the Holocaust. On the side wall near the *aron hakodesh*, hinged on a piece of railroad track from Poland, is a Torah mantle made of blackened steel. This steel mantle is pocked with holes. In the steel are the words from Isaiah, *"Atem edai, neum Adonai"* ("You are my witnesses, exclaims Adonai"). The spaces form the four letters representing God, *Yod, Hei, Vav, Hei*. This is the Ineffable Name, but in the Holocaust, God is not to be found for Jews and others on earth except in hollow spaces. Inside this metal mantle is a single piece of parchment, the only one surviving from a full Torah scroll taken from a Berlin synagogue during World War II. Miraculously, this single piece begins with the words with which the Moabite prophet Balaam blessed the People of Israel, *"Mah tovu ohalechah Yaakov,"* "How beautiful are your tents, Jacob."

This scroll is held up by two *atzei chayim*, trees of life (the wooden dowels on which the Torah parchment rolls). One is taken from the scroll Dr. Elk brought to Palestine in 1935, a gift from Dr. Leo Baeck (see Chapter Two for the story of its rescue). This scroll, likely the only one from Rabbi Baeck's synagogue to survive the war, is now in the *aron hakodesh* in the Ohel Avraham Synagogue in Leo Baeck, and one of its original *atzei chayim* holds the parchment in the Holocaust Memorial.

The other *etz chayim* to hold that piece of parchment is taken from a Torah scroll that was brought to the dedication of Ohel Avraham in

1978 by Dr. Albert Friedlander, a Holocaust survivor and the rabbi of the Westminster Synagogue in London. The scroll was among those rescued from a Prague basement following the Nazi Occupation. Ours is from the Czech town of Rudnice. As we began the dedication ceremony of Ohel Avraham in 1978, Rabbi Friedlander brought in the Rudnice scroll.

These *atzei chayim*, trees of life, represent the only artifacts remaining of those synagogues in Berlin and Rudnice. We attached a piece of metal taken from the building of the Berlin *Hochschule*. It is a very powerful symbol, sitting along the wall, but whenever there is a congregation, the axis is moved so that this torn Torah faces the congregation and both it and the congregation are witnesses as an eternal memorial for the victims of the Holocaust.

Another powerful symbol is a recess in the concrete exterior wall of the synagogue. This is the work of the kibbutz artist, Yochanan Ben Yaakov. It spells the words *na'aseh v'nishma* ("We will observe it, and we will hearken unto it"), the response of the People of Israel when Moses descended from Mount Sinai the second time with the two tablets of the covenant. The symbols within those meter-high letters represent the movement from slavery to freedom; the ascent toward God; the symbols of Shabbat and the festivals; the coexistence of Judaism, Christianity, and Islam; the priestly benediction; the crown of Torah; and the dove of peace.

The Congregation

Gil Nativ in his youth as a Leo Baeck student and later at the Technion had been my chief support in the many early student Reform Judaism projects. Gil had now been ordained, and he readily accepted my invitation to become the first rabbi of Ohel Avraham. Many were the spiritual experiences of the first members of the new congregation, especially those students who joined our youth group.

Rabbi Nativ left Ohel Avraham and Leo Baeck in order to study for a doctorate in Talmud at HUC-JIR in Cincinnati, where he was also a rabbi of a Conservative congregation. Upon his return to Israel, he became the teacher and supervisor of our Judaic Studies department. Rabbi Nativ is now a distinguished rabbi of the Israeli Conservative Movement, having served congregations in Haifa, Beer-Sheva, Karmiel, and in Poland. His wife, Ziva, was a student in that first ninth grade class I taught in 1962. She is now a veteran teacher of Torah cantillation, especially with special needs children.

Some predicted that Leo Baeck would fail where it was located, on the French Carmel, too far from *The* Carmel. History has proven them dead wrong. If it is a place of quality, people will come!

This is not exactly the case, however, with Ohel Avraham. In 1977, while raising the funds and completing the interior of our synagogue, Dr. Hanoch Yaakovson, professor of the Sociology of Religion at the Technion, predicted that Ohel Avraham would never have a significant membership, as the local population, which is at a low socio-economic level, would not be progressive. Though Ohel Avraham always had fine participation in worship services and has had seven outstanding rabbis, it has never reached the membership that Or Hadash, first in the Central Carmel and now on the heights of the Carmel in Ahuza, had from the very beginning. It is true that for a person or a family to seek membership and pay dues to a progressive congregation, they must have a progressive world view, and they tend to be better educated and more successful economically. Progressive Judaism, by and large, reaches poorer and less educated people through its social action outreach projects rather than through its active membership.

In the early days of Or Hadash, too often we had just a handful of adults for our Friday night services. I augmented that by founding a youth group for the congregation. Made up almost exclusively of Leo Baeck students, *motza'ei Shabbat* (Saturday evening) was the time for their main weekly activity, but we got them to come to the *Kabbalat Shabbat* service every Friday evening at five-thirty. They sat in the first three rows of the congregation. Following the service they met in the courtyard of Beit Rothschild and determined where and for what purpose they would meet that Friday night. Many adults sitting behind them attended the services because of their spirited singing. It was indeed a special *ruach*, spirit. In Ohel Avraham on the other hand, many youth come to the service, but they do not see themselves as a unified *chavurah*. Scattered throughout the congregation, they do not have the same impact.

Bar and bat mitzvah, as in many congregations in the West, has saved *Shacharit*, the Shabbat morning service. Secular Israelis will come to synagogue on Shabbat morning for a progressive service only if they are attending a bar or bat mitzvah. For many of these attendees, the beauty of the service is a wakeup call for their Jewish identity, a powerful experience. Yet there is a nucleus of members who attend out of a deep faith in our traditions. This nucleus is small indeed. This is not true in the Masorti (Conservative) Movement. Moriah, the Conservative congregation on the Carmel, has no *Kabbalat Shabbat* service but a Shabbat morning prayer service, where Western immigrants (whose tradition it was) meet *sabras*, many of whom learned to love that tradition while studying or working in the West.

All of the rabbis of Ohel Avraham have led a three- to five-month preparation program for bar and bat mitzvah. They create and lead a beautiful service, always for one child at a time. One of those rabbis, Dr. Edgar Nof, is probably the world champion of such ceremonies with over two hundred such ceremonies a year. He often officiated at four, or even occasionally five, such ceremonies on one Shabbat. He actually balanced the budget of Ohel Avraham through these services. He has been most successful in this in other congregations he has led.

The Appelbaum Beit T'filah is used for other occasions as well. Since the space is not only for *t'filah*, prayer, but is a *beit midrash*, a House of Learning, the interpretation of Jewish and humanistic values is of no less value than prayer. Consider this: second graders in elementary schools in Haifa come into Ohel Avraham to receive their first Torah book. It is truly a thing of the spirit, with their parents and grandparents *kvelling*. All the sixth grade girls who did not have a religious bat mitzvah ceremony have a group ceremony, confirming their identity as Jews. The seventh-grade students gather for a discussion on "Me and My Parents"; the eighth grade on "Me and My Body"; the ninth grade, a Bible contest; the tenth grade, the forty Arab villages created since the establishment of the State that have not been recognized; the eleventh grade on "The Status of Women"; the twelfth grade, "Ethical Dilemmas in Serving in the Military." The finals of the annual debate in Leo Baeck, on a subject in contemporary Judaism, are carried out in Ohel Avraham. This was established by the Gelb family, Rabbi Saadia Gelb of Kibbutz Kfar Blum leading, followed by his son, Professor Ehud Gelb, and led so ably and passionately by our veteran teacher, Leora Hammer.

Ohel Avraham, established in 1978 in the confines of a non-Orthodox state school is fulfilling its mission of prayer for those who desire it and values education for all. Every educational institution should have at least one sacred space. Leo Baeck has three: Ohel Avraham, a memorial room for our fallen graduates and students, and a *beit midrash* (Torah study room and an additional prayer room) now named for Annette and me.

Chavi Simonovich captures the comprehensive approach and unique spirit of Leo Baeck so well in an article he wrote for a Jewish Communal Services journal:

> *The Community Center at the Leo Baeck Education Center has left its imprint on Haifa for the last 30 years as part of an education process that the Education Center has been pursuing for more than 70 years. It is unique in that it sees the whole community as its responsibility: those who want to come into the Center for their own enrichment, those who need help in their neighborhood, and those throughout the city who are rejected by others. It is deeply committed to Progressive Jewish values and principles, fulfilling them every day in each program and activity. This practical Judaism is a way of life. The fact that its programs are initiated by a Progressive Judaism organization is seen as a guarantee of good quality service. The Community Center, as part of a peculiar organization that fits no other model in Haifa or in Israel, should not only be studied in depth but reproduced in other cities and locations as a way of bringing Progressive Judaism to the masses in Israel.*

Javier Simonovich, *Journal of Jewish Communal Services* (Vol. 84, No. 3/4, Summer/Fall 2009, pp. 307–312)

CHAPTER 5
CONTINUING THE VISION

The Successor

Rabbi Michael Marmur joined the Leo Baeck family in 1991. Michael is one of the most serious minds and spirits to be ordained by HUC-JIR in Jerusalem. From a prestigious rabbinic family, Michael went to all the right schools in England and excelled as an intellectual. He is a spiritual man. His work at Leo Baeck as the rabbi of the Ohel Avraham congregation and a teacher of Judaic Studies was outstanding. He had prepared himself well to become a leader of a great educational institution.

In 1995 he and I spoke about my retirement at age sixty-five in 1998 and his succession. He took on new tasks to prepare himself, including leading a two-year process in determining the Jewish liberal educational and communal culture at Leo Baeck. The only problem was that after his first year at Leo Baeck, he had told me, "I love this institution and can see myself spending the rest of my life here with a single caveat: if I ever receive a call from HUC-JIR, I would consider that seriously." Lo and behold, the call came in 1998. So I decided to delay my retirement by one year and go into a serious process to find the person who could carry forth Dr, Elk's and my work of sixty years. Unlike many leaders and institutions who in fact do not prepare, Leo Baeck insisted on a serious process of selection and a year of *chafifah* (overlapping learning period). When we announced my retirement, over a hundred candidates applied for the job, the great majority recently retired military men. A search committee was appointed, consisting of three members of the board of directors, Tzeira Trifon, and myself. The committee quickly narrowed down the acceptable candidates to twenty, and then, through a serious process, to four, two from within the institution and two from without. We sent those four to an evaluation institute to determine their leadership qualities.

While a number of viable alternatives were proposed and seriously debated, including educators working in the US, in the end the board selected Dani Fessler, my preferred candidate. Dani had worked with me for eleven years. I knew him to be a man of superior leadership ability, infused with the Leo Baeck spirit, and a graduate of our school who had always taken leadership roles.

In retrospect, the choice could not have been better. I recommend that every leader go through such a process. "Ours is not to finish the task," said Rabbi Tarfon. He might have continued, "But if the task is truthful, honest, and spiritual, one must find someone new to carry it on, at least on the same high level."

The first task Dani took on in the year of succession was to integrate the junior and senior high into one pedagogic and social school. His leadership was forceful and brilliant, and by the time I retired in the summer of 1999, Dani had proven himself as a leader. Leo Baeck's future was assured. Indeed, the years of Leo Baeck's development since Dani became its head have been phenomenal. That will be his story to tell.

The other four necessities for a good retirement have also been mine. My health has been good for nearly fifteen years despite some serious episodes. I have fine medical care from excellent physicians and the Maccabi HMO. My health has allowed me to play golf, coach baseball, and travel extensively. The money from my pension and from national insurance has allowed Annette and me to maintain our home and to travel and enjoy nature and other cultures throughout the world. Annette and I have shared common interests and mutually supported separate interests. Professionally, I have also been active since retirement in the things in which I believe.

The Leo Baeck Spirit

Upon the retirement of Shimon Khalifa as chairman of the board, I was chosen to succeed him. As chairman, and therefore the person most responsible for the proper management and finances of the institution, I have had a fine relationship with Dani, allowing me to help him successfully integrate new programs and branches into the institution. As Leo Baeck has expanded and sought to take on other schools in other communities, I have had the opportunity of counseling and partnering with Dani.

We attempted to become the management and to bring the Leo Baeck spirit into the WIZO School for the Arts in Haifa. We succeeded for two years, until the world financial crisis at the end of 2008. The World Council of WIZO told us they could no longer supply the $700,000 a year necessary to subsidize the school. The Leo Baeck Board of Directors felt we could not take on the required half of that financial burden, and so we had to drop that opportunity.

When the secondary school at Kfar Galim Youth Village at the southern outskirts of Haifa turned to Dani with a request that the renewed school come under the direction of the Carmel Coast regional district rather than the Haifa Municipality, we jumped at the opportunity. At that point, I was chosen as the chair of the board of directors at Kfar Galim. Leo Baeck had to back out of the partnership, but I remained as chair and am currently aiding Pini Agranatti, the general manager, with the transformation of the Kfar Galim school, dormitory, and farm into an institution for enhancing the environment and teaching "green."

I have had many opportunities to help in the advancement of women in Israel. Our hiring at Leo Baeck was gender-blind, and women earn as much as men for similar tasks. We rented our former facilities on Hillel Street for organizations for women's rights. I have been privileged for ten years to be the only male and the only person over forty on the board of Nisan, an Arab-Jewish organization for the creation of women's leadership.

I have had many opportunities to write about and to participate in the advancement of civil liberties and civil rights since my retirement. I believe deeply in the integration of Jews and Arabs in Israel and have taken a leadership role in helping the Arabs who live in formally unrecognized villages established since 1948.

This was the case for the Arab village of Ein Chud, above our residence in Ein Hod, as referenced in an earlier chapter on building our home. Because the Arab families settled there after the War of Independence, the authorities did not want them on the land and made their life quite impossible. No recognition meant no road, only a mountain trail. The families had great difficulty getting in and out of the village. They could not get building permits for infrastructure, homes, or a clinic. Their school was one of the worst in Israel, as teachers hesitated to travel there. The elementary school students could not even get accepted into Arab high schools in Faradis, the successful Arab town to the south, or the Arab-speaking schools in Haifa. I helped them get recognized, and now their children are bused to fine schools in Haifa.

In addition, the Muslim cemetery on the outskirts of my village has been neglected and overgrown with hedges and trees since 1948. To the chagrin of many members of my village, but with the support of others, I initiated a project of cleaning the cemetery and identifying the graves so that former members of the Arab village here, who now live in Bahrain or Kuwait, could come to visit the graves of their grandparents or know they are cared for, just as the Jews of Lodz, Poland, and Ziezmariai, Lithuania, want to have the cemeteries maintained despite there being no Jews left in the community.

One of the major tasks Annette and I have taken on since my retirement is that of helping new immigrants. I officiate at the weddings of Russian-speaking couples who for one reason or another cannot get married officially in Israel. Perhaps 300,000 of the million Russian-speaking immigrants to Israel in the last twenty years are not Jewish according to halachah. These 300,000 people have put their fate and their life into living in Israel, most of them for all the right reasons. As noted previously, thirty years ago the American Reform Movement accepted the recommendation of then UAHC President Rabbi Alexander Schindler that membership in the Reform Movement and recognition of a person's Jewishness should be through patrilineal descent as well as matrilineal. The Movement decided that a person is Jewish if at least one parent is Jewish, and the person was raised as a Jew and is not a member of another religion.

Consider this: Boris came to Israel as a fifteen-year-old in 1996. He studied in an *ulpan* for six months and then in high school, where he majored in mathematics and physics. Upon graduation at age eighteen, he was drafted into the IDF, where he served as a tank commander for four years. After completing his military service, he entered the Technion and now has two degrees, one in electrical engineering and a second in computers. He lives in Haifa and works in Matam, the high-tech center of Haifa.

He also fell in love with Olga. She has a Jewish mother, but her father is Russian, did not come to Israel with the family, and lives in St. Petersburg. Olga came to Israel when she was seventeen. She had a high school diploma from Kiev, served in the army, and is now studying textile design in the Shenkar College of Fashion Design in Ramat Gan. The couple met on the Internet and had been living together for three years.

Wanting to share their lives, they decided to get married. Olga and Boris flew to Prague to be married in a civil ceremony. In Prague they found several other Israeli couples in the courthouse, where a dignified ceremony took place and they were given an official marriage certificate from the Czech Republic. Olga and Boris brought this certificate to Israel and registered with the Ministry of Interior as a married couple. They sought me out because they wanted to have a Jewish ceremony. They speak Hebrew, want to make their permanent home in Israel, raise their children as Jews, go through the Israeli educational system, and celebrate the Jewish and Israeli national holidays. I met with the couple, counseling them both for marriage and as Jews. We created the text of a *ketubah* (marriage contract) together, and I taught them for two or three sessions.

I believe the possibility of increasing the Jewish people in this fashion far outweighs the danger of watered-down Jewish identity. Most of my colleagues in Israel do not agree with me. I prefer to be in the House of Hillel rather than the House of Shammai.

The immigration of more than 100,000 black Jews from Africa has been and continues to be for me one of the main tasks our generation. I have always asked whether it is possible for the Israeli nation to lift blacks out of Ethiopia, bring them to a highly industrialized technological and sophisticated civilization, and also make them freer and better able to cope in their new and very different environment. We have had the privilege of helping many along their way as they struggle to integrate into Israel.

We helped *Eliaz*, a sixteen-year-old. He decided he had to leave school in order to support his unemployed mother and five brothers and sisters. I was able to encourage him to stay in school by offering a monthly subsidy to the family, which I could afford, making life sustainable for them. Eliaz is now out of the military and has a responsible job and a beautiful wife and child.

We helped *Shlomo*, who needed a loan for the purchase of an apartment for him and his new wife. He has had a meteoric career in Israeli politics.

We helped *Almaz*, whose mother died in Ethiopia and who came to Israel with her father and stepmother. Because of the stepmother, Almaz was totally rejected by the father and was, in effect, a teenage orphan. I befriended her and helped her through the University of Haifa, where she met Zechariah. Both studied education at the university but have been blocked from getting jobs that could give them a living wage. We helped this couple purchase an apartment.

Bosana, whose first daughter was born when she was fourteen, was in a marriage arranged by her parents with a fifteen-year-old boy, who was abusive. Bosana is now twenty-four and has two daughters, ages ten and seven. She is successfully managing a family while working in food services at a hospital and studying as an adult to get an education for the first time in her life.

Yitzhak, one of six children, was a discipline problem in Leo Baeck's preschool center. His mother works two hours a day caring for an elderly person, his father does not work, and the family was living in a two-and-a-half-room apartment with no beds. They now have beds, desks, a television, and a computer, and all the children will have a high school education, most of them at Leo Baeck.

Reuben is a young man with one deformed leg who has successfully completed university and is now teaching in an *ulpan* for new immigrants from Ethiopia. The immigrants are called Falash Mura, a category somewhat like the Marranos of Spain, who were forcibly converted to Christianity a few generations back but secretly kept many Jewish customs. For many years, the Israeli authorities refused to bring them to Israel, but because of the interweaving of families, the last of the Falash Mura are now coming to Israel. Reuben is married with two children. His boy has two perfect legs and is a fine soccer player. I have assisted Reuben in his efforts to create cultural activities for Ethiopian Israelis living in Kiryat Yam, a suburb of Haifa.

Democracy and Civil Rights For All

A democratic government has the responsibility of protecting its citizens from harm. It must ensure that the roads and buildings are safe and match professional standards, so as to prevent harm. It must also defend citizens from the aggressive impulse, whether in family abuse, road rage, or attacks by enemies. But at the same time, it must not engender fear and hate in its citizens. It must ensure a general atmosphere of calm so that people can go about their daily lives with assurance of their safety and well-being. A government that does not protect adequately is irresponsible, but a government that needlessly engenders fear and hate is undemocratic.

Government also has the responsibility of treating each individual equally, regardless of color, sex, social and/or financial standing, religion, or ethnic background. This is a hard task, as people of wealth always wield more influence. Governments tend to give preference and more attention to whites than blacks, to men than women, to the majority religious group than to the minority, to rich than poor, to the more educated than to the less educated, to natives than immigrants. It is the government's responsibility to make those with less status feel equal and respected. There are governments that treat those in the second category as "almost equal." This is much better than some other governments, but not good enough, for if you are on the downside of almost equal, it means one thing only: unequal.

A woman who has the same task as a man with a high-tech company, but who is paid $1,000 a month less than her male colleague, does not consider herself equal. A Sephardic child in a classroom who is not given the same caring and affection by his teacher as an Ashkenazic child does not consider himself equal, though he may have pulled himself up by his bootstraps and reached the same achievement level as his fellow classmates.

Governments tend to be more influenced by wealth, social status, and power than by responsibility to every citizen. This was blatant in the 1960s and caused the great social revolution in America known as the Civil Rights Movement. People of color in America who were the children and grandchildren of slaves were unequal, abused, and kept down in that society. Growing up in the Houston of the 1940s, my black friends could not go to school with me; they had their own schools. If we got on the bus together, the blacks had to sit in the back, and I was considered weird by my white friends if I sat back there with my friends. Blacks couldn't drink from the same water fountains or use the same toilet facilities. They couldn't live next to me. As a young rabbi, I took an active role in the Civil Rights Movement. I went to Selma, Alabama, to join Martin Luther King and Abraham Joshua Heschel in the march for civil rights for blacks. I became a member of the NAACP, the National Association for the Advancement of Colored People. This was a legacy from my mother.

Upon arriving in Israel, I joined the League for the Abolishment of Religious Coercion, which morphed into the Israel Civil Liberties Union. I joined Shulamit Aloni in her political role as the most powerful advocate for consumers' rights, the rights of women, the rights of gays and lesbians, the rights of Arabs, and the rights of Reform Jews. If the leaders of government, both executive and legislative, do not live up to the highest standards of civil rights, civil liberties, equality, and pluralism, they must be challenged by those who chose them to lead to live up to the most basic concepts of democracy. This should not be a matter of left or right, but often is. I consider myself a center-of-the-road civil libertarian, which unfortunately places me pretty far to the left on the Israeli scale of justice and equality.

But one does not have to blame only leaders of government. The blame starts in the smallest nuclei in society: in the family and in the school. What is a democratic family? Parents must treat their children as equals in spite of their size or lack of knowledge. They must be given the privileges and responsibilities the parents give themselves. Just like at our dinner table in Houston, a democratic family is one where all the tasks in the home are divided. The children learn from the example of their parents that shopping, cleaning, laundry, the kitchen, and the clothing closet are everybody's responsibility, not just Mom's or Dad's or the maid's. Parents must train their children to give respect to those at the bottom of the socio-economic scale in their community—the yardmen, the cooks, the housemaids, the bus drivers. The Talmud says you must treat each person with respect, including "the non-Jew in the marketplace." As a parent, you know you've done a good job when your child greets the street cleaner with a smile and a "Shalom."

A school is a large family. It is not a public institution that only has the responsibility to impart learning into the brains of its pupils. It has the responsibility to help create loyal, intelligent, sensible, motivated, and socially conscious citizens. Just as parents cannot influence their children only by telling them what to do, so, too, a school administration and staff cannot create good citizens by ordering pupils to abide by the rules the adults have set. Nor can they expect to make good citizens by teaching civics. Children will become good citizens when they are adults if they are taught to be good citizens while still in school. They must be part of the process of establishing the rules. They must be given the privileges and rights of determining the social atmosphere and values that permeate the school environment.

Educators who have not done this would be surprised to see how first graders can focus quickly on the problems at their school. I counseled with staff and parents in the Carmel Vayam School on Kibbutz

Ein Carmel on the Carmel Coast. We chose two students from each class from first to sixth grade to be a school council and to learn the principles of the *Amana,* or social contract, a way of conducting ourselves ethically and morally that we had introduced at Leo Baeck (see Chapter Four for more about how *Amana* works at the school).

In explaining to the children, staff, and parents that we were beginning a process whereby they would determine the rules of behavior in the classroom, the courtyard, and the playing-field, we then asked them to name one problem they thought so significant that we should deal with it immediately. A first grader raised his hand and said, "Our biggest problem is on the buses that transport us to and from our villages. There is violence on the buses." So we began a process by which the students themselves would determine a sensible solution and also be responsible for setting an example. Through that process, the students collaborated in writing a social contract, and there was no more violence on the buses to Ein Carmel for a sustained period of time.

An educator willing to share with children can trust the basic ethical instincts of a six-year-old if we give each child the opportunity for independent cognition and communal responsibility. Rabbi Baeck was correct. Teachers at school and parents at home can make a partnership across the generations to solve the problems of today and tomorrow.

Praise for achievement and, after missing the mark, encouragement for *tikkun* (repair) are essentials in the democratic home and school. Seeking the opinion of students on intellectual and social matters is crucial. Children and adults will often not live up to the desired standards. You yourself do not always live up to these standards. Everyone should know that the effort and the search are as important as the achievement and are to be respected and encouraged. The home and the school are always in process. They never reach full achievement. The students are both the active participants and the future. If they are trained to be responsible citizens, the future is assured.

In America, whites had to learn that blacks are people, like them. In Israel, Jews still must learn that Arabs are people, just like them. The sociologists used to say that the goal of American society was a melting pot, to mold all groups into one American identity. The task was to make everyone into as much of a WASP (White, Anglo-Saxon Protestant) as possible. Blacks could not become white; Central Americans could not become Anglo-Saxons; Jews who kept their religion could not become Protestant. Today, American sociologists know that the best form of democracy is not the melting pot but rather a bouquet of flowers, each with its own fragrance, color, and beauty, coming together to make a fine esthetic bouquet.

In the Civil Rights Movement, the mantra became "Black is Beautiful." In Israel, Arabs must be able to have pride in their own language and traditions. At Leo Baeck, I wanted to have as much of the gamut of Israelis as possible: men and women, whites and blacks, Jews and Arabs, Ashkenazic and Sephardic, *sabras* and immigrants, Israelis and foreigners, children across the intellectual range, young people and old people. The challenge is to make all feel equal, cared for, and wanted. I cringe each time a child of Ethiopian origin is rejected by a mostly Ashkenazic religious school. I am appalled by the discrimination against women in the rabbinic courts. Israel is a multi-lingual, multi-religious, multi-ethnic, and multi-belief society. As long as all believe in the common welfare and in achieving a society of felicitous human relationships, all of those individuals and groups must receive the respect and opportunities available to others.

Religious Coercion

My studies in the United States were in the years of the rise of civil rights and the demand of black leaders for equality for people of color in America. I was a part of that movement. I believe passionately that every person, without regard to gender, ethnic background, financial status, or religious persuasion, should be considered by the civil authorities as equals and should have the same rights and responsibilities as any other citizen. When we arrived in Israel in 1962, I already knew from my experience as a student in Jerusalem that Israel was developing politically, ethnically, and religiously as a nation of unequals. Ashkenazic Jews discriminated against Sephardic Jews; men discriminated against women; Orthodox Jews discriminated against non-Orthodox Jews; and all discriminated against Arabs.

Upon arrival, I quickly joined the League for the Abolishment of Religious Coercion. It was here that I met Shulamit Aloni and debated Professor Eri Jabotinsky on issues of religion and democracy, as related in an earlier chapter.

I taught my students to care for the issue of who is a Jew for purposes of the Law of Return. In that first year, Brother Daniel, the

Catholic monk who had been born Oswald Rufeisen in Poland, applied for citizenship under the Law of Return, stating that his mother was Jewish and that he believed in Jesus but was a Jewish national and therefore should be considered Jewish under the Law of Return. Nine Supreme Court Judges determined that the halachah could not be the standard by which people were considered Jews in Israel. They established different, more common-sense criteria. What would the man on the street say when looking at a Catholic monk in a flowing gown, a member of a Catholic Christian order? That he is not a Jew.

Then my students and I debated the issue of Rina Eitani, a woman born in Holland to a Jewish father and a non-Jewish mother who was sent to Bergen-Belsen, survived, came to Palestine in 1946, fought in the Hagana, and met her eventual husband there. After the state was established, they moved to the development town of Upper Nazareth as pioneers. When in 1962 she decided to run for the municipal council in Upper Nazareth, she was denied citizenship. On the basis of the Brother Daniel decision ("What would the man in the street say?"), Rina Eitani's passport was ultimately returned to her.

In 1964, when I founded Or Hadash in Haifa, we had great difficulty finding a location for a liberal religious service because of coercion and discrimination. Then in 1965, I requested one of the memorial Torah scrolls that had been stored by the Nazis in Prague and was assured that one would be sent to us immediately. When after six months I hadn't received it, I called Rabbi Albert Friedlander, in whose synagogue the scrolls had been carefully repaired by a scribe. He told me the memorial committee had sent fifty scrolls to Israel, to Minister of Religion Rabbi Zerach Warhaftig, with instructions to give one of the scrolls to congregation Or Hadash in Haifa, one to the IDF, with the other forty-eight to be distributed according to the needs of congregations in Israel, When the member of the Westminster synagogue in London who had purchased the scrolls from the Czech government heard we had not received the scroll, he immediately called Minister Warhaftig, informing him that he was flying to Israel the next day to pick up the scrolls and bring them back to England. Israel would never see any of those scrolls again. Rabbi Warhaftig told him the scrolls had been *pasul,* and therefore buried. The man said, "I want you to take them out of their grave and put them in boxes. I'll take them back to London." Warhaftig called him back ten minutes later, saying he was mistaken, and he'd be happy to give Rabbi Samuels any of the scrolls he'd like. The next day I drove into Tel Aviv to the Ministry of Religion and picked out a beautiful scroll from the city of Rudice, where a vibrant community once lived, but where there are no Jews left.

I was involved in the famous case of Dr. Helen Zeidman's conversion as one of the three rabbis who converted her under Rabbi Moshe Zemer's leadership. Helen Zeidman was an American Christian with a love for Judaism and the Jewish people. She became a member of Kibbutz Nachal Oz on the border of Gaza and married a member of the kibbutz. They arranged their marriage by proxy in Mexico, and then went to register it. She did not go to the chief rabbinate for her conversion, as she lived in a non-Orthodox kibbutz that could not serve her kosher food, a requisite for Orthodox conversion in Israel.

The Israel Civil Liberties Union took Dr. Zeidman's Reform conversion to the Supreme Court to have it recognized. The National Religious Party, which was part of the governing coalition, threatened to leave the coalition if her Reform conversion was recognized. In order to prevent the fall of the Israeli government, Rabbi Shlomo Goren, Chief Rabbi of Tel Aviv at the time, drove down to Kibbutz Nachal Oz in the dead of night and converted Dr. Zeidman on the spot. Rabbi Zemer wrote a now famous article in *Ha'aretz* entitled, "Rabbi Goren Converted with a Reform Conversion."

To me, this is the most immoral, unethical, and unseemly Judaism possible. When religion is hand in glove with the political establishment, it becomes corrupt and corrupting. I have fought all my professional life to separate the Judaism of the spirit from making Judaism such a devious political entity. But such a caricature of Judaism continues to reign supreme in Israel, way into the twenty-first century.

The forced conversion of Ethiopian Jews and the prevention of their coming to Israel while under the extreme pressure of poverty and ill health is one of the blaring crimes of such a Judaism. The secret contract between the Jewish Agency and the National Religious Party before Operation Moses, which brought the first large group of Ethiopian Jews in 1985, stating that all Ethiopian children would have to study in Orthodox boarding schools, was another criminal and cynical pact. It prevented the children from living at home. They were discriminated against and kept apart from the *sabras* in those youth villages, and they were given an inadequate education for becoming citizens in a democratic state. I applied to the Minister of Education to let Leo

Baeck become a center for the absorption of Ethiopian children. He turned me down flat because of this secret pact. It has become a crying shame that for twenty-six years now the Ethiopian children have not been able to benefit from the tender loving care and serious education of humanistic Judaism and civil citizenship that hundreds of other immigrants from all over the world have experienced.

And many couples have come to me demoralized after experiencing the humiliation of non-acceptance of their status because one member of the couple has a non-Jewish mother or because of the status of *chalitzah* (unmarriageable childless widow) or *agunah* (abandoned married woman). The rabbinate wants to make the Jewish people into an exclusive racial club, mostly Ashkenazic. Foreigners are not welcome, both as Jews and as residents and citizens of Israel, and the darker their skin, the more humiliating the treatment they receive.

I have fought for a broad acceptance of people who are ready to throw in their lot with the Jewish People and raise their children as Jews. All together, the Jewish People numbers thirteen million, going down to twelve as assimilation and freedom eats into our numbers. When I was a child, we numbered six million Jews in the United States. Today, depending on the criteria, we are down to some five million. Israel today has absorbed over five million Jews since it was established. That means there are only another three million in other places in the world. The Jews of North America will not come here as long as America is accepting of people of difference. If the pool of Jews who come from places where they are not wanted is drying up for Israel, Jews who live in freedom will not come here unless they are Orthodox, and Orthodoxy is not growing outside of Israel.

I predict that if the unholy alliance between the civil government and the religious hierarchy of politicians and rabbis is not broken, there will be an exodus of liberal Jews from Israel to the freedom of the West, and the number of Jews in Israel will begin to decrease. If the economic infrastructure that secular Jews have successfully established in Israel is not maintained by them, who will pay the subsidies for the large Orthodox families?

I propose that the humanist Israeli middle and left join together in a new coalition and pass several new laws to stop this process before it's too late. There must be a basic law, like the First Amendment to the American Constitution: "The Knesset shall make no law establishing religion nor preventing the free exercise thereof." Yes, we want to have a majority of Jews in Israel, but Christians, Muslims, and any other person of religious faith should be equal before the law with all the basic rights of a citizen.

Israel must have a new law regarding family subsidy. Every couple should receive a substantial subsidy when their first child is born, half of that when the second child comes, half of that for the third child, and nothing after that. Increasing the subsidies for multi-child families, especially those where the father cannot work as he did not serve in the military, is so retrogressive as to be absurd. If Orthodox couples want to have large families, they must take financial responsibility for raising those children to become responsible citizens.

Israel must pass an education law that states categorically that in order for a school to receive government funds, it must teach (1) civics, including a positive respect for the three branches of executive government, legislative parliament, and judicial courts; (2) respect, including upholding the rights of minorities; and (3) basic skills of learning, including math, language, and science.

The government must prosecute to the full extent of the law any Israeli who attacks, harms, or discriminates against another Israeli citizen or resident. Such a government must break the unholy alliance between an ultra-nationalist right wing and an Orthodox settlement movement.

Israelis must be lured back home to Israel from foreign territory and, in order to prevent a civil war, Israel must get the cooperation of the rabbis and settlement leaders to bring their people home. There is no alternative. The occupied territories, where the settlements have been established since the Six-Day War in 1967, are not Israel and can never become Israel for demographic reasons. Breaking the alliance between the political and the religious bodies in our country is the key to solving both the conflict between us and the Palestinians and the conflict between a democratic and a theocratic Israel. The dream of a greater Israel is not the expansion of territory, but the expansion of the humanistic spirit. This is the only sustainable formula for Israel in the long run.

Conversion

As a Reform rabbi in the United States, I was convinced that intermarriage between a Jew and a non-Jew was a loss for the Jewish people, especially if the wife was the non-Jewish partner. I felt she would have a stronger influence than her Jewish husband in the raising of children. I was an advocate for conversion, and during the two years I served as an assistant rabbi, I conducted conversion classes in which both the non-Jewish and the Jewish spouse participated. There were beautiful moments of acceptance of Judaism and Jewishness by the person not born a Jew in the formal conversion process and in the acceptance of the new Jew in the congregation and community. On the other hand, there were many couples that refused to go through the process because the Jewish spouse found Jewishness irrelevant and was deeply assimilated into American culture without the Jewish factor.

The whole phenomenon became irrelevant in my work in Israel. It was at best a side issue, as I was dealing with a community accepting of their Jewishness and accepted as Jews by their community. One beautiful exception was Doris Reichmann, a Christian woman from the American West who came to live in Haifa and began coming to my services at Or Hadash. She was an older woman, a widow, who came to Israel on her own. I taught her, converted her, and she became a devoted member of my congregation.

Another amazing experience. Annette and two of our children danced in a studio in Haifa that was run by a ballerina from Sweden, Liah Schubert. She had an assistant who had been a fine ballet dancer in his younger years and had danced in companies throughout the world. Kai Lothmann came to be Liah's associate, teaching in the studio. We became friends. In the mid-1970s, he came to me and told me he had fallen in love with a Jewish woman, an opera singer from France, and he wanted to convert. I accepted him as a student and gave him books in English and French. He worked with me for almost a year and was ready to convert. It was impossible to set up an accepted Reform *beit din* for conversion in Israel in those years, so I recommended that he go to England to be converted by a Reform *beit din* there. He and his bride arranged a flight to England, where he would appear before the conversion court. They would then fly to France, so that her father, a cantor, could officiate at their marriage. They planned to honeymoon in Sweden, the home of Kai's aunt, his only living relative. As the date for this process approached, the head of the *beit din* in London became ill. The couple decided to reverse their travel, going first to Sweden and staying with the aunt until the court became available. When they sat in the aunt's living room, the following conversation took place:

Kai: Aunt Marta, I would like to introduce my fiancée.
Aunt: Tell me about your background.
Fiancée: I'm from France. My father is the cantor in Metz.
Aunt: You are Jewish?
Fiancée: Yes.
Aunt: Thank God!

Then she revealed to the astonished couple that so was Kai. He was born of a Jewish mother and Christian father in Stockholm in 1943 during the war. His mother died in childbirth. His father and aunt decided that because of the Nazis, it would be unwise to reveal Kai's mother's identity. The father died when Kai was ten, and his aunt kept the secret. This man became a dancer, danced all over the world and was drawn to Israel, of all places, and to a Jewish woman from France without knowing that he, too, was Jewish. The couple went to the Office of Records in Stockholm, found his birth certificate, and immediately left for Metz, where her father officiated at their wedding.

Another experience profoundly influenced my future thinking about the Jewish people in the modern world. My niece, Charyl Bryant from California, lived with us for six months as a teenage exchange student at Leo Baeck. We came to love her as our own daughter. A graduate of Stanford University, she is today a brilliant pediatrician. While at Stanford, she met Bill LeBlanc, a young man who does not believe in organized religion. Charyl called us from California one day to inform us that she and Bill were going to be married and asked if I would officiate. I said to her, "What are you and Bill doing on the fourteenth of February?" I was planning to be in California that weekend, and I was interested in discussing it with them. She called me back two days later to say that she and Bill would take me to a lodge in Yosemite. I was delighted to discuss their marriage, their relationship, and the fact that one was Jewish and another wasn't. A week later, they called to ask if three other couples could join. Two were already married, and one was engaged. And so it was that we set out to discuss the implications of intermarriage in their lives.

Bill's position was that he did not believe in religion altogether but would support Charyl in her desire to uphold Jewish traditions in their home. Each of the other couples described their relationship. All of the non-Jewish spouses had decided they would not convert to Judaism, but all of the Jewish spouses wanted to remain Jews and to raise Jewish children. I argued that the influence of the non-Jewish spouse would be so powerful that the Jewishness of the children would be in danger. I left feeling that we were losing Jews.

Happily, I was wrong. Charyl and Bill have a profoundly Jewish home. They have a Jewish library. They are members of a Reform congregation in Boulder, Colorado, where they have lived for the last forty years. Charyl has been the chair of the congregation's education committee, and she is a substitute cantor when the cantor of the congregation is away. Bill has never converted but is extremely supportive. Both of their sons celebrated a bar mitzvah, and I attended the ceremonies. One of them became the bar mitzvah teacher in the congregation. They have Jewish symbols throughout their home, and they celebrate Shabbat on Friday nights. That marriage produced two sons whose identity was Jewish. They are carrying the Jewish tradition forward.

My experience has led me to believe that the Reform Movement's embrace of patrilineal as well as matrilineal descent for determining Jewish status, *as long as the parents raise their children as Jews*, is the right position. As Jews have been given more freedom and acceptance within modern society, in order for us to increase, we must be accepting of non-Jews who build families together with those born into the Jewish people. It is best if we can convince them to convert, but if conversion, including the acceptance of Jewish theology, is the only entrance into the Jewish people, we run the risk of decreasing the number of Jews in the world each decade.

A more profound influence for me as a leader of the Jewish people in Israel has been the incredible movement of Russian-speaking people to Israel in both the 1970s and following Glasnost and Perestroika by Mikhail Gorbachev in 1989. When the Berlin Wall fell and the Iron Curtain rose, over a million Russian-speaking people left Mother Russia to come live in Israel. At least one-third of them are not Jewish according to the halachah. They were allowed into Israel under the family unification law. That meant an influx of between 300,000 and 400,000 new Israelis who were not halachically Jewish. Their children, who attended Jewish schools, were members of Zionist youth groups, served in our defense force, graduated from our universities, but do not have Jewish mothers, are now picking Jewish partners to marry and raising families in Israel. It is best if such a person would convert.

My colleagues in MARAM, the Council of Progressive Rabbis in Israel, have determined they will officiate in marriages only if the spouse without the Jewish mother agrees to convert through the Progressive *beit din*. I have come to a different conclusion. Couples call and ask me to officiate at their marriages after they have already booked a hall and have gone to Prague or Larnaca to get married in a civil ceremony. They will marry without converting, whether I like it or not. I want to save the Jewish partner and his or her children for the Jewish people. I meet with the couple several times, and if I am convinced they will raise their children as Jews, I officiate at their marriage. Most of these couples are Russian speaking. It is a sub-group and a sub-culture in Israel that can assimilate outside of the Jewish faith if not encouraged in their desire to have Jewish tradition in their homes. I believe as a Jewish leader that this is a mitzvah for maintaining the Jewish people in a world leaning toward assimilation.

For two thousand years, the Jewish People has not had a national homeland. Conversion to Judaism has been a Diaspora phenomenon. The only way to become Jewish was through belief and acceptance of Judaism as a religion. Once the Jewish People regained independence as a nation, the question arises if halachic religious affiliation is to be the only civic entrance into the Jewish People. I'm convinced that living in a society the majority of whose members are Jewish and whose majority culture is secular Jewish requires nationalistic and cultural criteria for entrance into the Jewish People as a nation. Hebrew as a native language. The songs and dances of Israel starting in kindergarten and going through adult life. The literature of our writers. Our theater of Jewish and Israeli themes. Our relationship with non-Jewish citizens and our non-Jewish neighbors. All must be taken into account when constructing an identity within the Jewish State. Can we become Jewish without the approval of rabbis?

Furthermore, what is the meaning of "Jewish" in the Jewish State? Does it mean only a majority of Jews? Does it mean the acceptance of Jewish traditions? Does it mean a status higher than non-Jews in the Land? Or does it mean, as in the preamble of the Israeli Declaration of Independence, the principles of the prophets of Israel, that what is desired of the Jewish people in its own Land is to live decent, ethical lives with respect for the other? I believed fifty years ago that there was a correlation between "Jewish" and "democratic" in what we call the Jewish Democratic State. Most Israelis think those two factors are mutually exclusive. But if democracy is the language of the Emancipation and if Jewish is the language of Amos, Isaiah, and Micah, then the two are inclusive, and the Jewish state has a responsibility to be moral, ethical, and humanistic. We cannot do that by discriminating between our Jewish and non-Jewish citizens and by only accepting the ancient halachic definition of Jewishness. In a world of globalization and technology and communication that does not recognize borders, if the only definition of Jewishness is halachic, the Jewish people will shrink, and our influence in the world will become negligible.

Midrash and Halachah

The study of Judaism is a multi-faceted jewel. Bible, Talmud, rabbinic studies, medieval literature, history, customs, liturgy, Israel, Jewish identity, great Jewish ideas, philosophy, and theology all merge into a comprehensive picture of the Jewish people, our culture, and civilization. Students of Judaism are drawn inexorably into paths that fit their *Weltanschauung*, their world view. As one progresses in knowledge, the task is to integrate the fields of study into a comprehensive *gestalt*. When you have reached that, you realize that certain aspects of your study fit best with your world view.

This has been my path. My father taught me as a young child to love the message of the Hebrew prophets. My mentor at Brandeis taught me to wonder at the biblical narrative. Nechama Leibowitz taught me the wonder of biblical interpretation through the midrash. My teacher of Bible at HUC-JIR taught me to separate between the true and the false prophet. My professor of history at the College taught me to analyze the documents of the past and understand the dreams and prejudices of the writers of history in order to determine what actually happened in days gone by. Leo Baeck taught me to look more toward the future than to dwell in the past. I find myself going back to my books and texts as I focus more clearly on what I really believe. As I read the daily Israeli newspaper, I am impressed even more with the courage of Amos, Micah, and Isaiah in challenging the power structure and the basic way of life of their day as they tried to save their society from the unethical practices of those with power, the rich, and the political and religious leaders. I am more and more impressed with the approach of midrash in using ancient texts in order to get to universal and ethical principles. I find my search for truth in what I pray is supported by liturgy that has been written through the ages and is still being created. Reform Judaism is ever evolving, and women and men leaders are constantly creating new books and articles to help the perplexed Jew of the twenty-first century find truth and meaning in our day from our rich past.

Our Ethical Will

This is the half-century story of the first Reform rabbi who came to Israel to build a liberal Judaism and enhance Israel's democracy. I started this book with a description of my love for the game of baseball. My coach at Brandeis told us that concentrating on "hitting the ball" was the supreme test of success at the game. "Remember that if you succeed three times out of ten, you will be a star," he said. At Brandeis I had a .384 batting average over four years. I have tried to "step up to the plate" and maintain that average during these fifty-three years in Israel. There have been many failures, and I have had to dodge many curves thrown at me. But I have kept my eye on the ball and have had the satisfaction of hitting many singles, doubles, triples, and even homers.

Now in our eighth decade, Annette and I have prepared for the transfer of our material assets to our family and to those educational institutions that formed us. We have not been in the mode of accumulating wealth. But we have been able to help at critical moments in our community and to save a modest estate. The Radcliffe Institute (the successor to Radcliffe College at Harvard), Brandeis University, Hebrew Union College-Jewish Institute of Religion, the Leo Baeck Education Center, and Interlochen Center for the Arts have been the key educational institutions that have contributed to our and our children's and our grandchildren's education, skills, and values. We want to "pay forward" toward the future of each of these for the privilege and opportunities each of them has given to us and helped to make us what we are.

We leave behind much more in universal principles than in finances. Ours has been a life of enrichment and values, a life of a vision of a more humane and enlightened world. It is these that we bequeath to future life in our family, our neighborhoods, our nation, and our world. We pray that each person will sleep unafraid at night, wake in the morning healthy and with faith that the day will be secure and productive, know the thrill of warm human feeling to all and greet them with a strong handshake, or a hug and a smile. And this is especially true with "the stranger in the marketplace." Love is often requited, and we are burned by the uncaring, disrespect, and even hate and violence toward us. But love is more often returned to us when we treat others with respect, caring, and a pleasant countenance.

Our liturgy and our prophets command us to free the oppressed, to lift up the fallen, to give shelter to the homeless, to heal the sick, to clothe the naked, to give bread to the hungry, to revive the weary. To live by this is to feel the pain and fear of the fallen, the sick, the poor, and the hungry. These are not just those who are of a lower status among us. We are all "fallen" from the high goals we have set for ourselves, "sick" from the lost opportunities in our lives, "poor" in living up to our highest standards, and "hungry" for love and acceptance. We plead for people to be more accepting of difference, more bold in learning what makes for felicitous human relationships.

Peanuts' Charlie Brown once said in a cartoon, "I love mankind. It's people I can't stand." Charles Schulz had it wrong. Love is generated one person at a time, through empathy and caring. Our life might seem pleasant, but in the long run we cannot have a good life if others do not. A strong democracy cannot survive when many of its people do not have a good life. We cannot have two parallel societies, one middle and upper class with enough material wealth and another with not enough to have a basically healthy physical and spiritual life. Society must give opportunity to all to realize their dreams and have a decent life. It is this value that we must pass on to those who follow us. Never be satisfied that you "have it all." There is no "all" until all others have a good life too.

We bequeath to you a passion to follow and to lead, to follow your own dreams and the dreams for a moral and ethical neighborhood, and to lead your peers in the paths to realize these dreams. Leadership is the energy to help others to be energized, to reach toward their own dream, to move us along a path that makes life better for all.

Sixty years ago we, Annette and Bob, set out on a mission to have a life of blessing together, to help each other to realize our dreams. We are family; we are Jews; we are Israelis; we are liberals who believe in constant reform; and we are teachers.

We have produced the most amazing FAMILY, three children who have given us three partners and nine grandchildren. You are all good, intelligent, learned, and loving people. We leave you our values, which you carry in your innermost being, with the wish that you will continue to lift that torch higher and higher as you make your mark on this world.

We have remained faithful JEWS. Our library is Jewish; our day, week, month, year are Jewish; our table is Jewish; our way of life is Jewish. Our long life has been Jewish. We leave all of you the richness of a modern Judaism with the responsibility and the opportunity for each of you to make the choices of what content to put into your Jewishness, whatever your tradition.

We are proud ISRAELIS. We planted our roots in this earth; we built our home on this soil. We have worked hard to absorb the sounds and sights of this Land. We dedicated ourselves to the people of this nation. Those roots took hold, and the One who binds us together helped us to grow a tree so strong and with branches so wide and leaves so beautiful as to make a magnificent garden in Haifa. We have seen "Truth Spring Forth from the Land." Rabbis Leo Baeck and Meir Elk would be proud that their names are on that tree. We taught our people; we educated them; we gave them our vision of an Israel to love and to be proud of; we lifted those in need. We found deep friends and colleagues in this society. We made beautiful music in our home and our surroundings. We opened our tent to receive people of all colors, all languages, all backgrounds, all opinions. We leave you the challenge of continuing to plant your roots and grow your tree in any way you desire, as long as it adds to the beautiful garden of our country.

And we are LIBERALS, and we are for constant REFORM. There are Israelis who are not liberals and not for reform. In our democracy they have the right to their way of life and their opinions, as long as they do not coerce others through law or non-choice education to accept those opinions blindly. But we believe that the foundations of this Republic, this Nation, are liberal, open, challenging, and free choice. Jews want freedom; Arabs want freedom. Freedom is the right to choose! We bequeath this choice to you. Never let others decide for you the moral or correct way. Use your conscience, based on years of ethical struggle, to do the right thing, to follow the moral path.

And finally we are TEACHERS. Your whole life is a lesson; your every day is a lesson; your every action is a lesson. The way you greet the sad stranger, the dirty street cleaner, the gritty gardener, the angry foreigner, the confused adolescent, the abused wife, the underprivileged child, the hopeless widow—that greeting is your constant lesson. Giving a lesson in a classroom, in a music or dance studio, or at the computer may get the material across. But the real "teacher" is the *way* we teach, the messages we send through how we treat and relate to our students. We bequeath to you that countenance that will lift these and all human beings and give them hope for a better life and a brighter tomorrow.

Glossary

Av beit din—head of the three-rabbi court for the Progressive Movement
Beit midrash—study space, classroom
Halachah—Jewish law
Kabbalat Shabbat—welcoming the Sabbath
Kibbutz—agricultural collective
Kippah, kippot—head covering
Midrash—Jewish lore
Moshav—cooperative agricultural village
Sabra—native born Israeli
Seudat Shabbat—Shabbat dinner
Tallit—prayer shawl
T'filah—religious service
T'fillin—phylacteries
Ulpan—intensive Hebrew language course
Yekke—German-speaking Jew
Yishuv—Settlement
Z'mirot—Shabbat songs

www.ingramcontent.com/pod-product-compliance
Lightning Source LLC
Chambersburg PA
CBHW071658090426
42738CB00009B/1573